Phantom Village

This book is dedicated to
James Spring
1919-1969

Phantom Village

The Myth of the New Glasgow

Ian Spring

Polygon
EDINBURGH

© Ian Spring 1990
Polygon
22 George Square,
Edinburgh EH8 9LF

Typeset in Linotron Sabon
by Koinonia Limited, Bury
Printed and bound in Great Britain
by Redwood Press Ltd, Melksham, Wiltshire

British Library Cataloguing
in Publication Data
Spring, Ian
Phantom village: the myth of the new Glasgow
1. Scotland. Strathclyde region. Glasgow.
Social conditions
I. Title
941.4430858

ISBN 0 7486 6090 9

Contents

The Author

IAN SPRING was born in Dennistoun, Glasgow in 1955 and studied at the universities of Strathclyde, Glasgow and Edinburgh. He has spent the greater part of his life in Glasgow but now lives in Edinburgh with his wife and daughter, where he lectures in Media and Cultural Studies.

Acknowledgements

I am extremely grateful to my students and colleagues at Queen Margaret College for their friendship and incisive academic comments, and to the college management for allowing me the time and resources to undertake this project. I am indebted to all my friends from Glasgow whose friendship through the years has taught me more about the city than I can return in a book. They are too numerous to detail here but I would like particularly to mention John Cowan, Willie Gallacher and Chris Wellington. Several people commented on parts of the text and I would like to thank them all but especially Cairns Craig and everyone at Polygon for their editorial advice. Finally, I am indebted to my wife, Elena, my daughter, Louise, and my mother, Marion Spring, for their constant support.

I am extremely grateful for permission to include textual material and illustrations in this book and I would like to acknowledge the following individuals and institutions: 7:84 theatre company, Thomas Annan and Co., The British Film Institute, The British Council, Corgi books, Ken Currie, Matthew Dalziel, Adam McNaughtan, Alasdair Gray, Great Scot International, *The Glaswegian, M8,* The Mitchell Library, Pete Murray, the People's Palace, Scotsman publications, Stephen Mulrine, Strathclyde Regional Council, Underwood and Co.

Part of chapter ten appeared in *Cultural Studies,* volume 4, no. 2, and part of chapter two in the *Scotsman* in May 1989. An earlier version of chapters three and four won the essay section of the Scotia Bar Writing Prize in 1989

Series Preface

Scotland's history is often presented as punctuated by disasters which overwhelm the nation, break its continuity and produce a fragmented culture. Many felt that 1979, and the failure of the Devolution Referendum, represented such a disaster: that the energetic culture of the 1960s and 1970s would wither into the silence of a political waste land in which Scotland would be no more than a barely distinguishable province of the United Kingdom.

Instead, the 1980s proved to be one of the most productive and creative decades in Scotland this century – as though the energy that had failed to be harnessed by the politicians flowed into other channels. In literature, in thought, in history, creative and scholarly work went hand in hand to redraw the map of Scotland's past and realign the perspectives of its future.

In place of the few standard conceptions of Scotland's identity that had often been in the past the tokens of thought about the country's culture, a new and vigorous debate was opened up about the nature of Scottish experience, about the real social and economic structures of the nation, and about the ways in which the Scottish situation related to that of other similar cultures throughout the world.

It is from our determination to maintain a continuous forum for such debate that *Determinations* takes its title. The series will provide a context for sustained dialogue about culture and politics in Scotland, and about those international issues which directly affect Scottish experience.

Too often, in Scotland, a particular way of seeing our culture, of representing ourselves, has come to dominate our perceptions because it has gone unchallenged – worse, unexamined. The vitality of the culture should be measured by the intensity of debate which it generates rather than the security of ideas on which it rests. And should be measured by the extent to which creative, philosophical, theological, critical and political ideas confront each other.

If the determinations which shape our experience are to come from within rather than from without, they have to be explored and evaluated and acted upon. Each volume in this series will seek to be a contribution to that self-determination; and each volume, we trust, will require a response, contributing in turn to the on-going dynamic that is Scotland's culture.

General Editor: Cairns Craig

Because there is no nonsense in Glasgow,
there is little talk of culture.

Colm Brogan,
The Glasgow Story, 1952

Introduction

Why write a book about Glasgow? Many scholars will know far more than I do about the city's past, many writers of more advanced years will have a store of reminiscences, anecdotes and stories. There are already scores, perhaps hundreds, of volumes about Glasgow, its past (there is a project currently to write a major multi-volume history of the city), its present, its architecture, its people, its peculiar ambience. I have presumed to venture my opinion on a variety of topics. I cannot claim to be an expert on any of them and I certainly would not claim to speak for any group of scholars or interested parties. Neither have I written an account that can be called in any way autobiographical – although constantly, perhaps more than I would like, I have referred to my own memories of a childhood in the city, hampered by a very imperfect recollection of any of the details. Notably, also, there is a manner in which this essay, as it approaches its conclusion and present day, becomes more subjective, personal and recondite. The reason for this is that this structure reflects my own encounter with not only city mythologies but also the difficult problem of personal identity. I have also tried, as best I can, to preserve the instantaneity of the writing – which, belongs, in my view, very much to my own personal perspective, and to a significant moment in time.

I am well aware of the paradoxical nature of this approach, and of the necessity to carefully qualify my conclusions. There is no excuse for believing that my own personal reminiscing about Glasgow has any greater truth value than the popular communal memory I try to analyse. Both are mythologies inflicted by nostalgia – which weakens remembering. Yet both are fundamental to the structure of the essay and for me, at least, the interaction between the academic and the personal discourse and the tension between personal and communal memory has been illuminating and made the experience of writing this book worthwhile. It is a conceit common to most writers that their personal experience has something of particular importance to say. I have no idea to what extent my own childhood memories may be seen as typical of or relevant to Glaswegians as a whole, but they are my own, and directly inform the feeling of this book. For Glasgow to me is associated not with a wealth of recountable memories but with an overwhelming sense of loss – a sense which I can also relate to the overall compulsion of New Glasgow mythology to attempt to grasp, sometimes desperately, a spurious communal past.

I have also eschewed the traditional academic essay format of a linear argument in favour of a more fragmented approach in which I try to draw on impressions and make a variety of connections between different things. Some of these ideas are presented in their gauche original form, unadulterated by reflection, in an attempt to preserve the freshness of the ideas, but I hope that they also serve to make my overall argument clear. The main points I am trying to make are as follows. Firstly, I have shown, I hope, that the New Glasgow is a mythology in the sense that I have outlined in parts three and four. I have also, along with many others, challenged the assumption that the New Glasgow is in every way a good thing for the people of the city as a whole. Secondly, I have tried to show the peculiar way in which Glasgow is reconstructing itself and, particularly, the use of pastiche and nostalgia to inform this process. Lastly, I have tried to suggest that the particular discourses identified in this process can be explained in a historical context. In this sense this book can be seen as a correlative to the Kinchins' book *Glasgow's Great Exhibitions* – the difference being that my concerns are ideological rather than purely historical. The historical perspective is itself important because I want to make it clear that the forces at work on the New Glasgow are both a part of a more general shift – the development of heritage culture, the rebuilding of the post-industrial city – and also specific to the city of Glasgow, building on the nature of its own peculiar ideologies.

Of course, it will be clear that, despite the subtitle of this study, there *is*, in every sense, a New Glasgow. In the last twenty years which constitute my own adult experience of Glasgow, I have seen the city change utterly. In 1972, when I did a housing survey in Shettleston and Dalmarnock Roads, there was deprivation equal to any favela in South America, or any other inner-city slum. As many as twelve people living in one room, backcourts running with rats, central stairwells dripping with water and walls covered in slime. Dalmarnock Road, I remember, had backcourts with both the round external stairtowers and the more recent square brick version photographed by Oscar Marzaroli; often windowless and lacking electric lighting. Through one close, surprisingly, I discovered that there was only a small enclosed courtyard with a solitary gas lamp standing in a puddle. Leading immediately off the yard was another tenement building, of three storeys, obviously precedent to the larger neighbour now blocking its light. While I took a photograph a young woman entered, pushing a pram through the rutted mud. Further down Dalmarnock Road, past a flattened roadside stretch of damp black earth there were corporation caravans, prefabricated in an era of greater housing demand and never replaced. Further still, on a corner, stood a one-storey public house called the Piazza, above the cracked walls and flaking paint, around the flat roof, were ornate plant pots devoid, in the sparse, smoky atmosphere, full of the dust of demolished, crashing sandstone, of any form of plants.

It is important to consider what these memories might mean. A legacy of poverty, deprivation. Surely no-one can be sorry that these slums are no longer with us? But, somehow, there is a great wish in me, in all of us, to revisit these scenes. Walk down either of these immense thoroughfares today and there is no sense of the new, of replacement, of organic development, only of emptiness, loss. The slums are gone, but their meaning remains. Recently, I was thumbing through Christopher Tunnard's book, *The City of Man* , and I came across these words: 'the sight of humanity enjoying itself is a heartening thing. You may turn and look at the slums behind, shaking your head... but remember, the evil of the slums is only the evil of poverty, which can be cured.' My answer to Tunnard is that it is not, it cannot. Glasgow for me is a city irrevocably shaped by the dusty, muddy legacy of Dalmarnock Road.

And yet, in many ways we still return here, drawn by some powerful nostalgic impulse. But why do we long for the impossible, to revisit the past? To some extent, the contents of these few pages are dictated by my attempts to arrive at an answer to this question. And why have I written this book? Perhaps because all I can get from Glasgow is a sense of loss, rather than a sense of belonging. Or perhaps they are both the same thing – in the words of the song 'I Belong to Glasgow' there is no great joy, only acceptance or defiance, a prolonged plea for personal identity. To belong to the city that only exists, it seems, as its own partial reflection in the bottom of a pint glass. Perhaps, after all, the only reason that I have written this book, is as a farewell to Glasgow, to exorcise this empty sense of belonging.

Finally, let me say that this is an essay about representation and not about economics or politics. I have not backed my sometimes contentious opinions with a barrage of statistics and factual examples. It is my personal belief, however, that, whereas I am willing to acknowledge that the New Glasgow has made a real contribution to the lot of the average Glaswegian, I doubt that it has made any more than the most superficial difference to the economic and social reality of the lives of the poor or unemployed in the city. Similarly, although I have no special knowledge as to the destination of the supposedly large sums of money that Culture City now pulls in, I doubt very much that any significant amount ends up in the pocket of the average Glaswegian. No doubt facts and figures can be produced which will decimate my argument and leave me dumbfounded. At the moment I remain unrepentant. Neither do I know what the future really holds for the city of Glasgow. There are some who believe that, as London and the south-east deteriorates, the old industrial cities of the north will come into their own. Others that Glasgow will inevitably face some sort of backlash as the Year of Culture comes to an end. Both of these scenarios may be partially true. I must also say, as one fortunate enough to be employed in what might be called the cultural industries, that I have fallen prey to the ultimate heresy. I don't believe that the culture in Culture City is all that important after all. I don't give much of a damn about a new opera hall. I believe that our own popular culture is worth preserving before anything else, and I have every confidence that literature, music and art will survive without gross municipal interference. In the end there are things every bit as important as these - such as housing, jobs, education and self-respect. As I finalise these few pages, I am continually plagued by a sorry parade of media Glaswegians, and hour after hour of television debate chews over such vexed questions as to whether the denizens of Castlemilk really want free tickets to see Pavarotti. There is much talk of the culture in Culture City and its relevance to the mass of the population, but no voice states the obvious - that the relevance of the New Glasgow to every Glaswegian lies not in the few blockbuster events organised for the Year of Culture, but in the continual media bombardment and cultural hype that invades public and private discourse. In this way, there is no escape - we are all New Glaswegians now.

As this book goes to press, New Glasgow mythology tightens its grip on the city each day. Walking up Argyle Street one day, on those now rare occasions when I revisit my home town, I saw a t-shirt in a shop window. Framed by the words 'I Belong To Glasgow' in large black letters, an illustration in pastel tones featured the torso of a man, naked, handsome yet muscular, his features not striking yet well-formed, his eyes lacking clarity, hidden beneath the faintest suggestion of a Neanderthal brow. Behind him, towering into the clear blue sky, was the familiar lattice of shipyard cranes or girders from Glasgow's now mythical industrial past. This image of the New Glaswegian, the city innocent, barely out of his swaddling clothes, in his nursery of repossessed industrialism, is, for me at least, a rationale for writing this book.

Deathwatch

How can one visit the home of one's childhood? Some, I suppose, will never have really left, but for the rest of us, separated by space and time, or class and culture, it is a testing journey to a strange land. One day I tried, in Dennistoun in the east end of Glasgow, walking up the path on the brae where Dunchattan Street stood, standing there, at the back of the close entrance to 65 Eveline Street, head tilted to the sky, but at a lesser angle than it was, thirty years ago, when I could view the distant wet slates and the twirling slatted chimney piece that was called, for some reason, a granny (in my five-year-old mind the shape, somehow, became inexorably confused with the image of my grandmother), and the immense expanse of backcourt middens forged from crumbly sandstone and black, black mud, with its plateaus, its gorges, its precipices.

But this is merely the topography of a dim, inefficient and fickle memory. These tenements and backyards are long gone, replaced by a new enclosed housing development in a sort of mock Scottish vernacular style. I never visited these smoky tenements again after one day in the early sixties when I left, with my parents, to begin a new life in the smarter, cleaner housing estates on the eastern periphery of the city, although they may well have stood for years afterwards – until the early seventies when the rotting dank tenement slums of the east end, of Dennistoun, Calton, Shettleston, Dalmarnock Road were, for the most part, erased from the city's volatile urban present and my own capricious memory of the homeland remained, with others, as the most substantial record of these dirty, lively streets.

My journey through the Glasgow of today does not, cannot, begin here. I can, however, begin at only a little distance from here. Round past Broompark Drive, into Ark Lane, to the corner of Circus Drive at Golfhill Primary School (my first school). Opposite the school, at the bottom end of Firpark Street, older than I am, and older too than the few remaining tenements or their forerunners, is a small patch of waste ground, once sparse and rocky but now landscaped and benched. Here, now buried, are the remains of underground air shelters from the war, and here too, the children from the school played for generations and, I presume, still do, hunting, hiding, gambling, arranging secret assignations and bloodying occasional noses as they did in my childhood. At the furthest extreme, old as the ground itself, stands a solid high sandstone wall, dandelions growing from the cracks, the pointing rotted, pitted surfaces lichenous – for all I know constructed of thin timeless strata, aeons old, fossils suspended in the heart of the stone. This was the very boundary of my childhood kingdom. The wall was too high, too insuperable to penetrate, by action or thought. Yet behind this wall, only a few paces from the ground I trod as a child, lies another world, a different Glasgow. A world of which I remained unaware until much later, when, as a teenager, I climbed the wall from the other side and, perched atop, looked down from the heart of Glasgow, then, at another Glasgow, the foreign quarters of the past, an infinitely more personal land.

This is the perimeter wall of the Necropolis, the old dome-shaped burial yard overlooking Glasgow Cathedral, Cathedral Square and Castle Street. A landmark obvious to both native Glaswegians and outsiders – the historian, the tourist. And herein lies the difference between the two worlds. One is both illusory and inaccessible – the primal geography of the imagination. The other not so. It exists in history, or mythology. This area, the Necropolis and the cathedral precinct is symbolic, emblematic, part of the common lot of every Glaswegian. No-one comes here unaware of its history and its part in a legacy of Glaswegian lore and tradition.

So here the wall, I take symbolically. Viewed from either side the absolute boundaries of two distinct realms of knowledge – both my own, man and boy; meeting like two lost twins on this exact but invisible plane. One remains personal, the other is part of a discourse that lives outwith my meagre experience. This essay is about the other Glasgow – the Glasgow of representation. As strange and immediate as this task is to me, sometimes the first Glasgow of my own childhood remembrance may force its way through.

The Necropolis is a quintessentially Victorian creation. It is a monument to monuments – a massive realisation of the peculiarly Victorian obsession with death. The cemetery dates from 1832 – although the large monolithic finger that commemorates John Knox (the great Protestant reformer is not buried here) dates from a little earlier. Most prominent Glaswegians of the mid-Victorian period are buried here and several guides to their graves have been published. To the Victorians, and since that period, the Necropolis has served a distinctive purpose as a viewpoint on the city, ideal for a stroll on a Sunday afternoon, a strange combination of pleasure garden and grand monument. In the late twentieth century it has fallen out of favour, although lately some attempts have been made to resurrect some interest in it as a local historical walk or a tourist attraction.

Sitting on the perimeter wall, the panorama is impressive and vast, so much monumental granite and so many obelisks, so many epitaphs, stone tears, so many crypts honeycombing the hill, crosses, eulogies, families aggregated through distant years. A black pock-marked stone angel stands at one corner overlooking the greater panorama of the city – possibly struck by lightning at some indefinite hour, only one arm remains. Crypts sport rusting iron grilles like teeth, noseless limestone caryatids shoulder enormous porticos. Few visitors could remain unimpressed by this strange deathly landscape, its twists and corners in spirally ascending paths, its combinations of monuments, of individual interests, ever-changing, perplexing, enigmatic from any perspective. Perhaps every visit to the Necropolis should be accompanied by a camera – if only a camera of the imagination; the grainy texture, the subtle changes of perspective, the stark silhouettes, present startling visual images, continually changing as the light varies and the mood changes.

This visual aspect has been employed to some purpose in the film *Deathwatch*, directed by Bertrand Tavernier. This is a strange sort of science fiction thriller. The plot is about a young television reporter, Farrow, played by Harvey Keitel, who has volunteered to have a television camera implanted in his eye so that he can document, for transmission, the last days of a young woman dying (conventional death has been replaced by euthanasia in this society). It was almost entirely filmed in Glasgow. The opening shots of the film, to an urgent, stringy sound-track, consist of a few brief cuts of grouped gravestones, followed by a longer shot of a young girl playing, among the gravestones, with a skipping rope. At this point, the most impressive moment, the camera rises, the cityscape appears, the Cathedral, the Royal Infirmary, the University of Strathclyde, tower blocks, industry, wasteland.

We cut to the hospital, a spot is concentrated on Farrow's eye. It is switched off and Farrow momentarily panics (at the end of the film he deliberately switches off the lights and blinds himself). We switch to a reverse shot, the Necropolis from the hospital, from Farrow's perspective. Death as subject.

Farrow turns to confront a nurse: 'Why did you let them do that?' 'Let them? This way I'll never forget how beautiful you are.' At this point the complete complexity of Tavernier's manipulation of point of view becomes clear. For the shot cuts from Farrow's view of the nurse to the same view clearly mediated through a television screen, the implanted video camera in Farrow's eye, then again to the multiple screens of the control room where the company producers

are viewing the scene. The same triple perspective is adopted in the
next scene. Farrow goes out onto the street, pans the scene of the
Barony Church, Provand's Lordship. Again we cut to the multiple
screens.

Farrow goes out into the town (we first see him crossing the road
in front of the infirmary with schoolchildren crossing in the foreground)
and a voice-over is introduced which is meant to be the voice of
Farrow's wife recalling, at some future time, his experiences of that
day. There follows a montage of fairly static scenes of Glasgow streets
and scenes – Tennent's brewery, Royal Exchange Square (now
Nelson Mandela Square), Montrose Street, Hope Street, Waterloo
Street. Finally, we cut from Farrow's view of a synecdochal detail of
a poster advertising the eponymous 'Deathwatch' television
programme to Farrow who is playing with children in an admirably
decaying children's playground with a vista of dockland cranes in the
background. This really ends the initial part of the film, the children
clearly reflecting the more symbolical skipping girl in the graveyard.

There are several remarkable things about this piece of film
footage. Firstly, Tavernier has clearly employed the unique ambience
of Glasgow, especially the area around Cathedral Square, to great
effect – a feat never achieved, to my knowledge, by any Scottish
filmmaker. Secondly, the complexity of Tavernier's mediated point
of view shot has an effect which is not reproduced in any other film
I have ever seen. When, for example, we view the montage of city
streets we clearly see a scene from the point of view of Farrow but
mediated not once, through his extraordinary eye/ camera, not twice,
through the multiple screens of the control room (we are made aware
of their existence even if they are not pictured) but three times,
through our own experience of the scene. This is especially powerful
if these are scenes that constitute a common or everyday part of the
reader's diet of images. What I find so extraordinary is the effect of
being presented with these very familiar images of Glasgow so over-
mediated, so completely reformed in their context as to give them
totally new and powerful connotations.

It is like seeing Glasgow for the *first* time, (what the Russians call
ostranenie – making strange, freeing the everyday from its habitual
ordinariness) but the overwhelming feeling, the inner meaning of the
text, seems to reveal something that has been there all the time, that
in the city there is something akin to death.

As Roland Barthes has said, there is something in every photograph
of death. In Farrow's living snapshots of the city there is a moving
element of the unworldly that so perfectly fits into the theme of the
film. The 'Deathwatch' of the film is just that, an essay in looking, an
extended gaze at death, at someone dying. The initial shot, of the

small girl in the graveyard as the camera extends the scene to present a panorama of Glasgow, makes it quite clear that the city is the arena of death. Farrow's eye is an elaborate metaphor for this slow death, condemned, as he notes at the beginning, to eternal remembering, or blindness, which is much the same thing. Farrow will give everything, or nothing, for just a little illumination. And yet from Farrow's few enigmatic words we can tease another clue. For as he directs his gaze towards the horizon from the hospital balcony, Farrow's comment is that 'this way I'll never forget'. Why is this ? Only his sensory organs have been modified, not his memory. Of course, *filming* is, if you like, a metaphor for making permanent – but consider it this way: Farrow's gaze has now shifted from the personal to the representational. Farrow's experience becomes more than individual. At this point, for Farrow, perhaps, the two Glasgows – the Glasgow of personal remembrance and the Glasgow of popular mythology – become one.

I would like to trace this very peculiar gaze or interpretation of the city a little further back in time, to 1858, not so long after the Necropolis itself was founded, to what may in some ways justifiably be termed the first truly *modern* representation of the city. In that year a small volume entitled *Midnight Scenes and Social Photographs* by 'Shadow' (a pseudonym for Alexander Brown, a small-time printer and would-be social reformer in Glasgow) appeared.[1] The book consists of some general observations of the slum areas of the east end of Glasgow and a revelation of the distress and widespread depravity of its inhabitants. These ingenuous prose passages are, however, very carefully constructed. They form seven days (Monday to Sunday) of perambulations through the 'night-side' of the city by Shadow and an acquaintance. That the whole thing is supposed to be the work of an anonymous observer is made clear by a simple etching, somewhat in the style of chapbooks and ephemera of the time, that adorns the cover of this edition. It shows two women, presumably prostitutes, slouched under a streetlight. Just appearing out of the gloom in the background is a silhouette ('shadow') of a man in a top hat. So explicit is this that we can only presume that the author or publisher was totally unaware that, in the age of the 'other Victorians' (an age troubled by the night-time wanderings of outwardly respectable womanisers, roues and worse – such as the notorious Charles Carrington, 'Walter' of *My Secret Life*) this is not really the pose of the *reformer* but of the *voyeur*.

Shadow's peculiar role as observer in this underworld is characterised very particularly in the foreword to the book:

> The writer of the following sketches does not wish the reader to imagine that their appearance arises from any supposed literary

excellence, but rather because it is presumed they will be found to contain facts and observations not without value on a subject of great and increasing interest, viz., the condition of the poor, and the classes generally inhabiting the lower depths of society. Should the 'Photographs' present a tone painfully dark and gloomy, it will be remembered that most of them have been taken by moonlight, from the 'night side' of the city. They are not creations of the brain, but so far as the writer's knowledge of the art extends – they are truthful. Highly-wrought pictures, and more exciting incidents, gathered from the experience of a week, month, or year, might have been produced; but as they occurred, so they have been given...with many imperfections.[2] The point about Shadow's collection is that the book, although published several years after the first popular photographically illustrated text, Fox Talbot's *Sun Pictures*, when, presumably, the technology was available, does not employ photographic illustrations at all. In fact, as can be gleaned from the tone of the introduction, photography is employed simply as a metaphor for his observations (in the form of what are often called sketches – also metaphorically). This use is primarily for one purpose, to emphasise the *truth value* of the contents – at a time when, with the popularisation of the calotype and portrait photography, the photograph itself was inexorably associated with a true, *unmediated* representation of reality – literally 'the pencil of nature'. With this in mind, at a period when the action of the camera was not the product of the creative artist but literally, as one early pioneer commented, 'a sunbeam in...a manoeuvre', we can see the point made in the introduction that these 'photographs' are images from the other, 'night side' of reality – 'taken by moonlight'.

The metaphoric function of the art of photography is exemplified in the astonishing etching by George Cruikshank that forms the frontispiece to the book. In the centre there are featured several scenes of depravity supposedly associated with the east end of the city and combined together in the same fashion as in popular etchings such as Hogarth's *Gin Lane*. There is a man lying on the ground with blood pouring from his head, a drunken couple, a man beating his wife with child in arm, a women being restrained by policemen in large top hats while a child clings to her waist, some lost children huddling together in the foreground. In the background, the only source of redemption, a preacher addressing his congregation, can be found, and a couple of ragged figures turn away from the frenzy towards him.

In the extreme left foreground, directly addressing the protagonists, stands a camera on a tripod capturing these scenes. To further emphasise the efficacy of this instrument to mirror reality and strip

Cruikshanks's frontispiece to Shadow's *Midnight Scenes and Social Photographs*

away the veneer to expose the truth another ploy is introduced. In the left background bounded by a wall, directly in the path of the camera, a section of the stone apparently melts away to expose the extremely debauched clientele of a rather downmarket tavern. Finally, the photographer himself (presumably Shadow) is again only revealed in silhouette, half hidden behind part of a set of curtains which frame the scene (another metaphor – 'the theatre of life').

That this metaphor is further developed explicitly within similar generic texts can be seen by the following fairly typical extract from a book inspired by similar excursions to the underworld – the Reverend D MacColl's *Among the Masses*:

> Our first visit was to an upper room, which we reached by climbing half a dozen dirty, crazy stairs. From the upper staircase window we could see the old crow-stepped gables of neighbouring tenements, and the broken chimney pots over many a roof. My friend without ceremony lifted the latch, and stood like the sudden apparition from another world before the startled group within. Standing in his shadow, I photographed the faces and fixed the impression. The room was large, but with bare walls, and without chair or table. A few bricks in the fireplace had been blackened by the occasional fire. The boards of the 'set-in' bed had evidently been turned into fuel, and only a few rags and a little straw lay in the corner. Three persons sat

on the floor with a broken bottle and a couple of broken tea
cups. They were drinking as we entered, and a cup hung
suspended in the hand of one to be duly photographed. The
householder – a little wizened man of fifty – sat opposite the
door; his wife, about the same age, with a draggled dress and
dirty mutch, from which her untidy hair escaped, sat close to
him; and with his back to us sat a stranger in good black dress,
and with thin silky grey hair falling over a forehead that bore
the marks of some culture. We learned afterwards that he had
once been well off, because well to do, with a dozen men in his
employment; but here, under the spell of the old tempting spirit,
he was in the midst of another spree. The old wizened face
belonged to the Mission, and needed looked after.[3]

What this example demonstrates is the quite literal exposition of this
metaphor in practice. Shadow's prose paragraphs are also specifically rendered as a series of snapshots, Man *as* Camera. Shadow, at
the beginning of the era of representational science, accurately
precurses, as a representational metaphor, Farrow's camera eye.

That Shadow actually physically employed the process of
photography, is suggested by another extraordinary passage – the
story of the Match Boy – which has a well-known provenance.

Before us (a considerable distance west), stands a poor bare-
headed, barefooted boy – his noble brow overhanging a face
wildly mixed with vice and intelligence. His clothes are in taters,
and his waistcoat, kept together with difficulty by three un-
equally-yoked buttons, hides his dirty little shirt. He implores
us to 'buy a bawbee worth o' matches'. Curious to know his
brief but apparently chequered history, we take him aside,
when the following colloquy takes place...[4]

What follows is a sort of fabricated interview of the type made
popular by Mayhew and others in the early nineteenth century – a
form that presents itself as seemingly natural or conversational, but
in effect serves the purpose of recreating the common speech of the
subject as, if you like, a form of sociological data. Shadow then
concludes:

We need hardly say that, after the recital of so painful a tale, it
was a special pleasure to relieve the moderate necessities of this
poor city Arab. Oh that a John Pounds could only have seen
him, and secured him! – who knows what an ornament he
might then have proved to society. We engaged him for the
following Monday at a photographer's, and he now stands
before us, poor boy, with one hand hid among his torn
garments, while with the other he holds his matches...a duplicate
of his photograph being presented to him for his mother, we

asked him the same day her opinion, when he said – 'She thought it *owre true*' – and well she might; for, as the benevolent founder of Ragged Schools would certainly have said, he was the *'worst of little blackguards!'*[5]

What is being described here is a fairly common genre of Victorian photography – documentary portraits of street urchins and low-life characters, perhaps taken on admission to a Ragged School or Mission and often accompanied, for the edification of the masses, by another photograph of the reformed youngster, engaged in some useful trade, to form a 'before-and-after' set (notably in the prints circulated by Doctor Barnardo's homes). What is peculiar, however, is that the description is of a photograph that does not exist, or cannot be traced – only defined by the literary portrait supplied, generously, by Shadow. The effect of this is to incite an immense curiosity. The reader is positioned as if to see, to peer into the past. The text creates a sort of envious longing for Shadow's own privileged gaze. This text typifies a particular mid-Victorian mode of representing Glasgow's urban poor and a particular ethnographic practice that has distinct implications for Glasgow today.

We Only Live to Take Our Ease

Some ten years after Shadow's wanderings, a real body of photographic texts featuring Glasgow emerges with Thomas Annan's famous photographs of Glasgow's streets and closes – a corps of work that is taken now to typify or symbolise nineteenth-century Glasgow as surely as other great photographers – Stieglitz or Riis in New York (there is an interesting exchange in *Deathwatch* : 'Who was that still photographer who made dirty kids and ugly alleys look beautiful?'/ 'Jacob Riis'), or Brandt in north-east England – seem to especially reveal their own time and place.

Thomas Annan was the founder of a family firm of photographers that still exists in Glasgow today (still selling prints from their original plates). Between 1868 and 1871, Annan took photographs of the old closes of the east end of Glasgow, mostly around the High Street, which were built around the decaying buildings of the medieval town. Bound volumes of these prints were produced for the town council and framed copies were hung on the walls of Glasgow University and exhibited in the Kelvingrove museum. An edition of one hundred quarto-size copies was published by the Glasgow City Improvements Trust in 1878 and further editions, with additional plates, followed up to 1900.[1]

Most Glaswegians are familiar, at least subliminally, with Annan's work, but there is one popular misconception that should be scotched. Although Annan's work was commissioned by the trustees of the Glasgow City Improvements Trust, their notable exposure of east-end slums was not, as many believe, instrumental in the plans for demolition and improvement of the area realised in the 1870's and 80's. Annan's work, therefore, cannot be compared to other photographic projects directly involved in the legal process of instigating slum clearance – for example, the contemporary photographs of the Quarry Hill area of Leeds, investigated by John Tagg.[2] In fact, the Glasgow City Improvements Act of 1866 – derived from the City Improvement Bill introduced by the publisher Blackie in 1865 – had already decided on these plans. The ancient slums around High Street were removed and replaced by new tenements (to degenerate into the slums of the late twentieth century) by the end of the 1880's. These plans were partly predicated by the benevolence of Victorian philanthropists, but were due, in no small part, to commercial concerns – with the increasing demand for city centre space and rented housing, especially with the development of the railway centred around the top of the High Street.

Annan's work was purely documentary, and must be read in this light. This was an attempt to record a piece of vanishing social history. To satisfy the immense curiosity for the strange land of urban low-life which Shadow, provokes. Annan belongs quite definitely to the same ethnographic tradition. His work was, quite literally, a curiosity, an exposé of the slum underworld for the Victorian middle-classes unwilling, unlike Shadow to venture into the depths themselves. His readers were comfortable middle-class Victorians like himself – one of Annan's earlier volumes of photographic scenes (not 'the closes') carries the epithet:

> For Christian merchants we make our plea,
> The pulse of the business world are we;
> with tenants and servants at our command,
> And spending ever with liberal hand.
> Yet e'en by us how much has been won,
> For the cause of right. See what we have done!
> And say, in view of facts like these,
> Do we only live to take our ease?[3]

In one respect, Annan's photographs are similar to Shadow's prose passages – they have no political dimension, they are mere representation. Yet in many ways they are totally different. Firstly, they are not Shadow's social photographs 'taken by moonlight', but require long exposures in daylight even in the least gloomy and oppressive closes and wynds. They have no access to the inner sanctum of the tenement dweller (thus giving the lie to Cruikshank's inordinate claims for the camera's power of revelation). Secondly, whereas Shadow had some familiarity with the comparatively new form of the sociological interview, Annan has no facility to let his subjects speak – or to put his words in their mouths. Whereas in Shadow the plight of the masses is exemplified through the peculiar sufferings of chosen typical or stereotypical individuals, in Annan's photographs they remain the anonymous (and sometimes regimented) masses.

The way in which the slum dwellers themselves appear in Annan's photographs is especially interesting. Some photographs merely show the closes deserted, but these are the exception. Most feature people, usually posed and directly addressing the reader – usually these are individuals, leaning on a doorway, or small groups, huddled together, as, for example, in the photographs of 80 High Street or 29

Gallowgate. In one particularly effective study, of 118 High Street, the inhabitants are grouped and posed together, children sitting in front, women standing behind, with one solitary teenage boy breaking the exact symmetry of the group, as for a conventional group portrait. The distinctive difference is that, in the narrowest of alleyways, they are squeezed between the two grey walls that frame them and define the focus of the picture – between indefinite dark spaces of doorways in the foreground and a vague murky sky in the background. In one well-known study, 65 High Street, a young boy in a shiny bowler hat (lit from above), like a refugee from a Ragged School portrait, stands leaning on one wall. His double seems to appear in 37 High Street, carrying a water jug, slightly blurred. Characteristic of all the photographs are the children, or dogs, or occasional adults, who do not appear. Unwilling or unable to pose for the lengthy exposure time required, they appear as blurred ghosts, in various degrees of detail. Phantom inhabitants of the dingy underworld, they give Annan's photographs, more than anything else, their strange, unearthly quality and remind us of the representational nature of these illusory images. Perhaps not surprisingly, attempts were made to erase these ghosts from later editions of the prints. On nearly all of the photographs, even those of deserted closes, the inhabitants are represented by their very vestments – the washing that is suspended from every possible window (washing tubs, jugs and other paraphanelia also appear frequently despite the supposed unsanitary nature of the slum dwellers). These often form fantastic shapes, occasionally blurred in the image by an infrequent gust of wind. They constitute much of the interesting texture and pattern of the individual images. What we see is an illuminating but highly constructed view of these people, bereft of action, the top lighting gifting them neanderthal brows and lost chins. They appear perhaps disinterested, posed in a fashion, and docile. Anita Mozley,[4] in her commentary on the photographs comments: 'Their presence in his photographs, while evidently not unwelcome to (Annan) does not seem, either, to have been especially sought, and was probably occasioned by the imposing presence of this tall man and his cumbersome photographic apparatus from the world outside the closes. Even sanitary workers, doctors and teachers feared to venture into these dens without protection.' Nevertheless (and media exaggeration of supposed inner city dangers is prevalent to this day), these people, constructed by a discipline and technology beyond their immediate ken, constitute the most interesting aspect of this body of photographs. What has been constructed, through the texts themselves, is the exact antithesis of Cruikshank's engraving – no vice, no drunkenness, no crime – merely an orderly people, husbands, wives, children preoccupied with one thing – their washing!

Although many of these photographs are exceptional, one that seems to me especially remarkable and representative of the strange nature of Annan's work, is that of 46 Saltmarket. Not only because of the number of people in it (thirty) but, to my mind, because of the extraordinary disposition of the people portrayed.

No. 46, Saltmarket, Thomas Annan

Barthes has referred to two elements of a photograph – the studium, or the general interest of the *mise-en-scène* . In this photograph there is a great deal of interest – the expanse of windows in the cliff of tenements above, the pattern of the shattered panes, the diagonal upwards stretch of the handles of the barrow. And also the punctum, an element that is unexpected or difference – that figuratively pierces the general overall coherence of the scene. In this photograph the standing figure of a girl in the centre of the photograph, standing proudly, erect, arms akimbo, positively *displaying* herself to the camera is, undoubtedly, the punctum. But is this because she is bare-headed, the only female figure, or because she refuses to appear cowed – the characteristic mode of address of the tenement dweller, the categorised subject, or because, for some reason, she is more in focus, more finely detailed than the others. Here lies the strange paradox, for, in those days of long exposures, the foregrounded seated figures are still blurred. That she isn't must suggest that she remained more still, more frozen. In order to appear more alive, more modern, the subject must adopt the rigor mortis of death! The undeniable truth of these images is that the people portrayed, or specifically the more substantial inhabitants of these long-lived dwellings (now also defunct), are confined and defined by the very crumbling sandstone walls that surround them. Figures buttress the walls, merge into them in the grainy texture of the collodion plate. (A strange feature of early photographers – and especially the Scottish photographers, Hill, Adamson, Keith – was that their subject matter invariably consisted of either stone or flesh – the first, in the form of monuments or ruins, slowly weathered by the insistence of external forces, often still with us today, the second much more fragile and transient, prey to a relentless internal canker, now long gone.) Edwin Morgan was referring to a more recent period of slum clearance when he wrote:

A mean wind wanders through the backcourt trash.
Hackles on puddles rise, old mattresses
puff briefly and subside. Play-fortresses
of brick and bric-a-brac spill out some ash.
Four storeys have no windows left to smash,
but in the fifth a chipped sill buttresses
mother and daughter the last mistresses
of that black block condemned to stand, not crash.

However, the sense implied is, I feel, the same. Here we view living, breathing Glaswegians resolved into statues, as substantial as the stony caryatids on the tombs of the Necropolis – and as silent.

Both Shadow's work and Annan's can be classified as ethnography, a particular practice or representing and delineating people or cultures that really derives, in its accepted form, from the classificatory sciences born in the late eighteenth and early nineteenth century. Ethnographical representation implies, as scholars such as Foucault and Said have pointed out, a particular power relationship between the represented and the representer. The most common tool of this practice is to represent and define the subject of the enquiry as, literally, the 'other' – a people or race exhibiting characteristics that are structurally opposed to the characteristics of the culture or race of the observer – generally the supposed dominant ideology and culture of the 'civilised' world (in this case the Victorian middle classes). Thus, it is not surprising that would-be reformers of the time should refer to their fellow Glaswegians as 'arabs' or 'natives' (Shadow notes 'no nautical explorer ever fell among savages who looked with greater wonder at his approach'). In order for this distancing process to work, however, a certain form of representation may be implied. Perhaps Annan is at a disadvantage because his form of representation, photography, is more suited to representing his subject metonymical, or partially, through examples of their demeanour or habitat. Shadow, on the other hand, represents his subjects metaphorically – and that is the precise value of the photographic analogy he employs. In both cases, there is clearly a bias towards a supposed verisimilitude, in Shadow's case, however, this is more directly constructed by the text. The clearly paradoxical nature of this representational metaphor is not obvious to some commentators on Shadow's work. John McCaffrey, a historian who wrote the introduction to the modern reprint of the book, comments:

> In his role as the Shadow he is keenly observing but unobserved (see how George Cruikshank brings out this aspect in his frontispiece illustration). He strives as far as possible to be present but not in such an obtrusive way, as would be the case today with a television camera and crew, as to affect the behaviour of those whose circumstance he depicts. Like a social photographer (sic) he seeks to give the reader the true and exact image he sees through the senses of his own senses (sic)...the word pictures sometimes flash with vivid detail...[5]

McCaffrey's exquisite confusion over the use of Shadow's informing metaphor (especially in the infelicitous comparison with the television crew) is, unfortunately, not untypical of historians of Glasgow (or even Scotland) and the way that they employ textual evidence. The error is twofold – firstly, to accept Shadow's supposed objectivity at face value – rather than as a construction of the text itself. Secondly, to accept Shadow's compassion as a kind of authorial intent instead of, as we can see, a construction of the particular kind of institutional practice he brings to bear on his subjects. The same problem seems evident in a more recent commentary by Andrew Noble, a literary scholar who sees Shadow's collection as 'where the realistic technology of the camera undermined the corrupt literary analogies derived from painting on which sentimental Scottish writing depended,' and who notes, 'the squalor, destitution, alcoholism and prostitution of the Glasgow slums seem near incredible. We have by this time the remarkable Annan photographs to corroborate Shadow's evidence... His is a quite remarkable book in terms of its detail and compassion. The 'photographs' he takes are of a heart of darkness in slum Glasgow which needed only nocturnal exploration to reveal'.[6] Noble's insistence on Shadow's comparative realism, his compounding of the photography metaphor, and his readiness to conjoin 'squalor and destitution' with 'alcoholism and prostitution' ('corroborated' by Annan – which they are not; Annan's characters being alcoholics or prostitutes only by implication!) show that his commentary only functions *within* the distinctive institutional discourse of the original text.

Ethnographic representations during this period were well established in Scotland, the primary impulse being, as Malcolm Chapman[7] has so clearly shown, directed towards the Celtic fringe in the Highlands and islands and intent upon shaping the inhabitants, within an established romantic discourse, into the residue of an ancient, barbaric but heroic race. Ethnographic investigation into the inner world of the city slums was, however, as carefully and fully constructed, but with distinct differences. George Stocking, an American anthropologist, notes:

> From the perspective of contemporary middle-class observers, the primitivism at the bottom of the social scale now had a dual character. On the one hand, there was the rural primitivism of the pre-industrial world, marginalized in England and still flourishing on the Celtic fringe; on the other, there was the urban primitivism of preindustrial London, metastizing in every industrial town and city. The first, which was to be the subject matter of the science of folklore, could still be looked at through an elegiac filter of 'soft' primitivism, the more so as the blood sports of the villages were outlawed and the raucous visitations of Plough Monday were transformed into Plough Sunday services. But there were no traces of 'Merie England' to be found in the new city slums, which provided the subject matter of the urban reformer's science of social statistics. They remained, even in the process of reformation, a disturbing and alien phenomenon – so far removed from the amenities and the morality of civilized life that many observers, including Freidrich Engels and Henry Mayhew, were impelled to use

racial analogies to capture the sense of difference. Thus for
Engels the working classes were 'a race apart' – physically
degenerate, robbed of all humanity, reduced morally and
intellectually to near bestial condition, not only by economic
exploitation, but by competition and association with the
coarse, volatile, dissolute, drunken, improvident Irish, who
slept with their pigs in the stinking slums of Manchester. And
for Mayhew, the street folk of London were a 'nomad race'
without 'the least faculty of prevision', flouting the middle-class
ethic of sexual restraint and hard work, reduced to the terrible
alternation of 'starvation and surfeit'.[8]

In the investigation of Victorian 'philanthropists' the urban masses
have no folklore, no customs, no life-style, no *habiliment* . They are
simply constructed, we could say, under the double yoke of the need
to work and the need to worship (and in a superficial sense, the need
not to offend). All differences, all personality, all real life is subsumed
under a label whose name, ever shifting, may be vice, misery,
vicissitude, destitution, immorality or (even) misfortune. Shadow's
objectivity and his *compassion* are real in the sense that, in real life,
Alexander Brown probably intended to be both and very possibly
succeeded. But within the text they are both constructed – objectivity,
as we have seen, through the metaphoric structure, and compassion
within a specific discourse of charity that has its roots in a peculiarly
Victorian ideology.

Victorian concerns with charity have been mapped out in some
details by various scholars. Axiomatic to the popular model is the
acceptance that industrial society at this time required that a percentage of the population accepted their own essential poverty and,
consequently, inner city squalor. Charitable institutions arise to serve
a twofold purpose – to salve the conscience of the middle and upper-
classes represented by the growing band of philanthropists and
reformers concerned at the immediate plight of the poor, and to
achieve at least the implied consent of the masses to the social
hierarchy. This was achieved only partially through coercion, but
predominantly through the process of hegemony and the two main
instruments were the class system and religious morality.

Within this hegemonic discourse, the self-same reformers were
unable to see any cause for the misery of the poor but their own vice
and drunkenness. This is made especially clear by the work of the
Mission movement of the time. For example the Church of Scotland's
Commission on the Religious Condition of the People of 1891,
'received from the superintendent of the Glasgow City Mission what
it termed 'interesting glimpses – some of them painfully interesting –
of certain conditions of city life'. These included references to the

large number of brothels in the centre of Glasgow, as well as to other houses which 'cannot be designated as brothels' but to which 'young women go...in the evening for prostitution'. It also noted the activities of an organisation which gave free breakfasts on Sundays to waifs and strays, including 'many girls of that class who are just between losing and winning' and commented that there was 'a sadder class still'. The Commission clearly was aware that prostitution existed on a large scale in the cities, and wrote that 'its victims are legion', but its intelligence was not good: it was not able 'to estimate the full extent of the social evil; it walks in the dark, and in the city its paths are not known'.[9]

It is also clear in these revealing examples of Stocking's 'science of social statistics', from William Logan's *Moral Statistics of Glasgow in 1863* , which succinctly map out the absolute distinction between the day and night side of the city:

The Moral Statistics of Glasgow
To cash yearly offered by professedly
Christian Glasgow to Bacchus,   £1,184,412
To cash yearly offered by professedly
Christian Glasgow to Belial,   £ 819,183
                                                 £2,003,595

'Hear, O heavens; and give ear, O earth' – six parts given to the devil, and one part to Jesus Christ! – six times more for hell than for heaven! by the commercial capital of the most religious nation in the world, by the city whose glorious motto is, – 'Let Glasgow flourish by the preaching of the Word', and at a time when one of her ministers, at the public meeting of the Benevolent Society, declared little children were to be seen gathering turnip skins with which to allay the pangs of their hunger. 'O that our head were waters, and our eyes fountains of tears, that we might weep day and night' for the madness of our people![10]

That the misfortunes of the poor could be commonly ascribed to drink, especially in the cities (sexual promiscuity was especially characteristic of the rural working class) and thus relatively easily prevented is, as here, the accepted nostrum of the times. The paradoxical nature of this type of textual evidence must be apparent to even the most hidebound historian. And it is exemplified in the fact that all these observations and statistics relate only to what might be termed the 'leisure' or extra-mural interests of the community. What always remains hidden relates to production. It is the work available and the wages paid to the people through those institutions whose interests are also close to the hearts of the businessmen, philanthropists (and publicans whose own weekly portion derived from the generous offerings of those devotees of Bacchus) which, through its self-evident inadequacy, disabled the working classes and divorced them from the exercise of self-help so beloved of the city missionaries. Ethnographic photographs of rural communities often associate the people with objects of labour – ploughs, or spinning wheels. The urban masses are not even afforded that small favour – they are clearly more directly thirled, as they appear in the photographs of Annan, to the battered, desperate wreckage of their own insufficient 'leisure' environment – frozen, as the collodion gells, in patterns of grainy grey against the pock-marked carcass of their own sandstone walls.

There is a message in this Mission literature that is not specifically political or sociological and is exemplified in a truly extraordinary novel called *City Echoes*.[11] This story is set in 'pagan' Glasgow:

> The localities where many of those Mission Halls are built are in most instances the very antipode of human civilisation... Glaring taverns, mysterious loan offices accessible only by stairs as dark and slippery as the lives and fortunes of those they aid with their momentum to misery and chaos, glare every-where with their lurid witchery. Closes gaping, black and grim in the sickly gaslight, have at their entrances little knots of suspicious looking characters. Young men closely shaven, bearing the unmistakeable prison crop, the greasy cap and muffler... bare-footed girls and half-naked women with disfig-ured looks, ragged children and barking curs, all mingle in a horrid melee.[12]

It is story of two newspaper vendors called Jim and Jock who sink to the lower depths of slum society. Jim is saved by the Mission and returns home one night from a meeting to find his drunkard mother lying dead on the floor. He sets the fire and makes his supper:

> There were two companies in that house that night from the extremes of the unseen universe – a deputation from Heaven and a deputation from Hell... Round the prostrate form of the mother whose soul had fled affrighted while she lay in her final drunken agony, there formed a circle of triumphant demons... Round that mother's son another triumphant circle formed...[13]

Jim says a prayer, coughs, and dies in heavenly transport:

> Jim's little storm-beaten body will henceforth rest in the employments of another City. He himself will grow evermore in understanding and in excellence – reaching evermore the higher, highest light within that City whose foundations have been from of old, and for ever.[14]

Jock, however, turns to thievery and has several adventures before he, too, is converted. He rejects his woman who 'was too ripe in old usages to take in "Washing" or turn a "Mangle", converts his criminal companions, and ends the novel as he looks out over Glasgow: 'There spread out beneath him the same familiar City and scene – but how changed! He saw with transfigured eyes.'[15]

I have more to say about this peculiarly Manichean view of the city transparently presented here – and exemplified in Shadow's day and night side of the city's character, but the main message of this type of literature is of the ready availability of redemption in Victorian Glasgow, a redemption that, despite the massive slum clearance and building programme of the 1870's and 80's, does not seem, in real life, to have proffered itself to the mass working classes of the city in any tangible form, or altered their common lot one whit. In one sense the improvements were merely cosmetic – the City Improvement Trust demolished far more houses than it built, rents continued to rise, and Irish immigrants continued to arrive. Yet, within a few years, by the year 1888, Glasgow, at least in popular belief, had been improved, or improved itself, to the extent that it could present itself to the outside world as the model of the Victorian city – an international centre of commerce, industry, and enterprise. In fact, the real starting point for my investigation of contemporary Glasgow is the year 1888 and this year is important for several reasons. Thomas Annan was in his grave only a matter of months, yet the major redevelopment of most of the east-end had taken place. It was the heyday of the grey sandstone tenement, Charles Rennie Mackintosh ventured on his career as an apprentice draughtsman, municipal Glasgow was thriving and the building of the City Chambers was complete, the first Rangers/ Celtic match took place and, more than anything, it was the year of the first International Exhibition in Kelvingrove Park. Glasgow, the second city of the Empire, was at the peak of its prosperity and achievement. The period from the first exhibition until the second, in 1901, has been identified as the apogee of Glasgow's industrial and commercial affluence.

We can only imagine what the Glasgow of 1888 was really like. If we pass by from the crown of Glasgow's Necropolis to Provand's Lordship and the High Street, possibly traversing the supposed medieval underground tunnel or the trickling Molendinar, streets away from the crowded travails of Annan's street urchins, we come upon the site of Glasgow Royal Infirmary. Here Lister pioneered antiseptic in the centre of the cholera-ridden closes. Modern medicine was born while the Molendinar stank from the effluent of Glasgow's industrial heyday. Millions died, a few, carefully selected, interned in the Necropolis itself. There is, however, no emotion in this scene. This is a monument to the Victorian institution – not to its inhabitants or victims. Today, the greatest physical momento of Victoria's Glasgow is the massive bulk of the new Royal Infirmary rebuilt, on the same site, in 1905. Dwarfing the cathedral. Built to an inhuman scale. The grey rectangular blocks, sooted from the innumerable chimneys of east end factories, support a honeycomb of interior rooms, cocoons of tiled anaesthesia. The major outlook from the serried ranks of windows – the monolithic mausoleums of the Necropolis. *Momento Mori*. Its anaesthesia, its white-tiled, high ceilinged theatres of anatomical display, its plastic bubbles, its permanence. It is, in many ways, the most impressive building in the city (although it is completely ignored, for some spurious arbitration of taste, in some major architectural guides to the city). And it is mysterious – its ways as inscrutable as those of the cathedral precinct, chinks in stone coffins through which you can peer, with stone-scraped knees, to glimpse the bones of saints, the mort-locked graves or the chiselled eulogies to whole families or generations of landed gentry. The trinity of cathedral, Necropolis, and Infirmary locked, from my perspective, in the self-same discourse.

There is something in the Victorian celebration of death that is a celebration of life itself, or, at least, of substantial things – of wealth or privilege accumulated during life. In a way, for the Victorians and Edwardians, Glasgow's favourite sons, whether famous forebears preserved in noble tombs, or the city notables ensconced in positions with financial or political clout, are exactly equivalent to the sturdy stone faced edifices of the commercial city – the Trades' Hall, the Athenaeum, the County Buildings, the Union Bank, that narrate the city's success in enterprise – second city of the Empire. So, nineteenth-century volumes picture the city gentry metonymic of the city's success in plates engraved from steel – each portrait in full face but slightly angled to avoid direct address (the profile is only the signifier of the criminal, the outcast, the deviant). In 1888, *Tweed's Glasgow Handbook* [16] was published. Notably, it portrays the city's buildings in slight perspective, in the same fashion. Relegated to the adverts in the addendum (printed on coloured paper) are pictured the commercial or industrial institutions, Campbell Blair's Wholesale and Retail Establishment (tea, coffee, sugar, wines and spirits) or Stewart's Steam Dyeing and Cleaning Works, represented in inaccurate perspective, its chimney spouting a plume of black smoke, 'blacks dyed for mourning in three days'.

Absent from Tweed's celebration of Glasgow's Victorian edifices, however, are the actual dwellings of the Victorian Glaswegians. More than any single development, the arrival of the classic Glasgow tenement made its mark on the city's landscape. The shape, the character, and the omnipresence of the tenement type has informed and shaped the experience of Glaswegians over more than a century.

Frank Walker comments:

> The tenement is woven into the fabric of Glasgow, held fast in
> the 'pleached alleys' that cross and recross the urban landscape.
> No-one brought up in the city before the end of the last war can
> forget a childhood lived out beneath its sandstone cliffs. It has
> been like that for generations: football, peevers, or 'kick-the-
> can' in the streets, cries of alarm or admonition ringing across
> the back courts, washhouses to climb, coal cellars to hide in,
> toilets on the landings, worn pipeclayed steps, wally tiles, the
> first cuddle in the close. As the *mise-en-scène* of urban life and
> experience it is the 'foursquare' tenement block that tessellates
> the mosaic of Glasgow's robust culture. Hind, Sharp, Gray, and
> others, have all needed something of its security as the grid on
> which the patterned play of character and narrative might be
> plotted. The canvases of Eardley and Morrison have held and
> honoured its hugely palpable presence. But there is, too, an-
> other picture, another reality. A crumbling world of spalling
> sandstone and damp walls, torn sheets flapping in the grimy
> drizzle, wind gusting through doorless closes, rats and vagrants
> picking at the middens, blind and bloody violence or sullen
> *Weltschmerz* on the street corner – the dilapidated tenements of
> the slums.[17]

That the peculiar architecture environment of the tenement cannot be
separated from social and cultural life is a consideration that has, to
a great extent, escaped the examination of architectural historians.
Frank Worsdall's interesting book, *The Tenement as a Way of Life*,
despite its title and the sections on the social, economic and legal
background of the tenement, has very little real consideration of the
tenement as a concept, as a social and cultural structure for living.
Instead, his detailed study is based on a single historical precept, the
destruction of tradition, and his style is elegiac – suggesting an overwhelming sense of loss:

> Tenement, these days is a dirty word and is used almost
> exclusively to describe a slum property. It is this attitude of
> mind which has been responsible for the destruction of so much
> of our heritage…this policy of destruction, that something new
> is always better than something old, is wrong and can be clearly
> seen to be so in the vandalism, the lack of community spirit, the
> general hopelessness and helplessness of life in a high rise flat or
> a monster housing scheme.[18]

There are several half-truths evident in this approach. Certainly,
Glasgow has been typified over the last twenty-five years or so, by an
undue regard for the new. For various reasons, the meticulous
preservation work that has enabled some other towns and cities to

maintain much of their architectural heritage has gone by the board in Glasgow. The city has suffered from a tendency to continually start afresh, forsake the past, and follow, blindly, the particular architectural fancy of the time. However, to blame the Modernist housing estate *per se* for many of the social problems confronting the city is not quite fair. It is generally understood that many of the housing schemes of the 1950's and 60's employed, as their basic unit, a version of the tenement style of three or four storey blocks with close access. The idea that this form of high density housing would function well in the fresher, more open environment of the planned housing schemes on the outskirts of the city proved notoriously wrong. There is a potent narrative that informs all Glaswegians of their collective tenement experience. It is that tenement life was the essence of the collective community, friendly, coherent, supportive, etc. The coming of the housing schemes, notably the high rise flat, destroyed this community spirit and it has never returned. In one of Adam McNaughton's most popular humorous songs, this message is perpetuated:

I'm a skyscraper wean, I live on the nineteenth flair,
But I'm no' gaun oot tae play ony mair,
'Cause since we moved tae Castlemilk, I'm wastin' away,
'Cause I'm gettin' wan less meal every day

Oh ye cannae fling pieces oot a twenty storey flat,
Seven hundred hungry weans'll testify to that,
If it's butter, cheese or jeely, if the breid is plain or pan,
The odds against it reaching earth are ninety-nine tae wan

The truth is somewhat different. The tenement system is not particularly suited to community life or close relationships with neighbours (even less so than the open close or vennel system it replaced). Devices constructed to ensure better communication – such as 'windae-hinging' or 'piece-flinging' – were more the efforts of a determined community to protect a way of life against the architectural hostility of a rigid system than anything else. The high-rise flat has its common spaces as well – for example the lifts – and so do most dwellings mistakenly based on original tenement designs. Whatever social or cultural developments led to the breakdown of the so-called 'tenement spirit' have much more complex origins than in mere architectural innovation.

The Glasgow tenement is not, in fact, a particularly egalitarian or uniform system. Tenements flats have many different styles and sizes. The smallest, squeezed behind the stairwell, are called single-ends. The very tenement facade is a sham, with various devices employed to hide the fact that, in the perfect elevation, the windows must be different sizes. Tenement schemes, in their own way, preserved and

perpetuated social inequality. The vital point about the tenement
type, as Walker is aware, is that it is not merely a building but a kind
of machine for living, a form of social engineering that cannot be
considered apart from both the social and ideological determinants
of its conception and, more importantly, its development and use
within the actual living tradition of Glasgow in the last hundred
years, and its part in the mythology of the city that I will examine later
in this essay. This point has been made clear by the work of the
sociologist Jaques Donzelot on urban housing in nineteenth-century
Paris:

> [there was formulated] a second objective: to design a housing
> unit small enough so that no 'outsider' would be able to live in
> it, yet large enough for the parents to have a space separate from
> their children, so that they might watch over them in their
> occupations without being observed in their own intimate
> play...The objective was to reduce the 'social' part of the
> lodging in favor of spaces set aside for the parents and for the
> children. The bedroom was to become its virtual center, one
> that would not be seen by the children. According to
> Fonssagrives, it was 'the little capital of the peaceable kingdom
> of the household'. What was needed for the children was 'a
> room adjoining that of the parents, which would deprive secret
> observation of the oppressive aspect it might have were it more
> apparent, while preserving its effectiveness.'[19]

Similarly, the rationale of Glasgow tenement design can be described
in terms of 'social' space and personal interaction within the context
of the family group. However, in Glasgow, one further step was to
shape the city's distinctive form. The tenement as a system was a
product only of the last quarter of the nineteenth century, developed
simultaneously with it was the first seemingly rationalised planning
of the city centre, the grid-iron system set east/west and north/south
and commonly known as the Glasgow grid. This was a radical
departure from the more organic growth of the medieval city, built
along the natural lines of the river. Anyone walking in Glasgow's city
centre today cannot fail to be aware of the strict directional nature of
the byways. Because of this, perhaps, Glaswegians have, above all
city dwellers, a heightened perception of the absolute values of the
points of the compass. Glasgow clearly has an east end and a south
side and main thoroughfares are seen as strictly following compass
points – Duke Street, Eglinton Street, Argyle Street, Ingram Street –
giving the popular conception of the city's topography a distinct
structure. Along most of these streets and many others, the tenement
landscape still informs Glasgow's townscape in 1988, but, because of
the two-dimensional nature of the tenement terrace, there is an

unfortunate by-product – the gable end. More often than not the product of demolition, it lays bare the fundamental, unornamented nature of the living space – graphic, naked cross-section. It is hardly surprising that some years ago, artists were commissioned to paint these naked spaces (some now well-known, such as John Byrne and Alasdair Gray). They adorned the gable-ends with geometric patterns and trompe d'oeil. With this display, on an extravagant scale, the wound is cauterised, the circle made whole, a thin veneer of culture covers the transparent stone membrane (In 1990, the city authorities plan a more transient display – several artists will be commissioned to produce images on photographic slides which will be projected on to gable ends).

This is the urban text employed as a cloakroom for clever or clichéd representational modes, but a much more fundamental and serious attempt has been made in recent years to alter the cityscape. Slowly, inexorably, at an unknown cost, without an articulated cause, attempts have been made to tinker with the Modernist land-scape, to fill in the naked slabs, the spaces, the principles of modernist architecture.

The award-winning Basil Spence flats in the Gorbals have been drastically altered – strange, occasionally arched pitched roofs perch like party hats on their summits, the vast verandah spaces invaded by brightly coloured shafts, the cantilevered terraces, the real guts of the design, denied their structural inevitability by painted designs. The Sauchiehall Street Centre has an added tubular and glass porch, its interior remodelled to make it equivalent to the true 80's shopping mall, without the integrity of the real thing. Elsewhere, the pitched roofs, the fake dormers, the brightly coloured tubes and painted concrete shapes abound. Like the gable-end (but infinitely more serious in purpose) painted shapes reaching skywards, narrowing or widening to deny the true vertical, try to break up the vast rectilinear slabs.

This is fine, if we can afford it, but one wonders what exactly the purpose is. It serves as pure design, a conversation piece, splashing colour onto the monotone cityscape. What two-dimensional design cannot do, however, is truly alter three-dimensional shape. Nor can a facade reshape an interior, or a pitched roof make a multi-storey block into a pre-war villa. The truth is, that the great Modernist project has so little to do with design that such facile innovations have little or no effect on the overall schema. Modernist housing in the sixties and seventies was, as was its predecessor in the late nineteenth century, an exercise in social engineering. Whether we talk of panoramas or cityscape or the perspective view of schemes or buildings, what remains hidden to the observer, the outsider, is the internal perspective, the living space, the experience of existence, of being there. Quarter of a million city dwellers who have little or no say in the shaping of the urban cityscape, have only their private lives to design within the ineluctable logic of the city environment. They are the anonymous, invisible protagonists of city style. Thinking back to Morgan's poem, what the 1970's and 80's have perfected is this metamorphosis to stone, to fabric, to concrete. The perfect invisible inhabitants of the painted city.

Perhaps, then, there is not so much of a difference between the Glasgow of 1888 and the Glasgow of 1988. We know, at least, that one is inexorably shaped from the other. I know, too, that sometime around 1888 the all-encompassing Glasgow grid extended itself unremittingly over the plains and drumlins of what is now the city centre until it met the irregular, older area around the High Street and the Necropolis. Its message was carried further to the east by the unwavering filament of George Street leading on to Duke Street, into Dunchattan Street, and up the stepladder past McIntosh Street, Fisher Street, and Edmund Street, to Eveline Street. And so a new tenement estate was born, on the old lands of Dennistoun, and there also, I was born, some sixty-odd years later. And so the Glasgow of 1888 is also a part of my personal heritage.

The Glasgow that I Used to Know

Round about 1975, Glasgow Corporation Housing Department published a book called *Farewell to the Single End*.[1] The subject was the massive slum clearance undertaken at that time and the replacement of the traditional tenement with new Modernist housing schemes. Ominously, with the peculiarly Scottish propensity for hubris, the new housing pictured and lauded in its pages as the height of modern chic – notably the notorious Hutchesontown E blocks, since demolished – have themselves degenerated into slums, or at least ghettos of underprivilege, poverty and unemployment. The greatest mistake was that the front cover portrayed a new, fashionable four-in-a-block housing development with, superimposed in the centre, one of Annan's photographs of old closes. The single end was not a product of Annan's Glasgow, but of later tenement plans. The lesson not learned by the planners and developers was that one generation's grand plan grows into the next generation's social problem. It is a lesson that has still to be learned.

However, it is in the late eighties and early nineties that the Annan canon is finally recontextualised. Today, in Glasgow shops you can purchase Annan's photograph of No. 65 High Street in postcard form. Notably, the photograph is bleached and rendered in sepia (unlike the straightforward black and white of the original prints). As if to quell any doubts, the reverse gives some details under the heading 'Art Cards'. One generation's misery incarnate becomes another's consumable style. Today, shop windows are stocked with Annan prints framed for domestic consumption and countless city centre pubs and restaurants mount Glasgow's old streets and closes on their walls.

The potent force that enables the recuperation of these images is nostalgia. The original meaning of nostalgia, as given by the Oxford English Dictionary is 'a form of melancholia caused by prolonged absence from one's home or country'. In fact, the term derives from the work of Johannes Hofer who diagnosed the condition in 1688 (although the German *heimweh* and the French *maladie du pays* were already established) as 'a continuous vibration of animal spirits through those fibres of the brain in which the impressed traces of ideas of the Fatherland still cling'. Symptoms included not only 'a bemused look...the near impossibility of getting out of bed, an obstinate silence, the rejection of food and drink, emaciation, marasmus and death', but also the adhesion of the lungs to the thorax. Treatment included leeching, purges, emetics, blood-letting, hypnosis and opium.[2] The pathological definition has, however, in the not too distant past, been pre-empted by another. The word has been translated to the synchronic, as opposed to the diachronic mode, to mean, in general terms, 'longing for the past'. Accompanying this shift, from the geographical to the temporal, is also a disassociation of nostalgia with 'melancholia' or disease, and a clear reassociation with the concept of pleasure. As Robert Hewison points out, 'the emotional equivalent of pastiche is nostalgia, which deliberately falsifies authentic memory into an enhanced version of itself. It is a strangely powerless emotion, a sweet sadness conditioned by the knowledge that the object of recall cannot – indeed, must not – be recovered.'[3]

Possibly the most blatant use of nostalgia in a Glasgow context is in another song by Adam McNaughtan, an English teacher, local historian and powerful folksinger whose own songs have been popular since the sixties:

Oh where is the Glasgow where I used tae stey,
The white wally closes done up wi' pipe cley;
Where ye knew every neighbour frae first floor tae third,
And tae keep your door locked was considered absurd.

Do you know the folk staying next door tae you?
And where is the wee shop where I used tae buy
A quarter o' totties, a tupenny pie,
A bag o' broken biscuits an' three totty scones,
An' the wumman aye asked, 'How's you maw getting on?'
Can your big supermarket give service like that?

And where is the wean that once played in the street,
Wi' a jorrie, a peerie, a gird wi' a cleek?
Can he still cadge a hudgie an' dreep aff a dyke,
Or is writing on walls noo the wan thing he likes?
Can he tell Chickie Mellie frae Hunch, Cuddy, Hunch?

And where is the tram-car that once did the ton
Up the Great Western Road on the old Yoker run?
The conductress aye knew how tae deal wi' a nyaff –
'If ye're gaun, then get oan, if ye're no, then get aff!'
Are there ony like her on the buses the day?

And where is the chip shop that I knew sae well,
The wee corner cafe where they used tae sell
Hot peas and brae an' MacCallums an pokes
An' ye knew they were Tallies the minute they spoke:
'Dae ye want-a-da raspberry ower yer ice-cream?'

Oh where is the Glasgow that I used tae know,
Big Wullie, wee Shooey, the steamie, the Co.,
The shilpet wee bauchle, the glaiket big dreep,
The ba' on the slates, an' yer gas in a peep?
If ye scrape the veneer aff, are these things still there?

This is well worth quoting in full as it is a realisation of what has been
called 'stairheid' nostalgia *par excellence*. It follows the same line as
much of McNaughtan's work in suspiciously opposing anything that
is modern in favour of what seems older or traditional. This sort of
thing is easy prey to parody – as can be seen with this version by Jim
McLean:

Where is the Glasgow I used to know?
The tenement buildings that let in the snow,
Through the cracks in the plaster the cold wind did blow,
And the water we washed in was fifty below.

We read by the gaslight, we had nae TV,
Hot porridge for breakfast, cold porridge for tea,
And some weans had rickets and some had TB...[4]

And so on. Now notably, McLean's version has not been so successful
nor is as interesting as McNaughtan's. We can observe, upon examination, that, although the experiences mentioned by McLean are
invariably unpleasant, those related by McNaughtan are not necessarily particularly pleasant or inviting in themselves. Nostalgia is not
particularly fussy about such things. The pleasure to be gained here
is the particular pleasure of remembering – or the exercise of memory,
even in relation to a distinctly false or imagined past. In
McNaughtan's song the pleasure is compounded through the constant use of traditional dialect or slang terms – remitting pleasure
through the selective mouthing of the language of the past. This borne
in mind, it is not too far-fetched to suggest that McLean's version, far
from subverting McNaughtan's intended message, actually supports it.

Another gross example of the same process at work can be seen in a
play that has been popular and successful in the 1980's, playing
throughout the country and recently adapted for television – Tony
Roper's *The Steamie*. This musical play works around a comparatively
simple scenario. One Hogmanay, a group of women meet in the local
washhouse. Here they indulge in fantasy, camaraderie, and glasses of
sherry, discovering a sense of belonging and community that is appar-

ently lacking in their drab, unfulfilling everyday lives. The play is
savagely anti-misogynist, the men are shadowy background figures
incapable of selfless behaviour and constantly threatening physical or
mental abuse.

The setting itself is crucial. The steamie reflects not only the
compartmentalised physical nature of their tenement life, and the
women's thirldom to mindless repetitive labour (they never seem to
get any further on with their washing), but is itself a reflection of the
institutional nature of their life. The characters are representative, of
different ages and religions – the common bond is their work (Mrs
Culfeathers is praised because even at her advanced age she can do as
much work as the rest) – but they are each apportioned a stall, literally
a 'cell' in the play's parlance. Within their cells, they communicate
down the line in a linear fashion. In order, however, for them to really
join together they must move from their cells to a more open central
area where they dance together and where a chorus of washerwomen
echo their sentiments.

Although the play is arguably innovative and anarchic in the way
the women reassess their own situation and challenge the dominance
of patriarchy ('men are a' very clartie in their persons'), it also serves
to demonstrate the characters' thirlage within the overwhelmingly
powerful domestic paradigm. For the dreams and fantasies they
choose to indulge in cannot separate themselves from idylls of
domesticity. Therefore, Mrs Culfeathers's finest memory is of
Glasgow Green 'with the rows and rows of washing hanging from the
lines – yon was a marvellous sight'. Her image of community and
companionship is quixotically merged with this domestic reverie
when she imagines the men's shirts and the women's dresses waving
at each other. The young idealistic Doreen's only ambition is to get
a house with a washing machine and a view from the kitchen ('You're
no wantin' much, are ye?') She has, it turns out, put her name down
for a house in Drumchapel. Her desires are hilariously exemplified in
a dream parody of a Hollywood romance – *Dream Come True* – in
which, despite the classic romantic scenario (Doreen is a movie-goer)
the words of the song return to the limited perspective of tenement
domesticity making a perverse contrast between the idyllic images of
the Hollywood dream machine and the realised utopia of the
Drumchapel housing scheme.

The reader needs some extra cultural knowledge to appreciate this
point. As straightforward naturalistic drama *The Steamie* verges on
the dangerously banal, as a specifically *nostalgia* piece, drawing on
both a general move in the eighties towards fifties nostalgia and the
peculiar 'Shoes Were for Sunday' brand of tenement romanticism, it
clearly fits into a distinct genre. The only nod toward serious social

comment that seems to make this mixture more justifiable than sheer self-indulgence comes in the apparent challenge to the dominant values of patriarchy. But this is hardly developed in a real sense, and is finally subsumed by another, more fundamental, if also more hegemonic, discourse – the idea of the tenement dwellers as a perfect community ('None of us are better than a good and honest neighbour'), as they go off, somehow more fulfilled through the day's labour, to wish their neighbours a good New Year.

These same characters – frumpy housewives in aprons, curlers and headscarves, and their men, in braces and bonnets, populate the cartoons of Willie Gall which have appeared daily in the *Evening Times* for many years (following on from a tradition started by the legendary Glasgow cartoonist Bud Neill).[5] Arguably, Gall's cartoons, like *The Steamie*, are pro-women – in that the housewives are portrayed as long-suffering, naive in wordly matters, but perspicacious as far as their own affairs are concerned. The men are invariably stupid, indolent, and either boorish or inconsequential. Their typical posture is either slumped on an armchair with a can of beer wearing a vest and displaying tattoos and beer bellies, or slouched cowering in front of their mistresses. The comedy is invariably reductive. Typical ploys are either to gently mock the pretensions of ordinary working people ('How many times huv ah tae tell ye it's RED wine wi' pie and chips?', 'Am ah puttin' you doon fur a Porsche 924 or a pair of socks?', 'Ah tell ye this – ye widnae catch me goin' on a state visit tae Japan!') or often, to take a cue from current affairs and to reduce a potentially serious topic to inconsequence by contextualising it within the extremely limited perceptions of the characters ('Is it true, madame, that you once played bingo in South Africa?', 'Ah want a go-slow train set!', 'Don't panic if ye hear a bang, Jimmy, it'll jist be anither works shuttin' doon'.) As these examples make clear, the humour is not primarily visual other than to signal the obvious stereotypes – the be-frocked, slippered housewife, hair in curlers, or the slovenly husband, immobile in front of the television smoking a cigarette (or, more recently, the spiky-haired punk dropout).

This repetitive, occasionally witty, often predictable stuff may raise a muted laugh, but there is a more serious point. The typical inhabitants of Glasgow portrayed by Gall inhabit a very cramped universe indeed and view the comings and goings of the world from an extremely limited perspective. The obvious comparison is with the urban kailyard – a form of writing, derived from the work of the so-called Kailyard school of writers such as Barrie and Crockett at the end of the eighteenth century, whose world of narrow-minded, small-town characters is typified by couthiness and sentimentality. The development of a sentimental discourse within contemporary urban

representations is mooted by Cairns Craig – 'is the nostalgia of the
late 19th century for the harsh religious security of the parish echoed
by our own nostalgia for the harsh working class ghettos of the inner
city, the certainty of human warmth amidst violence and poverty in
the latter matched by the certainty of salvation amidst suffering in the
former?'[6] In this context, however, there is a distinct difference – for,
unlike the kailyard writers, who ensure that both they and the
putative reader are placed in a position of superiority, Gall doesn't
purely disparage or poke fun at his characters. In fact, to some extent
Gall's characters elicit sympathy, for their long-suffering ways ex-
emplify some of the trials of everyman. In their trite pronouncements
is something of the wisdom of the fool.

Generally industrial relations, international affairs, etc. are of no
consequence in Gall's cartoon world and flippancy is the keynote.
The same overwhelming tone is apparent in the foreword penned by
the Glasgow journalist Cliff Hanley:

> To be perfectly serious, and even solemn, the Industrial Revo-
> lution was one of the great forces in shaping Glasgow and the
> Glaswegians. What had started as a wee fishing village with a
> cathedral and a few weavers suddenly exploded into being the
> Second City of the Empire (though, as some irreverent keelies
> pointed out, it was also the First City of the Pavilion and the
> Theatre Royal).
>
> It was an up-and-down affair, of course. Industries came and
> industries went. In the first half of this century, it all had a
> spurious atmosphere of permanence. Heavy industry was here
> to stay forever. The hammer's ding-dong was the Song of the
> Clyde and all that, and paddle-steamer passengers sailing down
> the Clyde got as much excitement out of waving to the riveters
> as they would get from seeing the magic waters of the Firth.
>
> Beardmore's Forge was the centre of the industrial world.
> North British Locomotives, all that, and the rich sulphur-laden
> smoke that gave the tenements their proud patina and had
> generations coughing and spluttering proudly.
>
> So nothing stays the same, and just as well, you may say.
> Factories and shipyards evaporated before our very eyes. But
> that is all a bit of the great Glasgow saga too. Without
> consciously analysing it, the common five-eight Glaswegian
> grew up knowing that slumps and catastrophes were always
> liable to be waiting round the next corner, and it was that
> certainty, or uncertainty, that shaped him, and her. We go
> through life braced for the next disaster, so that every disap-
> pointment is a delightful surprise. On the other hand, when
> slump strikes we can say 'Ah telt ye', and feel quite smug.[7]

There is a fundamentally serious point here, but it is drowned in a deluge of clever journalistic impartiality. There is a great deal of mythology employed – the famous Scottish put down ('ah kent your faither'), the tenements' proud patina, the Glaswegian approach to adversity (between Kiplingesque stoicism and comic pessimism). Yet, Hanley's history of Glasgow may as well be a history of Toytown. There is nothing real. There is a degree of wish-fulfilment. Glasgow can be anything you like – but always fun, always wonderful, always an object of interest and of curiosity.

Hanley is an old hand at this style of clever lightweight writing – he first came to prominence with an amusing, semi-autobiographical account of Glasgow called *Dancing in the Streets* and now his particular approach has really come of age in the Glasgow of the eighties. An example of his somewhat crazed style can be found in the introduction to a unusual book published recently entitled *Glasgow: A Celebration*:

> It doesn't take a starry-eyed romantic to detect in Glasgow of the Eighties an urge to celebrate. Celebrate what is not entirely clear, in the way the old industries were right there to be weighed and measured. But the reality of Glasgow, once entwined with those industries, was something of its own, and not just a by-product of furnaces and forges. More than most cities, Glasgow was to its people a sensation, a twist of the mind, a quirky view of the universe and a cheerful tolerance of human failings...

It is fairly typical of Hanley and his followers to renounce material things and dismiss real problems (the collapse of Glasgow's heavy industry) and laud the more nebulous supposed virtues of the mythical (or mystical) Glasgow spirit. This paragraph exemplifies that approach. There follows an extravagant eulogy of contemporary Glaswegians featuring the merits of Billy Connolly ('outrageous, subversive'), Michael Kelly ('Has contributed dramatically to the sheer pleasure of the city'), Edwin Morgan ('no dusty academic'), Alasdair Gray ('impossible'), Liz Lochhead ('a bloodless, feminist revolution'), Jack House ('goes on for ever'). Encapsulated in these contemporary worthies, Glasgow is an image of the perfect land: 'But Glasgow is not only composed of its own, by the tough new wave of poets, the Leonards, the Mulrines, the McDougalls, by its own writers and pundits. It has a dangerously seductive influence on incomers who can't find what native Glaswegians can ever have to complain about. People coming in from the East, from Germany and France get quickly dazzled and conquered.' Carried into some sort of ecstatic dwaum with his own rhetoric, Hanley uses mock Scripture to elevate the city to truly mythical levels: 'Let us now praise famous

men, and our fathers that begot us. And let us celebrate the grim, grey,
glorious, gorgeous Glasgow that hath made mortal life a hilarity on
earth.'[8]

Cliff Hanleyism is rampant in contemporary Glasgow. It is
expressed in superlatives and hyperbole. It is the notion that the city
is a giant funfair. The feeling that we are all continually sharing a
grand joke. The interesting thing is that the postulator of this sort of
crude fare can both be of the common folk, but also, somehow, stand
apart from them as a greater representative of the city spirit – he can
be what has been sometimes called a 'Mr Glasgow'. Mr Glasgow was
originally a theatrical term – the sobriquet of Tommy Morgan, the
comedian – but in recent years it has also become a journalistic term.
The *Evening Times*, for example, runs a page headed 'Mr Glasgow'
– not, as you may think, the work of one writer but of a succession
of journalists. The term now has taken the meaning of an experienced
knowledgeable figure educated in the city ways – an elder statesman
of Glasgow journalism, the city cognizant. In this way there are many
Mr Glasgows – the erstwhile Pat Roller of the *Evening Citizen*, the
late acerbic James Sanderson of talk-in fame. Jack McLean, the self-
styled Urban Voltaire holding court at Heraghty's Bar could be one,
as could the late Charles Oakley, at his office desk with the captains
of industry, or Jack House, chewing mullet in his stall at the Rogano,
or the ubiquitous Cliff Hanley.

There are too many Mr Glasgows. I am instinctively suspicious of
them – or perhaps just jealous. Is it because their prose seems so
effortless, so disinterested, their memories so efficient – when mine is
so inefficient? But I wonder, of what substance are their memories,
those continual meetings and meals, those endless street-corner
anecdotes – what do they tell me? My own concern is not with the
trivial details of how things have been, but with what they might have
been. Glasgow to me is associated not with a wealth of recountable
memories but with a story that cannot be told or, at least, that I
cannot tell.

Yet still the Mr Glasgows hold sway, and this strange but powerful
mythology is potently present in the Glasgow of the 1980's –
compounding what can be identified as the New Glasgow.

What is the New Glasgow? Well, it has been practically impossible
to walk the streets of the city or open a page of the popular press for
the last few years without being told of the re-vitalisation of the city,
a new feeling of civic pride, the rediscovery of Glasgow's true self. In
the last couple of years, Glasgow has been lauded by the BBC,
featured by Allan Massie in the *Sunday Times Magazine*, splashed,
along with New York, Oslo and Madrid, on the cover of super-trendy
I-D. Real and honorary Glaswegians have rushed to its defence when

it was described by Billy Connolly as a 'hideous yuppie toilet'. Exiles have shed soft tears for their tenement childhood. Magazines like *The Glaswegian* (now a free newspaper) have created a widespread sense of urban identity, and a fortnightly newssheet reminds us that it is, now and for all time, *Culture City*.

Every page of the popular press has told us of this enviable rebirth. There is a feeling of something important happening. Something we should know about, be part of – although it is something we inevitably find difficult to grasp. One way of looking at it, however, is to suppose that we can take the New Glasgow to have several constituent parts which, aggregated, constitute a sort of movement. Amongst these parts is the revival in the arts – the construction of the Burrell Collection, the revival of other museums, the renaissance of theatre and night life in Glasgow, the advent of Mayfest, the popular arts festival, the increasing popularity of visual artists, the Glasgow school, feted in London and New York, whose most notable members have been Steven Campbell, Adrian Wiszniewski and Ken Currie (although there are many others equally worthy such as Calum Colvin and Stephen Conroy). Then there are the writers – notably Alasdair Gray, whose innovative novel *Lanark* spawned a new interest in literature from the city and has brought a whole pack of writers to the public attention on his coat-tails – James Kelman, Agnes Owens, and several others. There is the revived interest in Glasgow's past – notably in the 'wally close' nostalgia – and the recuperation of the Glasgow dialect – 'the patter'. There is also the rebuilding of the city centre; the discovery of the Merchant City as a source of yuppie homes, the development of new pubs, restaurants, wine bars, discos, et al; the instigation of enterprising projects such as the Garden Festival and Princes Square and a host of commercial innovations in the city centre, not to mention, at this juncture, the most important development of them all – the advent of the much-vaunted Culture City.

The list could go on, but the obvious important point is that these things do not necessarily form a coherent whole, or derive from one predominant cause, as the media may suggest. They are linked not in essence but in the popular imagination. They serve to define Glasgow as a locus – not only physically, but within the realm of representation, for the new. They are located in Glasgow, but Glasgow is also now, located, inexorably, within them.

It may be difficult to identify when this all began, when the New Glasgow first burst forth into the light of day. Well, for the purposes of this discussion, I would like to equate the birth of the New Glasgow with the year 1986. Not that many of the components hadn't been around long before, nourished in the fertile soup of the 'Glasgow's

Miles Better' campaign, launched by the Struthers Agency to improve
Glasgow's image in 1982. The fully-formed offspring of this effort
seems to have reached its apotheosis only some four years ago – and
it arose from what was at the time rather a non-event, Glasgow's
acceptance as European City of Culture 1990 in 1986 (no-one in
Glasgow had heard of this particular prize before that date). The
mechanism that led to this was rather circuitous. The award had been
in operation for only a couple of years although not widely publicised
in this country, when, in April 1985, the Convention of Scottish Local
Authorities requested Scottish nominations in anticipation of the
award finding its way to the United Kingdom in 1990. At this point,
Aberdeen, Edinburgh, Dundee and Glasgow expressed an interest. In
April 1986, Glasgow presented a formal submission – 'there is a spirit
of co-operation and common purpose amongst the cultural
community…Glasgow is confident that the city can mount a cultural
programme which will enhance the status of Cultural Capital of
Europe, will be a credit to Britain, and be good for Glasgow' – and
by August was shortlisted along with eight other British cities
including Edinburgh, Bath, Cardiff, Liverpool and Leeds. The oddly

Comedian Rikki Fulton and 'The Bright Side of Town'

Ex-Lord Provost Michael Kelly and the 'Glasgow's Miles Better' logos

declamatory 'Cultural Capital of Europe' seems to have become the preferred title at this time and has remained so since. Due, for the most part, to the considered presentation of the submission, the choice of Glasgow for the award was announced by the Minister of State for the Arts, Richard Luce, on 20th October 1986, and ratified one month later by the European Community Minister of Culture.

The press coverage of this announcement was distinctly Manichean: 'Glasgow has left no stone unwashed to transform its blackness into glittering grandeur'.[9] In fact, the metaphor of stone-cleaning (an activity now widely discouraged by architects) was used extensively to connote this major change – 'In recent years the true beauty of the city has been revealed by a massive stone cleaning programme...The City Chambers is a prime example of the beauty of building restored from beneath years of grime. The old merchant city has seen its palatial-looking warehouses and office buildings restored to their original pale gold. Many have been converted into flats, breathing new life into the inner city...' The trouble with this sort of prose is that it did not pause to consider how very superficial this metaphor is when applied to true urban renaissance. At its worst, this ultra-enthusiasm erupted into excessive hyperbole – 'Today the latest stage in the renaissance of Glasgow was revealed. Now it stamps the city as culturally the most exciting in Britain. The 'no mean city' image no longer exists. Today Glasgow can claim to rival Europe's top urban jewels such as Paris and Florence. The old Glasgow – perceived for so long as a place of drunks and tenements – has been transformed into a vibrant and confident city with a glittering future.' It does not, when reading this, require a great deal of cynicism to enquire as to whence the drunks and tenements have departed, apparently overnight, but this policy is self-publicising and blatant exaggeration has been taken to its preposterous extreme in a book produced by Struthers themselves in 1986 entitled (you guessed it) *Glasgow's Miles Better*.[10] The predominant tone of this farrago of inconsequential nonsense moves from comparative to superlative. It features photos of Glasgow shoppers that could easily have been shot on the Costa del Sol, apes the canals of Venice or Amsterdam with a contrived shot of buildings reflected in a car roof, and makes direct comparisons, signalled by apposite photographs, with Edinburgh and even Manhattan – 'there's an indiscernible, underlying explosive excitement about the place; an energy that makes it like Glasgow.' Of course, the Glasgow's Miles Better Campaign was roughly based on a similar venture called 'I Love New York' – as the *Glasgow Herald* commented, 'New York has a few assets unknown to Glasgow; it even has a more appetising nickname, the Big Apple, which packs more punch on a T-shirt than Dear Green Place. But if Glasgow has no Broadway at least it has no Bronx either...'. It consists of endorsements of Glasgow from a variety of unlikely celebrities – Jeffrey Archer, Jimmy Greaves, David Owen, Diana Rigg, The Queen, Bobby Charlton, etc – which simply provide so many hooks on which to hang sundry passages of purple prose (indeed the endorsements are brief and vacuous – Kenny Dalglish likes Glasgow 'because it is my home town' and Ian Botham because his wife once went shopping there). The collection commences, perhaps surprisingly, with a foreword by Margaret Thatcher inviting those who want to know Glasgow to *'talk to the people'* (sic).

However, *Glasgow's Miles Better* is almost totally devoid of the opinion of the actual residents of Glasgow – a feature which, although to be expected in a publicity exercise like this, can also be discovered in the popular press. Notably, a press feature heralding the success of the Struthers campaign gave the reaction of a selection of typical Glaswegians interviewed in the street. Examining their contributions we can see that they are all wildly enthusiastic, aged between 20 and 35, employed (civil servant, teacher, jeweller, etc) and predominantly live *outside the city boundary* (Kilsyth, Bothwell, East Kilbride)! Hardly, we may note, a cross-section of the Glasgow public.

There is obviously something extremely disturbing about this recuperation of the image of Glasgow. Firstly, the recent campaign is strangely paradoxical. It claims to be, at the same time, new and iconoclastic – looking to and building for the future – and yet based on tradition – obvious virtues that have not been recognised (especially the mythology of the friendly city, usually opposed to cold and uncaring Edinburgh, as if we can only recognise ourselves by sounding off others). Nostalgia, in its new sense of longing for an imaginary past, is rife – and tradition and heritage, such as the Annan photographs, are repackaged and presented for the edification and amusement of today's equivalent of the Victorian gentry – the consumerist middle classes. The New Glasgow claims to represent the people of the city yet, throughout the campaign, a whole section of society is elided – the forty per cent or so of the population of Glasgow who are mostly unemployed, poor, and live in the large soulless housing schemes created as modern slums by the great Modernist housing revival of the 60s and 70s. Thirdly, and, importantly, the New Glasgow is a city of rampant consumerism – like Disneyland, a magic world of eternal consumption without reference to the problematic notion of production. It seems almost as if we buy into the New Glasgow style. It creates an educated elite – who live the rhythm of the city – go to the right places, buy the right things. But who are they? Can the New Glasgow style be experienced in real life? Or rather, since style is both real and insistently contemporaneous, can it constitute a coherent complete lifestyle ? Is there abroad in Glasgow a native version of the New Man – at the cutting edge of the new, his iconoclastic itinerary resolved to the apogee of modernity?

An interesting example of this incessant hankering after style can be seen in the current obsession with art nouveau and, especially the work of Charles Rennie Mackintosh. Ten or so years ago, only the cognoscenti appreciated this work – the real legacy of what has been called 'the Glasgow style' remained hidden to the majority of the population. Now, however, art nouveau, experienced through the work of Mackintosh and therefore accepted as a native Glasgow style (the Austrian Secession, Wagner, et al are not rated in Glasgow) has come into popular fashion. Old Mackintosh designs for furniture and street lampposts have been unearthed and there are plans to build from scratch a complete Mackintosh design – *Haus eines Kunstfreundes*, House for an Art Lover. In city shops, art nouveau designs by Mackintosh and the so-called Glasgow School adorn postcards, fingerplates, teatowels, designer mirrors, etc. Some critics have doubts about the commercial revival of Mackintosh. Stephen Games referred to the tenth anniversary Charles Rennie Mackintosh Society's conference as 'a kind of Oberammergau, a redemptive act of worship, as much in expiation for the betrayal of Mackintosh as in celebration'.[11] Frank Walker has noted that 'what is being done is not, after all, restoration, conservation or preservation. In effect, it is almost an attempt at reincarnation'.[12] The question is, has the work of Mackintosh and the Glasgow School been interpreted in good faith? Is the art nouveau revival triggered by a genuine interest in design or is it simply a potage of fashionable cliches, commercialised by the nostalgia boom ? The importance is in the way that New Glasgow style repossesses the past to constitute an artificial indigenous tradition. And perhaps it is appropriate that art nouveau itself is the style that can be recuperated in this way, as, following on from *fin de siècle*, it is almost a style with built-in decadence.

So New Glasgow style can be purchased – at least in the form of pastiche – an eclectic selection from a ragbag of cliches. And, as hordes of urban Scots try to rediscover or repossess their ethnic roots, back into popularity leaps the bête noir of recent years – the Glasgow dialect. In 1985, a small thin volume of dialect words by Michael Munro, *The Patter*,[13] was released. It trod on long established ground – short comic glossaries of Glasgow terms – for example, Stanley Baxter's *Parliamo Glasgow* – had some currency as long ago as the sixties, sold as a curiosity, at best an hour's amusement for a train journey or a stocking filler. Yet, although superficially an exercise in humour – witness the cartoons that accompanied it – the book, a spurious academic credibility accorded it by dint of the publishers, Glasgow District Libraries, was an astonishing success in financial and critical terms. It seemed to find a new enthusiastic audience among the New Glaswegians – presumably mostly middle-class converts to the city patois.

What is *The Patter* like ? Firstly, it is distinctly non-scholarly ('This is not intended to be a scholarly work of lexicography. While having the serious intention of recording the language I could see no reason to scorn entertaining the native as well as enlightening the foreigner and have tried to maintain a lighthearted tone') although it is obvious that the origins of some of the terms beg sustained research (variously Scots, Anglo-Saxon, Norse and even French). It also professes to be an attempt to recuperate the language of the city – 'The speech of the Glaswegian has been much maligned. Even natives of the city have joined in yoking it with illiteracy and stigmatising it as ignorant corruption of the Queen's English. No help has been given by various jokey books about Glasgow parlance that contrive to present it as a language for inarticulate idiots' (presumably a swipe at the 'parliamo' books).

The words themselves are distinct, colourful, and interesting, for example: bahookie, molocate, pochle, rammy, gallus, hackit, laldy, clype, breenge, geggie, skite, randan, dunny, skoosh, nyaff, glaikit, etc. Many terms are derived from football: bye, blooter, body swerve, blinder, stoater, shy; several refer to dirt: hoachin, clarty, mingin, manky, and more than could be listed here refer to drinking and various states of drunkenness (although, as scholars such as Eric Partridge have pointed out, this is a common characteristic in all cultures in which alcohol is consumed). The most characteristic rhetorical form is hyperbole, especially common in phrases: bite an ear (verbally pester); away with the fairies (out of touch with reality), do you think I came up the Clyde on a bike (do you think I'm daft), I could eat a scabby dog (I'm hungry), his face trippin him (looking unhappy), hair like straw hingin oot a midden (untidy coiffure); but also in shorter form: no danger (not likely), desperate (for the lavatory), flit (to move house), not quoted (given no chance), scratcher (bed), to stay (to live somewhere), knot yourself (to laugh uncontrollably), dead pint (empty glass), hardman (tough guy), headbanger (idiot), oot the windae (ruled out).

These general principles are not, however, explained or developed in the book itself which, ignoring origins or structure, is deliberately shaped not as a study, a survey or an essay, but as a dictionary for practical use. However, it is not really aimed at the foreigner or the interloper but at the native Glaswegian for whom all these terms and expressions will be vaguely familiar or half-remembered but will require consolidation. It is an amazing turnabout for, as Munro states, less than a generation ago Glasgow dialect was widely detested – often presumed to epitomise lazy or ungrammatical English (although this was based on an imperfect understanding – for example, the dialect term is 'youse' not 'yous'). Recently most regional accents have been recuperated to an extent – but *The Patter* goes one step further, it almost returns to the New Glaswegian his lost birthright, a language in which to express his new-found identity, but a language subtlely recontextualised – no longer the language of the streets and the slums but the language of the cocktail bar, the business meeting, the restaurant or theatre, the language of style, and also of nostalgia, as with-it New Glaswegians vicariously encounter the *lingua volgare* of their forebears.

The Construction of Consensus

In much of this surmising I have referred to the 'myth' of the New Glasgow, and I would like to show that some of the grosser claims for the city have little grounding in reality. But I do not wish to employ the term myth in its restricted meaning of communicated falsehood. I want to demonstrate that the New Glasgow is a mythology – a system of images, ideas, signifiers that has its own integral, coherent structure, bound together by an ideological glue. There are two main elements in this mythology to consider which I have glossed under firstly, 'The Construction of Consensus' and, secondly, 'The Urban Bricoleur'.

The notion of the construction of consensus should be quite clear. The media clearly addresses itself to the population of Glasgow as a homogeneous 'we'. There is no attempt to suggest that what is good for one group, or area, or class within the city may not be equally good for another. It is taken as given that the New Glasgow, in all its multifarious aspects, must be good for the population as a whole. This is a constant and powerful hegemonic process – whole sections of society who will never see the Burrell Collection or the inside of the new opera house will defend these projects to the hilt. There is no self-evident notion of an alternative – or that capital, especially, can be employed in many different ways. Instead, we have a vague idea in the fashion of the government's noted trickle-down philosophy. (One could say, on a more cynical note, that most people have yet to see any record of where the money spent on the recent huge developments in the city actually goes.)

Related to this is the concept of the urban bricoleur – a peculiarly acceptable notion that Glasgow as a city is developing according to some master plan under the guidance of a mysterious benevolent dictator – or bricoleur. This is palpably not the case – perhaps more than at any other time there are seriously conflicting interests at work in the construction of the fabric and the ethos of the city. The creation of Culture City, despite the various powerful bodies involved in it, is not blueprinted, yet forces conspire to ensure it – these are arguably not the forces of unrestrained civic benevolence, even in the narrower sense of the promotion of supposedly desirable high culture, but the forces of capitalism and self-interest. Despite this notion, however, it must be remembered that one of the tenets of the new realism is the avoidance of the master plan – which, on many levels, has failed us before – especially with the redevelopment of Glasgow in the sixties, the construction of the urban motorway and the housing schemes in the grand utopian Modernist model. It is difficult to remember how pervasive this discourse once was. Yet from the late fifties onwards, when the received dogma was that we had never had it so good, there was a widespread general assumption amongst the working class, in Glasgow and elsewhere, that, despite their immediate problems, the future held for us nothing but hope. This spirit can clearly be seen in the important Scottish documentary film movement of the fifties, especially the work of the Films of Scotland committee, which employed a variety of techniques – both innovative metonymic techniques and montage editing and other borrowings from the Soviet cinema of the twenties and thirties – to develop a breed of short 'propaganda' films which have been characterised as belonging to a particular discourse nominated the 'Scotland on the Move' discourse. These films portrayed a Scotland and a Scottish people marching hand-in-hand towards a bright new future. This form of mythologising is clearly at work in the documentaries created to greet variously the urban motorway, the massive New Towns such as Cumbernauld and Livingston, new Modernist housing in the schemes, and in contemporary newspaper and magazine advertisements (not to mention the general *zeitgeist* of 50s/60s Glasgow). These enthusiastic little narratives with their idealistic and patriotic vision of the future could not fail to interpellate the average tenement dweller. For most Glaswegians at the time, my family included, Doreen's vision of suburban bliss in the housing schemes in *The Steamie* was a personal dream *and* a shared dream. The future seemed full of attractive possibilities. No-one, neither the customers nor the planners, knew how it would go horribly wrong within only a couple of decades.

It would be tempting to labour this point but a particularly succinct and emotive summary of the failure of the great Modernist plan for Glasgow is given by Ian Jack:

> ...the death of Glasgow, at least in the place's most important (and most celebrated) incarnation as an intimate city which made large machines, came suddenly in the 1960's and was confused at the time with the promise of new life. Glasgow councillors flew out to Los Angeles and thought they saw the future in its freeways. The same men hired Sir Basil Spence and pointed him at the Gorbals. (Le Corbusier was not then a dirty name, but tenements were).

Those were the days when not just streets but whole districts were staked out on maps and marked for destruction via a coloured overlay of 'comprehensive redevelopment' or clover-leaf traffic intersections. I remember the pen-and-wash drawings in the same display: spindly, untenemental ladies walked their dogs through greensward and potential trees while something like the Empire State Building towered in the background, white and noble against a friendly sky.

All this to give people bathrooms. But the ambition was so grand and the city's Victorian housing stock so awful that nobody objected. Today the consequences are generally lamented – sometimes royally – and we needn't dwell on the shabbiness, the damp, and the poverty of thought that those watercolour sketches turned out to contain when translated into concrete. The people in Marzaroli's pictures who stand bemused among the rubble of the old Gorbals couldn't have foreseen that as their future. They were queuing up at the housing department, hoping to be allocated a nice wee flat in 'a good scheme'.[1]

Despite the importance of the Glasgow urban motorway on the native topography of the city, it is the distinct developments in Glasgow housing over the years that are important to help comprehend the situation of the average Glaswegian. Arguably, the history of Glasgow's housing is the history of Glasgow. I have already discussed the importance of the concept of the tenement in relation to the particular forms of social engineering engendered by the Victorian era and afterwards. The particular failure of Modernism in the restructuring of Glasgow in the 1960's and 1970's (not that the same process did not take place in other cities) is also an important ingredient in the complex mix that constructs the Glasgow of 1990. The development of housing policy in the city is a crucial factor.

The fundamental problem posed by housing development in Glasgow (or any large city) is exemplified by a description of the city in 1840, the period of extensive immigration from the country and from Ireland, by Edwin Chadwick:

We entered a dirty low passage like a house door, which led from the street through the first house to a square court immediately behind, which court, with the exception of a narrow path around it leading to another long passage through a second house, was occupied entirely as a dung receptacle of the most disgusting kind. Beyond this court the second passage led to a second square court, occupied in the same way by its dung hill; and from this court there was yet a third passage leading to a third court and third dungheap. There were no

privies and drains there, and the dungheaps received all filth
which the swarm of wretched inhabitants could give; and we
learnt that a considerable part of the rent of the houses was paid
by the produce of the dungheaps.[2]

The problem is clear – the squalor and the disease is caused not by the
houses or the inhabitants themselves, but by the entire structure of the
whole housing development. Like the human body, the city has to
breathe and defecate. Any failure in this basic structure – in the case
the lack of proper sanitation and waste facilities, and the system fails.
Nineteenth-century Glasgow was swept by outbreaks of cholera,
diptheria and other fatal diseases created by the sanitary problem.
Child mortality was high. To the poor afflicted people it must have
seemed like Nemesis but it is clear in retrospect that the system itself
was to blame. The Victorians came to understand this problem to a
limited extent and the housing reforms of the later nineteenth century
came with their awareness if not of the humanitarian issues, at least
of the economics of health and disease.[3] What to do about the people
themselves, however, how to allocate adequate housing to a
workforce whom capitalism had failed so miserably, was not so clear.
Enid Gauldie points out the problematic of nineteenth-century
housing – that poverty affected housing in subtle ways – people were
often too poor not to pay exorbitant rents as by necessity they had to
remain close to their source of credit – rising rents in central areas
would discourage the moderately well-off, but the poor had no choice
but to remain. This complex relationship between housing and
poverty was not really appreciated in the nineteenth – and arguably
in the twentieth century.

Unfortunately, the great failing of housing planning in the next
century was that it was only to reprise some of these fatal flaws. In
the late fifties and sixties it became clear that a massive slum clearance
programme was required. However, it took into the seventies before
it could be fairly said that this policy had succeeded, in the inner city
at least. In 1965, around forty per cent of dwellings in Glasgow had
no bath or shower, over twenty per cent were without an internal w/c,
thirty per cent had only one bedroom and sixty-four per cent had at
least one person per room. Up to seventy per cent were privately
rented and tales of slum landlords, such as the infamous Rachmann,
were rife.[4] In 1965, I remember, my parents were moved from an
inner city tenement room and kitchen, their own, but still a slum, to
a new semi-detached council house. It seemed idyllic. The Modernist
planners lost in their Utopian dream, had a fairly perfect understanding of most structural elements of the housing system – sanitation, servicing, access, employment of space – but practically no
concept of the greater requirements of their customers. Again, the

inhabitants were stifled, not by the smell of their own excrement, but by their comparative isolation. Of the supposedly limitless possibilities, few were delivered by the schemes for, missing from the system were the outlets for conviviality, for variety, for expression of any sort. The schemes were machines for living but the people refused to be mechanised and these limited environments quickly proved insufficient.

Of course, there are elements here that are common to the worldwide failure of the Modernist movement – the same reasons why the cracks have festered in Le Corbusier's Chandigarh, or why the tenants have restructured L'Unité d'Habitation – and these hardly need to be stressed. There are also some elements that are particular to Glasgow. The notion, for example, that Glasgow was to become an automobile city proved disastrously wrong when it transpired that few of the inhabitants of the housing schemes could afford, or indeed wanted, motor cars. In the sixties and seventies, the schemes and the roads appeared but the transport system didn't keep pace – spasmodic and inefficient buses that went off the road in a severe frost linked the schemes with the city centre and created bottlenecks in notable access roads (service buses can't always use the urban motorway). The misery of commuting to work was, however, relatively short-lived, as a radical Conservative government of the eighties introduced mass unemployment (which currently runs at up to 80-90% in some areas of housing schemes), ensuring that vast numbers of scheme-dwellers had no need to leave the peripheral ghettos especially created for them.

What seems apparent, then, is that the failure of housing for Glasgow's citizens in the twentieth century was not all that different in kind from the failure of the nineteenth century – brought about by disregard for the real social and communal needs of the people and the dedication of the powers-that-be to the dominant discourses of the time. The particular form of the Glasgow housing scheme was inspired by the tenement model, and many of the social evils of the scheme were by no means new. Yet criticism of the schemes stressed the inhumanity and inflexibility of the Modernist housing block (as humorously portrayed, for example, in McNaughtan's *Ye Cannae Fling Pieces...*) as if the Victorian tenement was, in itself, a particularly natural form and not, as it was at the time of its construction, at the forefront of new technology. Of course, there was a genuine opposition to new housing from the more conservative members of the community as might be expected. But whether this was a genuine premonition of the future is doubtful.

At its worst this is exemplified in a distorting gross sentimentalisation of the tenement past – as in Duncan Macrae's sentimental pastiche of a music hall favourite:[5]

> Faur frae ma hame ah've wandered,
>   An ah never will return,
> Tae ma ain close in the Gorbals,
>   Juist alang frae Jenny's Burn,
> For they're pullin doon the buildin,
>   An ah doot ah canny bide,
> For they're gonnae mak the Gorbals,
> Like New York or Kelvinside.
> An it's oh, but ah'm longing for ma ain close,
> It wis nane o yuir wally, juist a plain close,
> An ah'm nearly roon the bend,
> For ma ain wee single-end,
> Fareweel tae dear old Gorbals
> An ma ain close...
> They'll never be forgotten,
>   The days that we lived through,
> When we hung aboot the Gorbals
>   An we sterved on the Buroo,
> Wi the lassies playin peever,
>   An the laddies sclimmin dykes,
> An the weemin gaun thir dusters,
>   An the polis gaun their bikes.

The humour stops just short of parody and the effect is maudlin rather than humorous, but the point is clear. Nostalgia or sentiment impedes a clear view of past failings. As in *The Glasgow that I Used to Know*, the song indulges in the exercise of remembering through language and thus elides the obvious point that the lauded single-end and multi-storey cell are, in both ideological and real terms, very near neighbours indeed. Yet mythology is an even more powerful force than we can easily imagine. Anyone can buy into a little New Glasgow style, and the fundamental nature of housing does not exempt it from this – rather the opposite. In the newspapers these days there are adverts for flats in Dorset Court in Finnieston – 'A Better Choice of City Style' – recreated in the best Postmodern tradition of pastiche as a massive Art Nouveau tenement block, illustrated for the potential consumer in elevation by a simple line drawing to emphasise the fine lines. This is hardly surprising, but in the same newspaper a smaller, less stylish advert catches the eye featuring new, lower cost housing in Springburn – a traditional working-class and slum area on the north side of the city. This advert features no new plans or drawings or extravagant promises of style or artifice. Instead an old photograph of the area with some tenements and a tram is featured. The caption reads 'Better than the Good

Old Days'. The message is, however, directly at odds with this
caption. For the advert invites you to purchase a little of the old days
– devoid, apparently, of their supposed association with poverty and
deprivation. And the people *will* return. Apparently, inner city areas
like Springburn are now attractive to Glaswegians from the periphery
who can (just) afford home ownership. Utopia having failed them,
the past turns out not so bad after all, re-evaluated through the
distorting lens of nostalgia.

So there is traditional Glasgow, or the squalid, sickly, sweaty
Glasgow we inherited from the Victorians, and there is Modernist
Glasgow, rebuilt in the now forsaken image of a future god, and there
is the New Glasgow. In the city centre, all three live as close
neighbours – which gives Glasgow its peculiar quality today. Around
and about the city centre today the uneasy alliance of these different
Glasgows is only too apparent. If you start at Anderston where, from
one vantage point, you can view traditional tenements, Modernist
tower blocks and resurrected Art Nouveau tenement-style flats, and
finish at the famous Barrows market where you can witness the same
tripartite relationship between the Cartwheel junk market, the
Square Yard and Quincey's antique market – all dealing in much the
same material in different states of repair and price range – you can
visit along the way either *Babbity Bowster's* – a chic bar and restaurant in an old banana warehouse – or, directly opposite, *The
Strathduie* – a traditional public house with down-market customers
who prefer playing dominoes or listening to Patsy Cline to supping
mulligatawny soup and swallowing Loch Etive mussels while viewing contemporary etchings. In this way the new Glasgow does not
merge with the old. It is merely superimposed over it – like two
ancient continental plates inexorably grinding over each other.
Whether this situation can continue is uncertain – for no city centre
gives such an impression of flux as Glasgow. This is, after all, part of
its excitement – or terror.

Yet, if we visit peripheral Glasgow – derived in style from
Modernism, or, in the experience of the people, from the weighty
traditional forces of hegemony and class oppression – there is only a
sense of stasis. If you visit this Glasgow, in Castlemilk, as I did, to take
photographs, one icy Sunday in late October, feeling rather ostentatious with my camera and choice of lens when everyone else was
carrying a carry-out back from the Castlemilk Labour club, you may
see, in a back street, a decrepit Ford Cortina half-covered in an old
tarpaulin carrying a window sticker with the legend *Glasgow – a
Great Place to Live and Work*. Around about, these twentieth-
century tenements are half-dead already – windows boarded up to be
sprayed with gang slogans, the supposed front gardens of Garden

City deserted by their putative owners, gone to seed, dumped with garbage, the railings bent and mangled, or gone altogether, the personal boundaries of property obliterated. A small hut, apparently windowless, slats covered in chicken wire and a bombproof metallic door, turns out to be a doctor's and dentist's surgery.

It is hard to make sense of this – for the New Glasgow is full of contradictions. In the Merchant City the yuppies swelter while in the schemes the OAPs freeze. From the West End to the Cross the city is determinedly international – wine or dine in *O Henry's* or *Chimmy Chungas*, search for *Orwell's* (the pub), *Oblomov's* (the bistro) *Gandolfi* (the cafe), *Fouquet's* (the wine bar), *Freud's* (the hairdresser), *Descartes* (the delicatessen), or *Bobolofski's Balloon* (a wine bar with an unusual line in art decor). Alternatively, the theatres have resurrected kitchen-sink drama. For the stay-at-homes, the bookshops are full of consumable Glasgow – Marzaroli's photographs, Colin Baxter's postcards, Annan's old closes, and Corgi have reissued a series of Glasgow books – some wally-close nostalgia in the *Shoes Were For Sunday* tradition, some novels, and, surprisingly, the old bête noir, McArthur and Long's infamous *No Mean City*. Like the others in the series, this edition has a specially painted cover illustration. It features the Gorbals tenements bathed in the rosy glow of sunset, against a midden wall languishes a lithe fair-haired female in a sort of flapper-style outfit like a 30s gangster's moll, in the centre, gazing at the reader, the Razor King, dark-featured and handsome, like a Glaswegian James Dean. This, independent of the textual substance between the boards, is Glasgow sanitized, pastellised. A legacy of squalor, deprivation and struggle subsumed in a fairy tale for the New Glaswegian.

What may be obvious from what I have said is that invariably commentators on Glasgow – including myself – have recourse to a dualistic model. As if the elements of the city – culture, industry, pleasure, poverty – must always be in perpetual opposition. After the initial euphoria of the Culture City farrago, some commentators have taken a more realistic view of the new Glasgow. For example, Sally Magnusson writes in *Scotland on Sunday* recently: 'And yet, and *yet*, the city has another face, a million miles but in some cases only a few minutes walk from the wine bars and the glitzy shopping malls. This is not the mythical 'old Glasgow' that you hear wet-eyed intellectuals wax nostalgic over in comfortably, seedy, yuppie-proof pubs. It is the Glasgow of the 12-year-old gangs...'[6] This is not new at all, but follows on from a very old tradition indeed. The notion of the 'two cities in one' is a Victorian invention – spawned by the onset of industrial society and is found quite plainly in Victorian novels and the strange genre of supposedly reforming tracts produced by various missions and charitable bodies and in the Victorian novels that mimic their moral tone –

for example, in *City Echoes*, or in David Pae's *The Factory Girl*. Pae's story has an illuminating descriptive passage:

> The slanting beams of the descending sun fell brightly on the Clyde, as it skirted the southern boundary of Glasgow Green...To the north and west lay the city in dense compactness – houses, chimneys, and pointed gables standing in thick array against the clear western sky...Across, on the south side of the river...were tall chimneys and long blocks of high square buildings, with many rows of windows... From these many buildings came puffing jets of smoke – the rush, rush of the engine, like great heart-beats, and the clanking noise of machinery, which uttered its voice in its iron-labour-song, harsh and uncouth as its own hard self.[7]

An almost identical dichotomy, strangely enough, can be found in the voice-over introduction to an unusual and extremely interesting film production of 1950, *The Gorbals Story*, adapted from the play by Robert McLeish, the son of a Gorbals shipyard worker born in 1912:

> A city of well-stocked shops and spacious stores, big hotels, comfortable restaurants, fine theatres, luxurious cinemas. In short a successful city...(camera pans from the west end across the river to the south side) but strangely enough the Glasgow I generally portray lies on the other side of the slow-flowing waters of the Clyde. The Glasgow of grey skies, grey buildings, depression, frustration, streets in which passers-by walk grimly on their predestined course. A course leading through the darkness of poverty to an almost inevitable end.[8]

It is interesting that the film version modifies the main message of the play – that there is no escape – by framing the story within a flashback from the point of view of the main character, Johnny, played by Russell Hunter, who has somehow miraculously escaped to a West End terrace. Other distancing techniques are also obvious in the film – the strange scene in which Johnny is shunned at a dance hall is absolutely silent, clearly indicating a representation of selective memory. At the end of the film, the actors appear one by one for the credits, in direct address – this 'curtain call' clearly indicating the fictional nature of the narrative and distancing us once more from the main impulse of the story. Johnny, the Johnny imprisoned by the slums and burning up with despair, is not presented to us more directly (as in the standard classic realist text). Instead, he is mediated by, firstly, the remembering of the older, wiser, 'saved' Johnny, and, secondly, by the clear contrivance of the actor playing the part – Russell Hunter.The stage play is less circumspect, but equally interesting. When it was launched in the forties, it was seen quite seriously as an antidote to the dominant kailyard mythology of the

The Gorbals Story – still from the film

contemporary Scottish theatre, a slice of social realism. Early reviews
commended it for this attribute – '...Glasgow, the slummy, swarming
core of it, presented with honesty, frankness and verisimilitude', 'the
memory of the crude, raw quickfire humour of the slums', 'the rich
oil of crude, native Glasgow humour', '...truth with a sting and a
smell; a tragi-comedy coming over the footlights like can after can of
rotting garbage'.[9] An early publicity leaflet describes it as 'a play
about the South Side and the people who live in rooms. Here is a
chunk of real life. It's funny, it's dramatic, it's heart-warming'. An
accompanying sketch by the cartoonist Bud Neill has the following
caption – 'Awfy touchy, the polis gettin'. Aye, Hughie's in Coort the
day for drappin' the heid o' an' iron bed on wan last night – fae only
three up, tae, imagine.' The black humour – in the vernacular style of
countless newspaper and periodical articles, such the famous 'Little
Stories from the Police Courts' series that featured in D C Thomson's
Weekly News until recently – disguises that fact that the play itself
accepts uncritically the supposedly endemic drunkenness and violence – witness the smashing of the public house, the *Green Man*, in
the best cowboy tradition – inflicting the otherwise couthy urban
kailyard portrayed. This is not unrelated to the ethnographic portrayals of the nineteenth-century denizens of Glasgow's underworld.
The Gorbals itself is viewed as distinctly different from the 'civilised'

world, with its own particular rules and mores. As with the 'real'
underworld of Victorian Glasgow, there is no escape – other than death,
or (conversion) which, as the Mission literature shows us, is much the
same thing. This is why Johnny's West End redemption, in the film,
seems so phoney within the context of the narrative. Similarly, the play
was lauded in its time as both an antidote to the insidious *No Mean City*
(several reviewers commented on this) and as a real exposé of the evil of
slum housing. This dubious value tends to be lost in the film version in
which Johnny seems trapped in a spiritual morass rather than in any real
socio-economic problem.

The Gorbals Story, dated as it may seem in this context, can also
be recuperated by the 80s boom in nostalgia, as a recent production
by the Citizens Theatre played to packed houses. The poster advertising the show portrays a selection of dated caricatures in bunnets,
braces and aprons engaged in acts of both camaraderie and violence.
To anchor the meaning more securely, the drawing is framed by the
names of streets in the Gorbals – Florence Street, Gorbals Street,
Cumberland Street, Lawmoor Street. While these streets existed,
consisting of real tenements, *The Gorbals Story* naturally remained
in an anonymous location. Now that they are non-existent, or

The poster for the 7:84 theatre company's revival of *The Gorbals Story*

derelict, after the massive demolition and redevelopment in the Gorbals, they have moved into the realms of mythology. That these streets did exist, and nurtured generations of Glaswegians, came across to me as, poignantly, I recognised Lawmoor Street as the childhood home of my father. What is particularly interesting, however, about *The Gorbals Story*, is the way in which one text, presented in different contexts over a period of fifty years, can shift in meaning – from an exercise in social realism, to a melodramatic personal tragedy to a form of nostalgic comedy.

The lineage of this Manichean vision of the city can be seen in continuation comparatively recently, for Glasgow has also been well represented by television. In 1982, the very year from which, according to my schema, the birth of the New Glasgow can be traced, Granada Television produced a four-part documentary entitled simply *Glasgow* which raised quite a furore when screened in Scotland. The formula for this brilliantly produced but ideologically dubious production was quite simple. An ingenuous (English) reporter would descend into the underworld of Glasgow, in the fashion of a Shadow, and listen with a spurious objectivity to the denizens of this deep. The voice-over is complicit in the mythologising – the 'barras' are 'a cut-price grotto of wishful thinking', the local inhabitants, 'denizens of a nineteenth-century underworld in the 1980's'. It takes us to the aptly-named Mecca Bar, 'the bar at the bottom of the slide', home to a variety of winos and dispossessed East-enders (now, incidentally, a more up-market wine bar) and provides a simplistic explanatory nostrum – 'if the present's a problem, the past hardly worth remembering about, the future must be better'. There are several familiar themes in this mythologising – the descent to hell, the dualistic nature of Glasgow, the community frozen in time (the nineteenth century), and the specious concept of the homogeneous community (as narrative links are drawn between the inhabitants of the Gallowgate area as if it exists, village-like, apart from the wider city). Perhaps these are the dying strains of an old song, superseded by the happier tune of the New Glasgow – but perhaps they are not – perhaps they constitute a language for describing Glasgow that will not, or cannot, be usurped. Interestingly, a more recent and sympathetic attempt to describe the city – a home-produced documentary entitled *Glasgow By the Way* – reproduces this structure to some extent.

Of course, one way of resolving the contradictions of the dualist model of Glasgow is to consider the city as a typical example of the Postmodern city. Postmodernism is not as readily identifiable as a movement as Modernism. As a buzz word, it accumulates meanings, some complementary and some not so. Critics have suggested three

distinct kinds of Postmodernism:[10] a sort of neo-conservatism that
fêtes tradition and opposes the concept of the revolutionary or the
new – as exemplified, for example, by Peter Fuller's *Modern Painters*
or Prince Charles's musings on architecture; an anti-Modernism,
opposed to the central tenets of the Modernist movement – the belief
in progress, in explanatory philosophies, the notion of subjectivity;
and a more critical Postmodernism – which attempts to situate itself
as a genuine movement (rather than a counter-movement) by apply-
ing itself creatively to the contemporary social and cultural milieu.
Almost all the senses of the term can apply particularly well to
Glasgow, or rather the way we look at Glasgow, as Postmodernism
is an aspect of a perspective or a way of looking at things, rather than
an attribute of the city itself. Glasgow is a city cursed with a rabid kind
of puritanical conservatism, a city ill-served by high Modernism, and
a city that seeks to reconstitute itself for the eighties. The identifiable
constituents of Postmodernism in practice which fêtes simulation,
pastiche, the ephemeral, the intransigent, and is typified by nostalgia,
can hardly be missed. Perhaps, then, if the city is the accepted stage
for contemporary or Postmodern culture, Glasgow is a prime example of that practice.

There is a more particular way of looking at Postmodernism.
Marxist critics, notably Fredric Jameson,[11] have described it as a
specific condition deriving from the third, or latest, stage of capitalism. Postmodern society becomes, in this view, a cultural consequence of capitalism. In this model, Postmodern society is typified by
rampant consumerism, and, seen in this light, the rebuilding of
Glasgow's old centre – the Merchant City – is emblematic. The
Merchant City – so-called because in the eighteenth century, the
period of the first blooming of Glasgow as a commercial centre, this
was the centre of commerce and the area in which the city merchants,
mostly trading in the importing of tobacco or other crops from the
New World, set up their homes. Subsequently, this area became
industrialised in the nineteenth century and was largely devoted to
warehousing, market trade, or office space. It became more run-
down in the first half of the twentieth-century before its resurrection
in the late seventies and eighties to provide private inner-city housing,
fashionable shopping and leisure outlets – taking over as the centre
of city style from the long-established West End.

Several conclusions could be reached about the nature of this
transformation, not least concerning the total eclipse of commerce
and the production of wealth directed towards consumption. There
is also the characteristic move from the open common space of the
city centre towards the preserve of the individual and the exercise of
his/her power (wealth). As in similar inner-city developments in

London, New York or Los Angeles,[12] the development of these old warehouses or offices into private housing concentrates on the interior space, the serviced flat, the private patio or roof garden. Inner-city living is characterised by the invisible inhabitant, who is situated within the earthy pleasures of city-centre living but aloof from, all-seeing but unseen, part of the city milieu but free from its worst exigencies, its torpor and crime.

Another completely internalised development in the city centre is Princes Square shopping centre. The shopping mall, in recent times, has completely usurped the functional Modernist shopping centre, and is seen by some as the epitome of the Postmodern consumer society. The mall is not, of course, for practical shopping, but for recreation – shopping is a new, culturally rich, leisure experience. Princes Square is characterised by its extravagance. Built from the skeleton of an old galleried warehouse, it has been adorned with mahogany and beech, brass, marble and glass, arranged in fanciful designs with the usual art nouveau motifs and flourishes. Entering into Princes Square, the shopper can feel dizzy for a moment. The scene is turned in on itself, focused on the central mall – the only escape is to gaze, high above, through the skylights to the sky. In the gallery there are windows painted with urban landscape scenes, no view over the city, the purpose of the overhead windows being to internalise the light. Suspended from the ceiling and constantly swinging over a dial in the basement is a Foucault pendulum – an instrument which is made to move constantly between two points by the rotation of the earth. This is something of a fraud – a device popularised by science museums which claims to demonstrate that, contrary to normal expectations, it is really the world that is moving while we stand still. This is also an illusion perpetuated by Princes Square and the Foucault pendulum could almost stand as a symbol of the complex itself, for the Square is full of constant movement, showering fountains, escalators set at a tangent to each other (for Jameson the escalator is a particularly Postmodern art form), sinuous staircase banisters and streams of wandering shoppers, and, forming street-level access to the top balcony, one moving staircase that passes, on the walls, a gallery of great Scots – Moore, Maxton, Mackintosh, Baird, Kelvin (the selection is more akin to a tourist guide than a Victorian monumental procession) painted on the walls amid twisting vines in perfect *trompe l'oeil* – so that they can *only* be viewed on the moving escalator, looking straight ahead. In some ways, however, this is all movement without a purpose – the escalator, for example, is a notably inefficient method of getting up and down, primarily designed for pleasure; the shops, if distinctive, are identical in ethos – they are expensive, aesthetically designed for display (most people who come here leave without buying anything – in a real sense Princes Square is modelled not on the shopping centre but on the museum; a pastiche of vaguely related past mores and styles), they often have short, trendy, cryptic names – *Saxs, Optical, Entice, Monsoon, To…, One, Jigsaw, Henrys* (sic) – which are usually presented tangentially rather than emblazoned – cut from iron plaques, painted in bizarre stylish lettering, or displayed vertically – demonstrably coy about the actual act of selling. On the top gallery, there is an eating area with a choice of different outlets to choose from – *Salter's Seafood* (with 'traditional' tiles and sea shells), *Mings* (with the sign of the painted dragon), *Elmo's* (where, quaintly, you get a little American flag on your sandwich) – there are a couple of bars – *The Penguin Café, Buzzy Wares, D'Arcy's* – to snatch a drink and sit outside to pause and observe. All in all, Princes Square is not about the banalities of shopping but the pleasures of style. It is a chance to wander in a luxurious setting in which the actual shop fittings have the appeal of expensive ornaments – an attention to detail that few commercial outlets can afford. It is serene, with perfect miniature trees and bubbling fountains reflected with skill in the artificial – thus trees and waves are also etched into the glass casing for the lifts, like gigantic Waterford crystal, *Crabtree and Evelyn* feature trees constructed from natural sponges. Princes Square offers a highly crafted and unique aesthetic experience. What the consumer will get here, whether they can afford the high fashions or not, is a little bit of New Glasgow style – or a least, a piece of that identity, of the fashionable elite. It is, if you like, thè jewel in the crown of a city that seems bent on resolving itself into one giant shopping centre. Add to Princes Square the new clothes stores in the Merchant City, the various markets in Argyle Street and Sauchiehall Street, the new Forge shopping centre, and the new massive, hi-tech St. Enoch's Centre, constructed in glass and aluminium under enormous transparent pyramids (inside are strange pointed pyramidic rocket-like structures with rotating veins and flashing lights) and it is hard to see where it will all end. The old commercial merchant town is transformed into a monument to consumerism.

If you cannot make the trip to Princes Square, however, some of this can be consumed at home, in the privacy of your own Merchant City penthouse or council flat. In 1988, a new glossy free magazine appeared in shops and pubs. *M8* is a style magazine, consisting mostly of glossies and fashion shorts with features that relate to either Glasgow or Edinburgh (the title refers to the motorway between the cities) but in impulse, ethos, content and format it has everything in common with New Glasgow Style rather than the city's more conservative capital cousin.

Mr Farrell begs to intimate that he has opened

THE DOLPHIN BAR

157 DUMBARTON ROAD PARTICK CROSS

*For the second hundred years in business,
the premises have been specially modelled to suit the trade, and
adapted to suit the requirements of the district.*

*Mr Farrell recommends the DOLPHIN Centenary blend of Fine
Old Matured Scotch Whisky to his patrons and customers, in full
confidence of deserving their continued patronage. He also keeps in
stock a supply of the best imported Wines and Spirits and the very
finest of Ales and Porters obtainable.*

Advertisement for the *Dolphin Bar* from M8

M8 is for the fashionable and the yuppie classes – who know, or want to know, what to wear, what to drink, where to be seen, and what names to know. This is not an uncommon format, but *M8* is peculiarly Scottish, if not Glaswegian. One of the most obvious determinants of its particular flavour is its obsession with football – well-known footballers from Scotland's top four teams (Rangers, Celtic, Hearts, Hibs) model clothes in each edition and a readership survey poses idiosyncratic questions – 'In which of the following fashion outlets do you buy your clothes? Which football team do you support? Describe your present haircut and name your hairdresser'.[13] Articles occasionally deal with topics of relevance – for example, a piece by Mike Cruikshank entitled 'Nae Mean City! (who's kidding who?)' looks at Glasgow mythology but with a notably topical or trendy twist: 'Glasgow the City of Culture 1990! The City that is Miles Better? Or is it? How many times have you heard the men in your pub discuss the Gay community as if it was dirt...' Mostly, however, the magazine works around a series of adverts or advertising features for typically fashionable New Glasgow bars, restaurants and shops with exotic names: the *Tuxedo Princess* (an art decor style cruising boat), *Buzz Carter's* ('on the walls, the city groans'), *Ichi Ni San, Katherine Hamnett, Chimmy Chungas, Faze2, Blitz, La Taniere, Navy Blue* (a nostalgia clothes shop), *The Drawing Room, Boutique Homme, Oblomov's, De Quincey's, California Tan,* or *O'Henry's* (sic). That these impute a lifestyle that is both selective and expensive and excludes the average working-class Glaswegian (except vicariously) goes without saying. Yet *M8* has its distinct flavouring of predominantly proletarian urban values – its obsession with sport, urban decay and local dialect, for example. If anything, *M8* connotes a city in continual flux – nothing is anything but brand new, not least the more fashionable boutiques and wine bars – yet one article in the second issue carries a totally contrary message. Entitled 'Sanctuary Amidst a Sea of Change', it purports to celebrate 100 years of the Dolphin Bar 'one of the last of a dying breed of 'spit and sawdust' working men's pubs' in Dumbarton Road. The article informs the reader that 'tradition remains a foundation stone of the Dolphin Bar', yet in the accompanying advert for the bar the interior is completely faked. A sepia photograph – recently constructed – features young models dressed in modern adaptations of 1900-30s clothing (of the sort you can now buy in the shops of Princes Square) seated around an incongruous domino table drinking pints of stout. In the background light filters through curtained shoulder-height windows and a framed image of Victorian patriarchy hangs, in soft focus, on the wall. Presumably, the genuine customers of the Dolphin Bar have been supplanted and replaced by some of the models who inhabit the fashion pages of the magazine. The purpose? Once more, to recuperate a little more working-class nostalgia and set it to the service of New Glasgow chic.

And so mythology continues its work in its subtle way and, with a blasé headline or a hazy photograph, erases generations of genuine (or at least long-established) history from the record.

Cancer of Empire

In the early 1920s, when the nation was just about coming to terms with itself after the terrible hiatus of the Great War, William Bolitho, an English journalist, visited Glasgow and potently described the Clydeside slums in a book entitled *Cancer of Empire*:[1]

> The Red Clyde, the smouldering danger of revolution in Glasgow, owing to the swift development of political affairs in Britain, has ceased to be a local anxiety, and become an interest and an alarm to the whole civilised world...There is something deeply wrong with the Clyde; the whole middle-class of England knows it...The Red Clyde will remain the focus of English politics, until it has been cured, or definitely appeased; or until first Scotland, then industrial England, becomes fully infected by it, with momentous effects on Britain, the British Empire, and the rest of the world.
>
> The mainspring of the trouble is, the root grievance of the Clyde, is Housing. This is a simple term for a cancerous condition which, starting from the lack of space and light in the homes of the workers, festers and complicates itself, in numberless vicious circles, feeding on their Scottish vigour of character.[2]

Bolitho goes on to develop the metaphor of the cancerous growth throughout the book, which is mostly an exercise in journalistic description but also, in its own way, an impassioned denunciation of the social and political circumstances from which the slums derive. His style is partly reminiscent of Shadow's sojourns into the underworld:

> Door after door as we knocked was opened by a shirted man, suddenly and softly, as if impelled forward by the overpowering slum smell behind him. It is this smell which is the most oppressive symbol of such lives: choking, nauseating; the smell of corrupt sweat, and unnamed filthiness of body...Sometimes it crept out at us past the legs of the householder, insinuatingly, as if ashamed; sometimes it brazened it out, full and pestiferous; once, in a woman's shilling boarding house, it leapt out and

took by the throat like an evil beast: the smell of the slums, the unforgettable abominable smell...In most cases the inhabitants may not notice it any longer; have grown used to it, like beasts to their cage. Whether they feel its deep humiliation or not in misery so deep of surroundings and food and life as no domestic animal in England knows, they keep their bits of brass polished. At one place there was an old man and his wife alone, with hardly a stick of furniture; but, on the mantelpiece, he had set up, as a child builds a cubist facade with bricks, a structure made of polished condensed milk tins, that shone in the flicker of the fire; but he had left them unclean within, and not cared to smooth their jagged top edge of opening.[3]

It is clear that Bolitho is creating a whole mythology here that is not simply contained within the Glasgow paradigm but has a wider significance and is to do with poverty, possession and a form of general degradation. However, there is feature of his style that is not typical of the Victorian 'anthropology' we have already seen. The attention to detail, the impassioned plea, the personal involvement and disgust – 'giving himself away' as an outsider – are more contemporary, reminiscent of Orwell's precocious literariness. As a journalist he is allowed the element of the personal without compromising his supposed objectivity. There is also, however, a clear symbolic structure developed throughout the work:

I was determined to see the bottom of this gulf, this sore in the Empire's heart: we went at past three to visit a woman's common lodging-house. On the street, the Close was supplied by a high prison gate, behind which a sooty gas-flare twinkled. At the third floor, on one of the doors, besides the painted iron ticket, was inscribed the word HOME...Here at last the smell that had been pestering us all night was at home; hideous living, unashamed. We passed steadily through lines of iron racks, strewn with sacks, baskets, clothes, rags; inhabited dustbins, the beds in this dormitory. Heads peeped out of the refuse, old head, with wisps of white hair; sleepy, inquiring eyes. One looked at me bashfully and tittered. As we passed through the kitchen, where everything lacked, where there was no brass, no hob, no built-in stove, I looked instinctively to see if *they* were there; and found the long row, four of them, rounded dish-covers, in tinned iron, rusty, unpolished. The rest of the absolute minima were starved off; these pitiful symbols of Hope or custom are as resistant as humanity itself.[4]

The ornamentation he finds in these poor hovels is given supreme significance. His personal philosophy is made explicit and is religious in nature: 'Bed, hearth and chair; humanity's minimum, as simple as the Parables...two china dogs, and between them curious shapes of solid brass...rough profiles of women's boots, cut and scored out of a plate of metal...Art...has left traces of itself even here...Even the poorest houses have this ornament: memento or symbol of Hope?' The condensed milk cans, the metal templates, have a special place in Bolitho's personal iconography; his writing is surprisingly passionate and full of conviction for a young man (Bolitho died at the age of 39), yet there is also something naive and condescending about his style. It must have seemed rather strange to Glaswegians themselves that it had taken so long, and Bolitho had come so far, to find a living hell in their midst, and, for a people proud of their craft and skills at work, it is probably insulting to suggest that the only tangible sign of their humanity, in their own homes, is their ability to fundamentally shape and polish pieces of scrap metal.

Still, Bolitho is determined on redemption which will come in the form, not of the Mission preachers, but of some sort of benevolent government. And, whereas the real clearance of the slums was not to come for some time, Bolitho's rather sensational style was effective in publicising the conditions in the Glasgow slums. It did this in several ways – the florid prose style was one, the composition of the cover illustration another. Designed in the 'Glasgow style' popularised by the illustrator Jessie M. King, it is an abstraction that would as well grace the cover of Dante's *Inferno*. The squat figures in the foreground are as vague and undefined as Annan's shadows, the dark walls of the tenements rise to the sky like the dark gloomy cleft of a deep gorge. Only a chink of light seems to enter its confines. The photographs that illustrate the book, all signed by James McKissack, are in distinct contrast. They are a peculiarly muted monochrome, 'arty' photos printed on yellow paper. They all have notable short titles: A Backland, A Back Green, The City Behind a City, The Turnpike Stair, Farmed-Out Houses, The Glasgow Tenement, A Glasgow Playground, The Washtub. In a way, they show the *best* of the city, without concentrating on rubbish or graffiti. They are primarily architectural studies, devoid, in most cases, of human forms. The point is that they are synecdochal – they represent the city through its supposed typical constituent elements. This is very important, for, because of this technique, the streets and slums of Glasgow in Bolitho are not personalised. Bolitho does not deal with real people, real houses, but rather with the representative, typical elements of the whole – or small cells in the greater organic growth. It is precisely this technique that enables him to fully develop his pathological metaphor, but, in retrospect, it is perhaps an unfortunate metaphor – for cancer is mindless, with no known root cause, it afflicts us unaware, and it cannot be cured.

The cover of *Cancer of Empire*

Apart from Bolitho's occasional condescension and heavy pathos, however, an interesting trend can be readily identified. For the Victorians the Glasgow underworld was a strange land, vaguely terrifying and disgusting but also interesting, exciting or exotic. In the twentieth century a different position evolves. Glasgow, in Bolitho's terms, is a cancer; in the title of Sidney Checkland's book, *The Upas Tree*,[5] it is the mythical tree of Scandinavian mythology that, in growing, destroys all around it, in Alasdair Gray's *Lanark* it is a spiritual cesspool that inflicts its inhabitants with strange diseases. Glasgow itself becomes some sort of creeping malady, an affliction of the body or soul – its significance shifts from the general to the personal; Glasgow becomes part of ourselves. In some of the writing of the twenties and thirties there is this heightened sense of personal disgust. One of the better known descriptions of the city of that time, for example, comes from the pen of Leslie Mitchell, better known as Lewis Grassic Gibbon:

> Glasgow is one of the few places in Scotland which defy personification. To image Edinburgh as a disappointed spinster, with a hare-lip and inhibitions, is at least to approximate as closely to the truth as to image the Prime Mover as a Levantine Semite. So with Dundee, a frowsy fish-wife addicted to gin and infanticide. Aberdeen a thin-lipped peasant woman who has borne eleven and buried nine. But no Scottish image of personification may display, even distortedly, the essential Glasgow. One might go further afield, to the tortured imaginings of the Asiatic mind, to find her likeness – many-armed Siva with the waistlet of skulls or Xipe of Ancient America, whose priest skinned the victim alive, and then clad himself in the victim's skin...But one doubts anthropomorphic representation at all. The monster of Loch Ness is probably the lost soul of Glasgow, in scales and horns, disporting itself in the Highlands after evacuating finally and completely its mother-corpse.
>
> One cannot blame it. My distant cousin, Mr. Leslie Mitchell, once described Glasgow in one of his novels as 'the vomit of a cataleptic commercialism'. But it is more than that. It may be a corpse, but the maggot swarm upon it is fiercely alive...[6]

Even more extreme is the vision of Glasgow constructed by the poet Edwin Muir. Muir, originally from Orkney, came to Glasgow as a young man and suffered a severe depression there accompanied by a heightened sense of mortality. His *Autobiography*[7] tells this story, and although it is notable for its sincere but somewhat ridiculous portrait of the depressed Muir wandering the streets of the city reciting Heine to himself, it has some powerful passages – not least when Muir, working in a meat factory, sees the swarms of maggots on the offal as a metaphor for the decadence of the city. Muir's excessive excremental vision is exemplified by his section on Glasgow in his book *Scottish Journey*:

> I have been told of slum courts so narrow that the refuse flung into them mounted and mounted in the course of years until it blocked all the house windows up to the second-top storey, and I have been given an idea of the stench rising from this rotting, half liquid mass which I shall not reproduce here. I have been told of choked stair-head lavatories with the filth from them running down the stairs; of huge midnight migrations of rats from one block to another, and of bugs crawling down the windows of tram-cars...The refuse that one finds scattered in the streets of an industrial town has always seemed to me to tell a great deal about it, and to be in a humble way a synopsis of its life. One finds there a miscellaneous and yet representative collection which is very revealing...scraps of newspapers, cigarette ends, rims of bowler hats, car tickets, orange peel, boot soles, chocolate paper, fish-and-chip paper, sixpences, broken bottles, pawn tickets and various human excretions: these several things, clean and dirty, liquid and solid, make up a sort of pudding or soup which is an image of the life of an industrial town...in this soup it is considered a perfectly natural thing for human beings to live.[8]

This development of the city as an image of hell fits within an international tradition, and relates to American literature of the time – there is a story that the poet Archibald McLeish moved to Chicago and thought it was hell, but on returning to Glasgow realised it was only purgatory – but there is also something peculiarly Scottish about this vision. Like Bolitho, Muir has the most obvious explanation for Glasgow's situation, although it not directly a political explanation – Muir's personal philosophy is based on the mythology of a lost Golden Age, which is fairly prevalent in Scottish literature:

> The division in the nature of these people was due directly to the corrupting influence of Industrialism...I felt all this very clearly, far more clearly than I could feel it now, but quite blindly. I felt at the same time something else, which was much more terrifying. The best way I can put it is that these people seemed to have all passed through the slums, and to bear the knowledge of the slums within them. On their faces, which were different from the faces I had known before, I thought I could see, quite clearly displayed, a depraved and shameful knowledge, a knowledge which they could not have avoided acquiring, I can see now, but of which they were for the most part unaware...

This depraved knowledge which I found in people's faces was
frightening mainly, I think, because the knowledge was con-
cealed from its possessors, and was like a dangerous thing,
always within them, whose existence they ignored.[9]
This is a poetical imagination, and a personal one. However,
whether, for Muir, the image of the Glasgow slums was merely a
reflection of his personal angst or whether it had more profound
roots in the very nature of city life is besides the point. Muir was
something of a visionary, and what we see developing as in the
thirties, with its appalling depression and omens of the holocaust to
follow, is a sensibility that projects Glasgow as the detritus of
industrialism, some awful cesspit of human depravity, and as a
terrifying personal view of hell.

And so Glasgow in 1938, fifty years on from 1888 and the
International Exhibition, may have appeared, on the surface, as very
like anywhere else in the Empire, or the civilised west. The razzmatazz
year of the last of the Golddiggers movies, *Golddiggers in Paris*, *The
Lady Vanishes*, and *Angels With Dirty Faces*, and schmaltzy hit songs
including *The Folks Who Live on The Hill*, *Someday My Prince Will
Come*, *Donkey Serenade*, *You Must Have Been a Beautiful Baby*, and
Sail Along, Silvery Moon. In 1938, if you smoked Players cigarettes,
you could collect a series of fifty cigarette cards featuring famous stars
– Fred Astaire, Dick Powell, Vivien Leigh, Myrna Loy, or Anton
Walbrook, Nova Pilbeam, Brian Aherne, June Duprez. 1938 – in
Glasgow the year of the Empire Exhibition: and some famous figures
were in town to visit the Exhibition at Bellahouston – Eddie Cantor,
Paul Robeson, Gracie Fields, Charles Laughton – and, in all the
papers, the major attractions at Bellahouston Park were enticingly
advertised – The World Revolving in Space, Mysterious Door
Opened By Invisible Ray, Putting the Eye in the Needle, Victoria Falls
in Replica.[10]

Glasgow in 1938 – the Empire Exhibition, the celebration of all
that was fine in the Second City of Empire may have seemed the best
of all possible worlds. It was, of course, twilight to the bloodiest of
dawnings. Glasgow in its finery in 1938 must have remained a potent
memory to the thousands of young Glaswegians – my father included
– who would not see their native city for several years – if at all – after
which the world would be transformed in a way they would never
have thought possible. At least not in the heady summer of '38.

In that year, to accompany the exhibition, the Edinburgh publishers Oliver and Boyd published a volume – *Scotland 1938* – which
was meant to capture the spirit of the nation at that time. The volume,
with its art deco letters on the spine, its championing, on the one
hand, of heritage and tradition and on the other, of the new

architecture and industry was totally in keeping with the ideology and the style of the time. The collection consisted of twenty-five pieces by various contributors from journalism and the arts. J R Allan, the editor, contributed the main piece on Glasgow:

Who would angle for the Leviathan with a bent pin, or try to describe Glasgow in three thousand words...

To begin with, no native of Glasgow could write about his own town in less than three volumes, and even then he would be afraid that he had missed out just one more instance in which Glasgow is superior to all other cities of the earth together. Or, and such is the temper of these days, he would find life too short a time for setting down the miseries of life by the dirty water of the Clyde. He would need a year to paint the smoke cloud that hangs so low upon the houses; another ten to describe the horror of mean grey streets; and a whole generation to examine the full wickedness of Glasgow bailies. The town breeds such an excess of love or hate in them that belong to it that I dare think there is a place for one who, being free from obligation to hate or love, can look upon the town with casual eyes.

But of course I am not casual about Glasgow; for, however lightly one may regard Heaven and Hell, Glasgow, that is part of both, cannot be turned off with a laugh.[11]

What we can see in this short piece is an attempt at a kind of balancing act. Deep down, the grotesque personal horror of Glasgow cannot be denied or ignored. But there are other redeeming features and virtues which can, for the time being, at least, allow us to thole it. The Empire Exhibition, too, is best seen as an attempt at this kind of desperate balancing act. The contrasts and paradoxes evident in the the presentation of the exhibition are massive – it was an exhibition devoted to industry on industrial Clydeside which had suffered hardest of all from the Depression, heavy industry was not the flavour of the year, the shipbuilding and metal-working industries were in decline, unemployment and poverty were rife; it was an exhibition with the stated object to improve international relations and emphasise the peaceful aspiration of the Empire at a time when such thoughts were far from the mind of our European neighbours; it was an exhibition that attempted to harmonise the country and city with kitsch displays of Highland 'tradition'[12] subsumed within the city context. Yet it was a success for all that, and is fondly remembered by many Glaswegians today – perhaps as a welcome peaceful interlude before the horrors of war, or perhaps as a rare chance, following the exposés of Bolitho and company, to display the virtues of Glasgow to the wider world. It must have been a time of great excitement – so much happening flavoured by the dangerous, distant omens of change.

For there was still, in the thirties, despite the travails of the Glasgow people, a powerful pride in the city itself that is evident in the popular press of the time. Because of this, Glaswegians had a very ambivalent attitude to the most notable work of fiction featuring the city of the time – the novel *No Mean City*, by McArthur and Kingsley Long, first published in 1937. *No Mean City* is a sensationalist account of the career and eventual demise of a hoodlum known as the Razor King in the seedy south side of Glasgow. The title of the novel is ambiguous, as befits the times, but the authors' motive was to display the seamier side of the Glasgow slums and the criminal underworld of the Glasgow gangs. Because of the contentious nature of its subject matter, the authors saw fit to justify it with a preface:

Though all the characters in *No Mean City* are imaginary and the book itself mere fiction, the authors maintain that they have not drawn an exaggerated picture of conditions in the Glasgow tenements or of life as it is lived amongst the gangster element of the slum population.

General readers, some of whom may find it difficult to believe this, may be interested in the following quotations:

'It is not uncommon for eight, ten, or twelve persons to be herded together in a single room. There are (in Glasgow) 175,000 'houses' without baths, and 105,000 'houses' have no internal sanitation.' – *News of the World*, 29/4/34.

'Glasgow's infantile death rate, which was mainly caused by tenement congestion, was 112 in the thousand in 1932 compared with 67 per thousand in London and Birmingham. The infantile death rate in tenement wards is four to six times greater than in residential areas where there are few tenements'. – *Daily Herald*, 16/8/34.

'John R___, 22, leader of the Billy Boys Gang, *and known as the Razor King*, was sent to prison for eighteen months at the High Court in Glasgow yesterday for having assaulted William R___ and seriously injuring him.' – Glasgow *Daily Record*, 17/12/30.

'The spear of a swordfish and a wicked-looking Gurkha knife were among the number of weapons taken possession of by the police following an alleged gang fight in Kerr Street, Bridgeton, yesterday afternoon. The 'battlefield' was strewn with weapons after the fight' ...extracts of the same kind could be quoted *ad nauseam* from the Glasgow and national papers of recent years.[13]

It is strange that a fictional work (and a reasonably well-written one at that) should have to justify the factuality of its content, especially in this formalised way, calling on the greater authority of the popular press. It is stranger still that conjoined in this introduction should be the twin problems of deprivation and crime – the former already studied, the latter largely hidden from the popular gaze until then. Perhaps what most offended the critics of the novel was the implicit suggestion that the two are somehow linked – and that violence and crime (not, you will note, the type of crime so readily identified by the Victorians – theft, prostitution, etc – but a kind of random yet organised mass warfare) should be the direct consequence of deprivation.

Whatever view we take of *No Mean City*, however, it was to introduce a theme that would not go away and, in doing so, perhaps constituted the thirties's major contribution to the mythology of Glasgow and set an agenda for subsequent discussion of the nature of representations of the city. The novel, despite various condemnations, was a success, and spawned a number of sensational and inferior copies in subsequent years. A typical example, published in the fifties, is Bill McGhee's *Cut and Run*. McGhee also feels obliged to justify his work:

> A number of publications on the same theme have already been slated by some of Glasgow's prominent citizens for giving a distorted impression of the city, for showing its citizens as foul-mouthed, razor-slashing gangsters or lazy, street-corner louts. Let me forestall any such criticism and put the reader straight about any misconceptions which might arise from what I say. The story which follows has nothing whatsoever to do with the ordinary people of Glasgow: high, middle or lower class. These are mere spectators – and that rarely – of the kind of violence I describe...but do not imagine that these furious and beastly outbursts of violence do not take place in Glasgow. Read a Glasgow evening paper dated to-day or a few days back, and you will read something which is so endemic and peculiar to Glasgow.[14]

There is something straightforward and factual about this that suggests a documentary flavour to the work, yet he continues in a very different vein which suggests that what he has in mind is a clearly fictionalised structure:

> Most of the lads spend a very short time in the company of the top-notchers. There are, of course, exceptions, such as the ambitious youth who appears on the horizon as a threat, picturing himself in the shoes of some well-known hard-case. Sooner or later one such youngster comes off best in the encounter, and the loser's career is on the wane... But the ordinary lad's term of gangsterism is short merely because he is

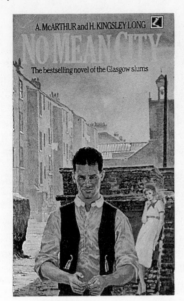 

Covers for the Corgi editions of *No Mean City* and *Cut and Run*

squeamish, and, although he may succeed in hiding this very
human failing from the others, he himself cannot ignore it…for
that squeamishness is the cosh-boys worst crime. To be a
success he must be prepared to 'take a liberty'…if he sticks to
that rule he will thoroughly enhance his reputation. Behind his
back others will refer to him (and what more could he ask for?)
as a 'nutter' or lunatic. Another term commonly used is
…HEAD-CASE…

Many gang-fights, through the years, have been caused by the
girls who run around with the 'chib-men', sometimes carrying
the offensive weapons which the term implies.[15]

This is a piece of mythology and not a piece of social commentary (nor
a piece of really imaginative fiction) which is not particularly Glaswegian, or even Scottish, in type (compare, for example, American
films of the fifties), and, not surprisingly, as Annan has been
recontextualised by the current boom in nostalgia, so have the
gangland novels of the thirties and fifties. Both *No Mean City* and *Cut
and Run* have been reprinted by Corgi. The blurb for the latter reads:

CUT AND RUN

is a story of the Glasgow slums, its streets, its people, its pubs,
gaols, betting shops, brothels, dance halls, and the teeming life
behind the grimy walls of the great grim tenements, where lust
and violence walk hand in hand.

Bill McGhee was born and raised amid the sprawling squalor
he describes, and there is a pitiless authenticity in his picture of
the seamy side of a great city seen through uncoloured glasses.[16]
Clearly the hyperbole and alliteration here are in a common tradition
of blurb writing, but there is also a fundamental misunderstanding
evident in the last sentence. McGhee's aim is not to elucidate or make
plain but to add 'colour' to his writing in the metaphoric sense. This
is made quite clear by the strange paradox that this very blurb is
overlaid on a commissioned painting that portrays the tenement
mise-en-scène in artificially rosy tints! More than that, the characters
depicted on the cover are clearly identical to those depicted on the
cover of the Corgi edition of *No Mean City* – despite the fact that they
are two separate novels, written at different times! What we can see
here is a spurious narrative continuity given to the corps of the
gangland novel spanning a period of decades, as if, again glimpsed
through the distorting lens of nostalgia, the subject, the imagined
gangland story, was now the object of dispassionate study. So our
representation of Glasgow in the thirties, through this mythology, is
presented as unmediated, and recedes further into the fictional past.
And as this process takes place the genre itself is resurrected, and new
gangland novels of the thirties are being written, in the eighties, by
those whose knowledge of those times is purely vicarious – for
example, John Burrowes, a Glasgow journalist best known for his
biography of Benny Lynch, has written several novels in this vein. His
'family is from the Gorbals and this gives him the highest qualifi-
cation to write about this renowned and colourful place' as the
publisher's hype tells us. As the recuperation of the grimy hell-holes
of thirties Glasgow continues through this process of 'pastellisation'
it is not surprising to see, in the same series, as well as the gangland
novels, several more sentimental reminiscences of the tenements –
such as Molly Weir's *Shoes Were for Sunday* – reprinted with similar
cover illustrations but featuring different characters, and even the
Cliff Hanley books – *Dancing in the Streets* accompanied by a cover
illustration that, with a very silly effect, takes the title literally.
Unfortunately, one of the best works of fiction to come out of
Glasgow, Alan Spence's excellent collection of short stories *Its Colours They Are Fine*, first published in 1977, is also included in the
series, and here a sinister ploy develops, for the painted cover of the
book is clearly based on a well-known press photograph of a razor
slashing on the corner of Renfield Street and St Vincent Street (the
victim was, in fact, a plainclothes policeman) originally published in
1971. The sensational effect is hardly worthy of Spence's finely
wrought stories and, inevitably, one small item of news of the once
real world, becomes mythologised in the cause of dreaming the New
Glasgow.

Just a Boy's Game

With the gangland novels of the thirties, we can see a peculiarly potent myth emerging – the myth of the Glasgow 'hard man', or the 'wee Glasgow hard man' as some would have it. A 'hard man', in this context, meaning a tough guy, or at least someone who can't be taken advantage of. One continuing popular embodiment of the mythology of the hard man can be found in the television dramas of Peter McDougall. McDougall's first television play, *Just Another Saturday*, was a revelation when first televised in the early seventies. Mixing actual footage of an Orange Walk in Glasgow with a dramatised narrative (in a sort of cinéma vérité style), McDougall's carefully-wrought script, based on an accurate observation of real Glasgow speech patterns, produces consummate drama. All McDougall's plays, in fact, have this carefully crafted illusion of naturalism which can be misleading – for McDougall is not really interested in real documentary or social comment or even particularly in the minutiae of everyday life. He is intent upon constructing urban mythologies. These narratives only work within a particularly rigid structured framework which must be clearly adhered to within the narrative discourse.

This is apparent in perhaps his most accomplished single play, *Just a Boy's Game*, first screened in November 1979, which created quite a furore at the time because of its uncompromising treatment of gang warfare and violence in the urban west.[1]

Just a Boy's Game is the story of a reformed hard man, Jake McQuillan, played by the rock singer Frankie Miller, who has, metaphorically 'hung up his guns' – McQuillan doesn't carry a 'chib' or any weapon, as opposed to McCafferty, the young contender, who has a fearsome-looking knife. This gives McQuillan a dubiously moral stance – although his past misadventures are never investigated. If the 30s hard man was clearly interpellated by the gangster movies of the time, then this play is transparently motivated by the cowboy or western film. The metaphor is most clearly elaborated by McQuillan's jovial car mechanic mate, Tanza – during the opening confrontation he refers to a 'gunfight in Sugar Hoose Lane' and he tells the police that McQuillan has 'hung up his guns years ago'. Similarly the 'game' is introduced early on with the boy's talk of football, McCafferty's cry of 'Young Team ya bass!', and the barman's retort to McQuillan – 'you know the rules' – which clearly doesn't refer simply to pub etiquette. This complex structure is further compounded by the fact that the major characters continually talk in metaphor – as if they have swallowed several copies of *The Patter* (despite McDougall's reputation as a naturalist, the more harsh, realistic dialogue is in fact reserved for the minor characters). McQuillan, of course, has all the attributes of the standard western hero, he is controlled, competent, cynical, tough, unhappy. There are the usual classic scenes, the stare out, when McQuillan reduces a young hoodlum to tears simply by looking at him, the moment when McQuillan, threatened by the youngsters, merely smiles. The final 'shoot-out', when McQuillan is forced to shape up to the baddies, and personally defeats McCafferty in a hand-to-hand battle.

There is, however, an equally powerful controlling paradigm made explicit in the title. The encounter and the build up to the encounter between McQuillan and McCafferty is, in fact, an elaborate but clearly defined game with its own specific rules. This is parallel to the unravelling of the generic narrative form with which the informed viewer is totally cognizant. Clearly, whereas the other characters carry on their random lives unaware of their previously determined fate, McQuillan has the extra knowledge, the overall omniscient understanding of the workings and eventual denouement of the text, of the reader. It is inevitable that however valid or just his moral standpoint may seem to be, McQuillan elicits the reader's sympathy.

The two-part structure of the narrative is particularly crucial in this respect. After the initial sequence, McQuillan forsakes the opportunity to go drinking with his friend Dancer in order to go home to his grandmother (he lives with his grandparents and doesn't talk to his mother) to support her as she copes with his grandfather's terminal illness. The grandfather, played by the late comedian Hector Nicol, is a particularly bad sort, who has spent a period in jail.

In the final sequence McQuillan has 'read the signs' that point to the showdown with McCafferty, and refuses to go home, even though his grandfather appears to be in his final throes. There is highly stylised scene in a snooker hall in which the frame of snooker acts metaphorically to demonstrate McQuillan's impending mastery of 'the game'. McQuillan appears to have no choice – 'You don't go back' he tells Dancer and Tanza when confronted with McCafferty's gang – he has to abide with the (unwritten) rules. McQuillan must triumph but Dancer, who, paradoxically, has the possibility of a settled family life but turns to drink (breaking the rules to which he should conform) is sacrificed as he is killed being chased by the gang. The final twist comes at the end when McQuillan confronts his grandfather on his deathbed. McQuillan, thinking he has a complete understanding of the 'rules' of the hard man game sympathises with his grandfather – 'Ah know the game, ah'm like yerself'. However, the grandfather, with a more perfect understanding of the rules, trumps him by whispering that he doesn't care for Jake and 'when ah wis young, ah could have taken you anytime'. The play ends with a close-up of McQuillan's emotionless face narrowing to the eyes only framed by a red background, and a song that makes the message more explicit still:

> And it's all in the rules of the game,
> Like a jungle of cowboys out staking a claim.
> The rules remain always the same,
> Boys will be boys, and men will be men.[2]

Another television drama scripted by McDougall that appeared at about the same time as *Boy's Game* and which drew on the same strain of violence and squalor was the adaptation of Jimmy Boyle's autobiographical *A Sense of Freedom*.[3] The career of Jimmy Boyle is now so well-known to need little elaboration here. Born in the Gorbals, he became involved in money-lending and criminal activities. After several acts of extreme violence he was eventually given a life sentence and became infamous as a particularly violent and uncontrollable prisoner. Eventually, in the seventies, he was 'rescued' by the Barlinnie Special Unit, and his rehabilitation was accompanied by a growing interest in art and literature. Now established as a writer, he has been released and lives in Edinburgh. Particularly because of the nature of his criminal activities – extortion, money-lending and protection rackets aimed at victimising his fellow citizens in the Gorbals (ie – directed specifically at working-class, ordinary people) – Boyle has never been readily forgiven by those Glaswegians who remember his reign of terror. Sidney Checkland comments on this ambivalent attitude: 'And yet there is a powerful moralism in Glasgow working-class life. Though Glasgow authors showed a good deal of sympathy with Jimmy Boyle, as depicted in the play *The Hard Man*, working-class opinion certainly contains a strong element that finds it hard to forgive him his violence on the ground that he was a victim of a vicious society, for they know the terror of such men. The Boyle story has provided a wonderful opportunity to project a Brechtian Glasgow: the television presentation, *A Sense of Freedom*, provoked from Stanley Eveling of the *Scotsman* the description of a 'Glasgow glowering back at us like a mangy, scruffy, savage alley-cat hopping with tics. You could smell the pee.' Richard

Last of the *Daily Telegraph* was left 'wondering uneasily if there may not be three divisions of humanity, male, female and Glaswegian.' Of this sort of projection (with its lack of understanding and sympathy for the fate of Glasgow), many working-class people are, with justice, deeply resentful.'[4] In fact, *A Sense of Freedom*, despite its portrayal of fairly extreme and gory violence which earned it the condemnation of many Glaswegians, is not particularly naturalistic in itself. It is, in fact, clearly a companion to Boyle's stage play, *The Hard Man,* co-scripted with Tom McGrath, which fictionalises Boyle's career, and which created a sensation on its first appearance due to the obscene language, nudity and scatology of the second act, which stylises Boyle's confinement in the form of a giant cage on centre stage.

In many ways *A Sense of Freedom* is similar to *Just a Boy's Game*. The iconography is the same, grim tenements, squalid pubs, gloomy rain-soaked streets. The violence is portrayed graphically and the metaphors are similar, especially as regards football – Boyle, planning a battle against a rival gang, talks about 'scoring' and 'getting an equaliser' – and weapons, or chibs, interestingly, are 'tools' in both. As *Just a Boy's Game* works to elicit the viewer's sympathy for McQuillan, *A Sense of Freedom*, especially in the second half of the play which deals with Boyle's prison experiences, generally sympathises with Boyle. The initial part of the play is earthy and pulls no punches with regard to violence, but it is full of contrasts. Initially we switch from a sordid scene of one of Boyle's 'clients' vomiting in a close mouth because of his fear of confronting Boyle, to Boyle visiting his mum and buying sweeties for children. He is, this seems to suggest, not such a bad sort after all and an integral part of, and perhaps created by, the Gorbals community to which he belongs.

There is an interesting version of an old but exceedingly complex mythology in the Boyle story – that out of the worst sometimes sprouts the best. The supposed rehabilitation of Boyle is really, in microcosm, the story of the New Glasgow. In another version this is, like the title of the popular ballet, the *Miracle of the Gorbals,* in that, as in Shadow's Glasgow, there is an easy redemption amongst the squalor. (In the words of William Montgomerie's poem, *Glasgow Street* – 'Out of this ugliness may come / some day so beautiful a flower'. I remember, as a schoolboy, my art teacher suggesting that I paint a picture on this theme and, after rendering the grainy tenemental backlands in my best imitation of James Morrison, I found it almost impossible to impose the colourful bloom, so evidently a creature of a different genre. The romance was shattered, even though the painting won a prize.)

However, the potency of the traditional portrayal of Glasgow as a city of squalor, poverty and violence peopled by aggressive gangs, constitutes the so-called 'No Mean City' image which the 'Glasgow's Miles Better' campaign went to such pains to counter. The hard man myth has been identified as a particularly regressive myth. Colin McArthur, the film critic, comments, 'Certain societies (the Germany of the Third Reich and the pre-Civil War American South are perhaps the best examples) are characterised by a noxious mélange of sentimentality and brutality. Modern Scotland displays something of the same mix. The sentimentality is evident in the decayed romanticism of tartanry and kailyard, the brutality in the emotionally retarded male heroes who lurch drunkenly across Scottish television screens and through the pages of most Scottish novels', and other critics have pointed to the lack of normal relationships between the sexes in Scottish literature, film and television.[5] As far as portrayals of the female sex go, of course, there is a tendency towards simplistic and regressive modes. Women are invariably either aged mothers, abused wives, or tarts. Whether this is a result of a certain narrative impulse or an innate Scottish sexism I do not intend to consider. In Scottish fiction especially of the 'hard man' variety, women have no independent personality – as McQuillan says, 'a maw's a good machine'.

There has been a lot of discussion concerning the real constitution of the hard man mythology. The novelist William McIlvanney has recently (on the BBC television production, *This is Me Since Yesterday*) stressed some of its positive attributes – '...if it was fed on the steroids of publicity, it did earn its muscles on the street...people who have hard lives – not a lot of money, not a lot of comfort to show for it. They tend to walk around on their own collateral. Who they are when they walk into a bar is essential to them' – whereas other critics, predominantly feminist, have condemned it as the residue of a macho patriarchal dominance. Despite these regressive characteristics, however, the more positive characteristics of the hard man stereotype have been developed, over time, to produce a new breed of almost avuncular hard men on the right side of the law in, for example, McIlvanney's novels featuring the police detective Jack Laidlaw.[6] Laidlaw is a hard man with a conscience, who inhabits 'Glasgow...the city of the stare' and who has the sort of streetwise understanding of the city that enables him to be, at one and the same time, tough and sensitive. In fact, a McIllvanney type of character – the rough, rugged, hard-bitten policeman with, beneath the bluff exterior, a heart of gold has been brought to the television screen in the form of Taggart, a Glasgow detective played by Mark McManus in the series of that name which has proved popular enough to be networked in the eighties.

In many ways Taggart is the stereotypical screen policeman, in the tradition of *The Sweeney*, cynical, obsessed with work, unable to sustain proper family relationships (pathos is introduced to *Taggart* in the form of his crippled wife), but his identification with Glasgow is a vital factor that the series plays to its utmost, employing genuine contemporary Glasgow locations and situations (such as the Garden Festival). For the southern viewer this link, both with the actuality of Glasgow and the urban west of Scotland, and with a distinct Glasgow mythology, must be a vital part of his reading of the text. This is made quite clear in the title sequence of *Taggart*. It begins with a panorama of Glasgow, identifiable but with a surfeit of harshly-outlined rectangular modernist blocks, a sky of travelling clouds developing above the title and name 'Taggart' and appearing in shiny moulded chrome letters as the panorama loses its tints and becomes monochrome. A succession of clearly identifiable images of the city – a multi-storey block, Glasgow University, a tenement – in high contrast slatted format are presented in an obvious attempt to further anchor the Glasgow connection with the series – and to demonstrate the diversity of the city precinct.

Then a line drawing of Taggart himself is superimposed. It is not animated, but a succession of different drawings is employed to avoid a stationary effect. The only movement is as the portrait tilts slightly into direct address. There can be no dubiety about the meaning here – the craggy, lined face of Taggart in representation addresses the viewer against the equally harsh background of the city landscape. Neither is completely at rest. We are invited to associate Taggart metonymically with the city of his birth. Taggart is Glasgow.

Finally, the camera pans away from Taggart to focus on the city panorama itself. We can enter Taggart's world. It is, however, a twilight world. The city becomes dark, the floating sky above is now a fiery red.

We can hardly fail to sympathise with Taggart, to identify with his morals, his dedication, appreciate his difficulties. The Glaswegian actor Mark McManus, who plays the part, has become something of a celebrity in his own right and has co-authored a book about the city that seems to deliberately confuse real and fictional versions of city life. It may well seem that there is redemption for the hard man – with the proviso, of course, that he is on the right side of the law. Within the criminal underworld of Glasgow, the hard man is a survivor – but he survives not only by his capacity for toughness but by his rigid adherence to a legitimated code that exists apart from the hard man paradigm or the peculiarly Glaswegian mythology that spawns it. This is, in fact, the real reason for the continuing popularity of the hard man stereotype – it is not to do with toughness, or macho posing, or excitement, it is to do with knowledge. The hard man is the only one who really understands the complexity of life in the city, he *knows.* Knows where to be, what to do, knows exactly how to react to each given situation. It is hardly too fanciful to suggest that the hard man stereotype precurses the whole concept of city style. And this is why the traditional hard man is still a figure regarded with some affection in Glasgow and why, for example, the comedian Billy Connolly is the 'big yin' – a notable tough exterior with a soft centre.

The complete recuperation of the hard man image seems to come, however, not with television drama, but with a different body of texts – a group of contemporary Scottish films that seem more difficult to place. If the development of the hard man can be traced to specific generic mores from popular culture, it is not so simple to categorise these – although the impetus possibly owes a great deal to the individual contribution of the film director Bill Forsyth. This corpus of films begins with Forsyth's *That Sinking Feeling*, a comedy in which the group of teenage would-be gangsters break into a warehouse and steal a selection of bathroom furniture. The criminality of these proceedings is negated by a farcical combination of circumstances (in the Ealing comedy tradition) whereby, for example, one of the youngsters manages to sell a battered sink and cistern as a piece of modern sculpture. In this way their criminal activities are subsumed by a comic tradition that labels them as merely harmless fun. This style reaches its apotheosis a few years later in a film not directed by Forsyth but which bears his hallmark, *Restless Natives*, directed by Michael Hoffman, set on this occasion in Edinburgh, in which two bored teenagers become media celebrities by robbing tourist coaches in fancy dress

In these and other films, such as Forsyth's *Gregory's Girl* and Charles Gormley's *Living Apart Together* and *Heavenly Pursuits* the hard man stereotype is turned on its head. If, in the established schema, the hard man exists in a totally malevolent world, vicious, unyielding, an underworld populated only by the lowest of the low, in which he can survive only by divesting himself of all human frailty, compassion, misgivings, or childish misconceptions, then the structure of these films is exactly the opposite – the world is almost totally benevolent and weaknesses and even criminal acts go unpunished, redemption is always available, the future is always rosy. The survivors are hardly hard-bitten but underdeveloped, childlike adults with foibles, inadequacies, illusions – in fact, soft men. Not that this tradition of the childish innocent hero had not existed before, nurtured by the Kailyard school (Barrie's *Peter Pan* is, of course, the epitome) but its application to a contemporary urban context seems new.

Bill Forsyth's *Comfort and Joy* is a good example of this tendency. Set in Glasgow, *Comfort and Joy* features Bill Paterson as a radio disc jockey Alan (Dickie) Bird who is depressed after the breakup of his relationship with his girlfriend and gets involved in a mafia-type battle between two rival families running ice-cream vans. The film has some clever touches, not least in the way that the absurdity of Bird's profession as a radio disc jockey is conjoined with the seeming absurdity of Bird's own life and a continuous background is added to the *mise-en-scène* by the voice-overs of radio reports on war, terrorism, a pregnant panda, a radio lookalike competition, and motorway traffic reports. This is all very well, but the film is so lacking in an overall narrative that one feels that Glasgow merely serves as a sullen and anonymous backdrop against which to parade Forsyth's tiresome childish jokes. The point about *Comfort and Joy,* however, is that, like all Forsyth's films, it elides true violence and crime through rather obvious humour. Thus at the beginning, when Bird encounters an ice-cream van attacked by two hooded hoodlums with large clubs, one of the men advances towards him menacingly only to ask for an autograph and a radio request for his mother. Bird approaches the stricken vehicle and asks 'Is that blood?' 'No, it's just raspberry essence'.

Later he comments 'People getting so angry about ice-cream, it's a joke'. Unfortunately, in the way that real life sometimes has the temerity to interfere with media illusion, the very real 'ice-cream war', upon which Forsyth tangentially based his story, came to prominence at the very moment of the film's release, with the particularly unsavoury murders of a family involved in the ice-cream van trade in Glasgow's Ruchazie. The actual 'ice-cream war' had, to the knowledge of the local people, been going on in the housing schemes of Garthamlock and Ruchazie (in such schemes, bereft of shops and other facilities, mobile vans are an essential service to the community) for years, with frequent violence and with the full cognizance of the police.

This unfortunate coincidence did not do any great damage to the film at the box office, but certainly brought home to many the rather paradoxical relationship between Forsyth's fictional wish-fulfilling screen world (praised by several Scottish commentators at its inception for its realism) and real-life.

The confusion of the naive and childlike, or under-socialised softman, Dickie Bird (his name itself evocative of Disney more than anything) is mirrored by the confusion of the film's plot. At one central point, Bird, intent upon making a serious documentary for his radio station, draws a plan on a wall chart that connects himself, ice-cream, the city, etc. by means of directional arrows. He can't make any sense of it, and neither can the reader. Likewise, the relationship of any of the comic book characters in *Comfort and Joy* to the city

environment is unclear. The city merely exists, but it doesn't inform
the narrative in any way, or grip the imagination – as in *Deathwatch*
or even *A Sense of Freedom*. Yet the new 'soft man' is, in a way, an
antidote to more traditional stereotypes and has, therefore, been seen
as potentially progressive. Like much of the New Glasgow, however,
it is an empty image, created not from the real world but by a strange
atavism – a return to a fantasy world only perceived through the eyes
of a child. Thus, despite various attempts at restructuring the hard
man myth – for example, through comedy, as in Carl McDougall's
popular song *Cod Liver Oil and the Orange Juice*, with its mock
religious structure ('From oot o' the east there cam a wee hard man'),
or in the imbecilic Big Tam in BBC Scotland's successful television
sitcom, *City Lights*, or in Bill Bryden's *The Holy City*, a disastrous
attempt to place the story of Christ in contemporary Glasgow – with
David Hayman, who played Boyle in *A Sense of Freedom,* as the
punter / prophet – it is the original unadulterated form that has been
most successful. There are several reasons for this – the mythology of
the hard man is strictly based on a distinct set of rules and, as such,
it attempts to understand or explain the ways of the city. It also, at
least in its best-known narrative form, 'talks' to the people in a
common and popular language – the parlance of cinema or football,
the quick-witted retort that is supposedly so typical of Glaswegian
wit. For all its unsavoury aspects, it is an important component of
Glasgow mythology

If the real world occasionally impinges on these almost perfect
fictions, then the opposite principle also applies – the real world has
tended to be fictionalised even by supposedly serious research into the
urban situation. The sort of stylised gang warfare that led to the
writing of *No Mean City* in the thirties, resurfaced in a slightly
different form in the fifties and sixties, transferred, for the most part,
from the inner city ghettos to the new peripheral housing schemes.
Once again, in the sixties, the violent activities of these gangs became
a source of media attention that was hardly to Glasgow's credit.
Several projects to counter gang violence – generally now, in a more
liberal society, seen as a consequence of urban deprivation – were
hatched, including the notable but ineffectual intervention of Frankie
Vaughan, the singer/dancer, in Easterhouse. A more scholarly attempt at understanding was the interpretive study undertaken by a
criminologist, James Patrick, and detailed in *A Glasgow Gang Observed*.[7] Basically, the rather unconvincing story is that Patrick, a
probation officer, adopts a new identity and is initiated into a
Glasgow gang with the help of one of his former wards. The book
details his experiences in an objective matter-of-fact style. Patrick's
prose is fluent and easy to follow:

...Saturday night. Frank Murphy, a boy with a crew cut and a large ugly scar stretching from the tip of his chin to his ear, was the centre of attraction. He had, I was told, fifty-nine stitches on the side of his face; he had been 'ripped' only a few weeks ago: 'It wis in the papirs'. Then my attention was directed to Tommie McConnell whose claim to fame was that he had punched a boy through the window of a large department store in town...I heard an old-age pensioner asking for a pint of beer and a packet of nuts. This prompted Pat to remark: 'Nice to see y'ir still gettin' yir nuts.' More laughter. In the toilet I read a large spray-painted slogan:

> Wild
> Young
> Catholic
> Team
> Rules
> O.K.

Around this notice gang members had appended their signatures, e.g. Mad Harry, Fry, Jim, Mad Mex etc. I re-entered the bar in time to see a labourer, while stretching for his drink, nudge Pat accidentally in the back. Pat immediately challenged him and his mate to a fight. I had noticed the two navvies earlier, standing beside us in the pub, two hefty six-footers in gumboots and donkey jackets. As voices began to rise, the boys in the pub (and there were roughly thirty of them there, with more next door in the signing lounge with their girlfriends) began to encircle them. Pat put his left hand into his top right-hand inside pocket where 'chibs' or weapons are normally carried. 'If you bring that oot, y'ir deid', shouted one of the workmen. 'Wee Midgie', whose hair looked as if it lived up to the sobriquet, and who was standing behind the two labourers, struck them over the head with a full lemonade bottle. As the men fell, Pat and Baggy kicked them mercilessly in the face and stomach while Tim lifted an empty bottle of Newcastle Brown Ale and cracked it over their heads.

This is, of course, hard to accept as objective description. Instead, the close attention to detail, especially to language, is reminiscent not of the traditional sociological text, but of narrative fiction in the gangland novel genre:

We were now walking up Sauchiehall Street listening to Pat criticising himself for having started the fight. 'Ah should hiv' ma heid examined. Startin' aw that an' me up in court oan Wednesday an' aw.' By now it was nearly ten o'clock and Baggy suggested going to the Granada Dance Hall...

The girls looked superb in the half light, their very young faces heavily painted and their eyes black with mascara. Some wore lime green trouser-suits, others daring backless dresses. Their skirts and 'sexy wee black froaks' were all very short. Pat commented, as he pushed forward and was pushed back by the girls, that some dresses were so low: 'Ye can see their breakfasts'.[9]

Patrick is, in fact, obsessed with the exotic: slang – 'going radio' (radio rental = mental), slogans – 'MYT' (Mental Young Team), 'YMF' (Young Mental Fleet), nicknames – the members of the gang are called Podgie, Gallie, Beano, Wee Midgie, Eldo, Big Fry, Wee Cock, Plum Duffy, Blinkie, Big Dim, Shug Wilson, Cocoa, Chancy Chalmers, Mitch, Baggy, etc. Strangely, though, although he displays the gang schematically around a core in a name diagram, he also confesses that the names – those I have just quoted – are fictional. It seems odd that, if the structure of personal relationships and the relationships themselves can serve to explain the nature of the gang's activities, then the very language they use – the names, the slogans, the slang – is not also peculiarly revealing. Perhaps it is a sociological conceit, but this sort of symbolic employment of language – the way the gang inscribe and reconstruct their own identity through their conversation or more physically carve their rubric on the city walls – is not really investigated by Patrick, although he includes a glossary of terms and explains slang terms, thus objectifying the language, an aim seemingly at odds with the immediacy of the semi-fictional accounts. Rather than looking at the way the gang's macho mentality or structured subculture has impinged itself on the popular imagination, however, he is intent more on dissecting the guts of everyday experience. Despite his recourse to theories of sociology or criminology, he is, eventually, fictionalising the gang, very much in the same fashion as Bill McGhee, although with a much keener eye for colourful detail.

The players in these reconstructions are not the traditional hard men of narrative fiction, despite the obvious similarities, and there is a very simple reason for this. The adolescent hoodlums encountered by Patrick are not constructed by an impartial narrative but are themselves the subject of a directed study. The keynote of the true hard man is his ability to understand the rules in any given situation – at least until, occasionally, his downfall. The subjects of Patrick's goldfish bowl study are obviously lacking in the ultimate knowledge – the controlling discourse belonging to the observer. They are emasculated, and this is particularly appropriate – because, in the sixties, the prime motivation of many such studies, although Patrick can be partially exempted from this fault, was to explain gang violence in specifically social terms. The gangs were seen as bunches of misguided and impoverished youths led into random violence by a few 'heidbangers' or psychopaths. This explanation ignores for the greater part the traditional structured nature of communal relations that actually typified the old Glasgow tenement communities, and the particularly unifying nature of the social mores and shibboleths of the Glasgow gangs, and, not least, the religious and sectarian motivation.

Sectarianism is an important ingredient in the 'No Mean City' image, although it is so sensitive a topic that it is often portrayed tangentially. The gangs of the thirties, the San Toi, the Derry and the infamous Billy Boys, etc, almost all arose from religious motivation – the Billy Boys apparently being formed to combat Catholicism after a riot at a football match – and were almost entirely sectarian in their membership (although there is evidence that this wasn't strictly observed – after the fashion, as some have pointed out, of Celtic football club, who do sign Protestant players). The mythology of the sectarian gangs has been publicised, for example, by Edwin Morgan's poem *King Billy*, describing the funeral of Billy Fullerton, leader of the Billy Boys – an event that attracted a crowd of over a thousand people years after the gang had faded into obscurity (the mythology has it that the English police chief Sillitoe, a blunt man who tried but didn't succeed in putting an end to Rangers / Celtic games, destroyed the Billy Boys, but, in truth, it was really the war that put an end to their activities). Sectarianism in Glasgow, of course, has a long pedigree, dating to the mass immigration of Irish (and some Highland) Catholics in the early nineteenth-century. Both the orange and the green still derive their impetus to some extent from Ireland but sectarianism in Glasgow has developed its own particular structure which does not admit on any major scale the type of violence and guerilla warfare associated with Northern Ireland.

How does sectarianism function in Glasgow today ? Nostalgia in the real sense of the word – as nostalgia for one's homeland – can truly be said to inform the everyday life of a significant proportion of the Catholic community of Glasgow. Inscribed in the fabric of the community – the names on the doors of the flats in the closes of the cloned blocks in the housing scheme ghettos of Glasgow echo the ethnic origins of the Irish immigrant community. Their homeland, however distant, or reconstructed is part of a national mythology – the Irish Club, Ceoltas piping competitions, the shamrock, ceilidhs in the James Elliot Centre, Celtic football club, St Patrick's day, etc. Strangely, many Glasgow Protestants are descendants of Irish immigrants (such as my own grandfather) but they do not preserve the mythology or the feeling of a homeland. This is an important factor in the maintenance of an insular Catholic community in Glasgow, and, whether you subscribe to this nationalistic mythology or not, there is a structured and intensely symbolic ritual associated with Catholicism that functions in the same way. Similarly, the Catholic church offers both rites of passage and everyday rituals – the communion, mass, confession, etc. that go some way towards constituting a Glasgow Catholic family.

The higher echelons of some Protestant sectarian groups, such as the Black Men, have their own structured mythology, but most Glasgow Protestants must look on the average Catholic's more intimate everyday and mythical communion with envy, for because of their very majority, their ethnic diversity, the historical inevitability of Scottish Protestant religious schisms – paradoxically a Scottish Protestant diaspora – identity is not a characteristic of Protestantism that brooks comparision with Catholicism as a real religious belonging.[12] Instead, Protestants derive their religious icons and characteristics from a second-hand history of another nation bereft of its genuine and motivating *mythological* content. Somehow, Protestant Kirk history, the Jacobins, Covenanteers, the Disruption, preserved in a hundred dusty Victorian tomes, has none of the fantasy or mythical and elemental flavour of the strange apocrypha of greater European Catholicism, with its Latin intonations, its strange saints, its personal embodiment of the notion of God, of family, of self. Nationalism (or rather Scottish nationalism, or even nationality) can have really no part in the religious substructure of Glasgow – especially Protestant Glasgow, which perversely takes its inspiration from Ireland – although, somehow, despite the travails of King Billy at the Boyne, historical inevitability dictates it is a battle they cannot win.

There is a mythology inherent in any Glasgow church – or the pastel-painted displays of plaster saints in the windows of Carruth's Grotto – that is strange, inexplicable, attractive and threatening to the average Protestant. Their lack, in face of the ethnic masses of the Catholic community is made more poignant by their failure to occupy the common ground of poverty, at least in a historical sense. The Protestant movement in Glasgow is typified by absence. There are Catholic schools, but there are also non-denominational schools – characterised by something less, rather than something different. The most radical, in religious terms, sects of the Protestant faith, the Wee Frees, etc, like the infamous Rechabites, practice their religion to perfection only through abstinence. As Bill Murray says, 'while Catholics are stuck with a hierarchy committed to sectarian education, Protestants are stuck with the Rangers Football Club'.[10]

Strangely, the esoterism of the Catholic rites are echoed by the shibboleths of the pseudo-masonic rituals of the Orange Order.

Because they cannot perpetuate the mock brotherhood of the professions to constitute their own family (as the original Irish immigrants could in their ghettos) the Orangemen resolve history into symbolism (in the mounted figure – warhead – of King Billy and the iconography of Rangers football club) and meticulously track their symbolic battleground on the topography of the city through their periodic marches (not merely once a year as some may think but, in certain parts of the city, nearly every weekend). The ceremonial nature of these occasions is vital, although their aggressive nature is not just a rallying call, but a direct confrontational display to the Catholic community (marching through Catholic areas and often playing loudly outside churches) and they are organised like a military campaign – with location, timing, content, volume, etc, all crucially important.

And yet, in the Protestant heartland of Glasgow, there has been a slow, significant change. If you visit today the largely Protestant suburb of Rutherglen and the rallying points – the *Twenty Club* or the *Old Quarry Bar* – you will see that, in recent years, the symbolic portrait of the Queen has been replaced by a series of soft focus and gilt framed family portraits of the younger members of the Royal family. This is a strange irony. All symbolic value is suddenly lost to the iconic power of the family bond. The banner-waving, baton-tossing, flute-playing blue boys of the Orange Order suddenly dewy-eyed at the prospect of their lost brothers and sisters of a foreign class, culture and nation.

What sort of system can harbour and sustain such paradoxes? Simply, one that relies absolutely on a symbolic order. In the eighties, religious bigotry exists merely for its own right, for the distraction of its aphocrypha, or the attractions of nostalgic remembering. There is no violence to speak off – at least not on an organised level. The days of the Billy Boys and Dans are gone and Glasgow, to its credit, has not succumbed to the attraction of the particular brand of bigotry endemic in Northern Ireland.[11] (In some senses, in fact, the bigotry remains within, but generally harmlessly, unspoken – one well known Glasgow joke tells of a Protestant Celtic player complaining to a colleague about being called a 'papist bastard' by rival fans. 'Don't worry', he says, 'it's been happening to me for years'. 'But that's OK, you are a papist bastard', he replies). And yet the bigotry is still with us in its more general divisory sense, if not exhibited on a personal level (very few sane Glaswegians will actually refuse to greet a neighbour or start a conversation in a pub despite his sectarian beliefs). To our shame, we still have segregated schools, although, if we ask the schoolchildren themselves, very few actually support this provision. The issue is, however, such a hot potato that no-one will really confront it. The sectarian problem seems to have faded into the background in the Glasgow of the eighties. One explanation for this may be that the social constituents of its birth – notably the competition for employment – have no more mileage in an era when employment is a non sequitur. In the New Glasgow, sectarianism leads only into itself – competition is the preserve of the individual, employment the victory of Kismet rather than the funny handshake. The sectarian institutions are now merely a hobby or a bad joke. Only the mystery survives and knowledge holds no quarter. We have moved some way towards the old adage, that in the kingdom of the bigot, the blind man is truly king. And, despite all I have said, at the extremes of fashion, perhaps, the excesses of bigotry may be creeping slowly back into prominence. On television the comic, Rab C. Nesbitt, plays a ridiculous extremist bigot, Mason Boyne, to some effect, and at the Barras stalls sell t-shirts with offensive sectarian slogans aimed at both sides of the divide.

In dealing with some of the hard truths of what might be called a traditional Glasgow mythology, I have looked at the hard man stereotype, gang violence and sectarianism. Another ingredient of this rather unpleasant mixture is the propensity, both mythical and real, of the Glaswegian for alcohol. Drinking in Glasgow is more than an occasional pastime – for much of the population it is a very serious hobby (this is a mythology itself but also, unfortunately, a hard truth – alcoholism, alcohol related crimes and health problems are particularly prevalent). Hugh MacDiarmid, in his essay *The Dour Drinkers of Glasgow*, discusses the particular nature of drinking in Glasgow:

> The majority of Glasgow pubs are for connoisseurs of the morose, for those who relish the element of degradation in all boozing and do not wish to have it eliminated by the introduction of music, modernistic fitments, arty effects, or other extraneous devices whatsoever. It is the old story of those who prefer hard-centre chocolates to soft, storm to sunshine, sour to sweet. True Scots always prefer the former of these opposites. That is one of our principle differences from the English. We do not like the confiding, the intimate, the ingratiating, the hail-fellow-well-met, but prefer the unapproachable, the hard-bitten, the recalcitrant, the sarcastic, the saturnine, the cross-grained and the cankered, and the howling wilderness to the amenities of civilisation, the irascible to the affable, the prickly to the smooth. We have no damned fellow-feeling at all, and look at ourselves and others with the eye of a Toulouse-Lautrec appraising an obscene old toe-rag doing the double-split...
> Our attitude is not inhuman. We are experienced men of the

world. We like what we like to be a little grim – in keeping with
the facts of life, and loathe facile emotions. We cherish no
illusions, and consequently prefer a mutual taciturnity to any
sort of social joy, standing shoulder to shoulder with other men
we do not know from Adam and do not want to know. We feel
no necessity whatever to indulge in any airs and graces, are not
fond of promiscuous conversation, at least of any sustained
sort, and if our risible faculties are moved at all by the human
spectacle, that movement only adorns our faces intermittently
with some sort of *risus sardonicus* that in flickering across our
features barely interrupts the emission of the dense smoke of the
black tobacco going well in our clay pipes.[13]

The exuberant Rabelaisian language disguises the more insidious
implications of this kind of thinking. The clichéd mythology of
Glasgow, the friendly city, is perhaps the most pernicious of all the
city mythologies. In a real respect the taciturnity of McDiarmid's
dour drinkers is the happiest of all Glaswegian character traits – a
healthy respect for one's privacy. But there is also something rather
disturbing about the Glaswegian habit of heavy drinking. At its worst
it is not a sociable habit at all but a type of personal confrontation
with the outside world. This is displayed by the special nature of the
Glasgow pub which has refused to be reformed since its origins in the
nineteenth century and still sticks, largely, to the sole purpose of
providing drink – with little else to amuse the customer.[14] Not surprisingly, one of the first principles of the New Glasgow has been to
develop city leisure outlets such as wine bars, cafes, restaurants. This
has substantially altered the image of the city's drinking spots but has
generally failed to penetrate the suburbs or the schemes – where
things go on much the same as before.

Perhaps the New Glasgow, as it reconstitutes its mythologies of
the recent past, would like to forget about the reality of the unholy
trinity of violence, religious bigotry and drink that so pungently
inform the so-called 'No Mean City' mythology, but, stubbornly, it
won't go away. Generations of Glasgow comedians – from Tommy
Morgan to Lex McLean to Billy Connolly to Gerry Sadowitz – have
made these unsavoury topics their staple diet. Today Billy Connolly
is recast as a reformed Glaswegian and advertises non-alcoholic
lager, but Glasgow itself cannot be so easily cured.

Unthank

Over two centuries there have been many Glasgow novels – the sentimental or morose redemption stories or mission tracts, the twee Victorianism of Guy McCrone's 'Antimacassar City', the gangland genre, and other attempts of varying merit. It was generally accepted, however, that Scotland's largest city had not produced one work of outstanding or lasting merit. Scottish authors seemed to find their voice in the rural or small-town idiom; the urban scene seemed to defy description for over two hundred years. Despite the variety and power of descriptive or documentary reports like Bolitho or Muir, no sufficiently flexible fictional discourse had been discovered to portray Glasgow in the form of prose fiction. There was no great Glasgow novel. At least not until Alasdair Gray published *Lanark*, an epic novel first conceived in the sixties, in 1981.

Lanark is written in two distinct sections – Books One and Two are a naturalistic account of the childhood and early life of a young man called Duncan Thaw in Glasgow of the forties and fifties. It is fictional rather than autobiographical, but some details are clearly derived from the life of Gray himself. Although well written, the style and structure do not noticeably deviate from a number of other similar novels and short stories. Books Three and Four, on the other hand, are distinctively new and innovative. They follow the adventures of the eponymous Lanark in a fantastical land featuring the nightmarish city of Unthank – which is clearly a perverse dystopian version of the city of Glasgow. Lanark, too, is a resurrected version of Thaw, and the suggestion is that Lanark is Thaw's alter ego in a sort of after life, Thaw having died, we are led to believe, prematurely by his own hand. Although there are many European precedents for this style of writing, the only comparable exercise in Scottish fantastic fiction might be David Lindsay's *Voyage to Arcturus*. Glasgow, as reflected in the grotesque vision of Unthank, becomes symbolic of a greater urban or personal nightmare in a manner that is both compelling and original.

Unthank, as we are introduced to it in Book Three (paradoxically this comes before Books One and Two in the novel) is both a recognisable version of Glasgow and a sort of blighted wasteland:

> The path went down a steep embankment between the two hills which seemed to be rubbish dumps. Where it twisted sharply I sometimes walked forward and found myself wading in what felt like ashes and rotten cloth. We crossed the dry bed of an old canal and reached the end of a street. The city did not seem a thriving place. Groups of adolescents or old men stood in occasional close mouths, but many closes were empty or unlit. The only shops not boarded up were small stores selling newspapers, sweets, cigarettes and contraceptives. After a while we came to a large square with tramcars clanging around it. The street lamps only lit the lowest storeys of the surrounding buildings but these looked very big and ornamental, and people sheltered between pillars on their facades. Some soot-black statues were arranged round a central pillar whose top I couldn't see in the black sky.[1]

The weather in Unthank is always cold, wet and miserable, and the sky is continually dark. Lanark, a misanthrope, has arrived here after a mysterious train journey (an established metaphor for death) and spends his time searching, in practice and metaphorically, for the light:

> The Elite Cafe was entered by a staircase from the foyer of a cinema. A landing two thirds of the way up had a door into the cinema itself, but people going to the Elite climbed farther and came to a large dingy-looking room full of chairs and low coffee tables. The room seemed dingy, not because it was unclean but because of the lighting. A crimson carpet covered the floor, the chairs were upholstered in scarlet, the low ceiling was patterned with whorled pink plaster, but dim green wall lights turned these colours into varieties of brown and made the skins of the customers look greyish and dead...A door by the bar opened onto a narrow outdoor balcony above the cinema entrance. This had room for three crowded-together metal-topped tables with parasols through the middle. Coffee was not drunk here because the sky was often dark with strong wind and frequent rain. The tabletops had little puddles on them, the collapsed cloth of the parasols flapped soddenly against the poles, the seats were dank, yet a man of about twenty-four usually sat here, huddled in a black raincoat with the collar turned up. Sometimes he gazed in a puzzled way at the black sky, sometimes he bit thoughtfully on the knuckle of his thumb. Nobody else used the balcony.[2]

Unthank is an extremely oppressive world of strictly limited possibilities. Gray uses fairly conventional techniques to achieve this effect, through his description of the city, details of Lanark's alienation, threatening scenes at a parody of a Social Security office. But Unthank isn't the all-powerful totalitarian state of *1984* or other futuristic fantasies. Such dytopias are built on a different model – the controlling paternalism of the state. Unthank is not particularly malevolent to its citizens, it is above all indifferent. Even Lanark's rather pathetic anarchism is tolerated as an amusing quirk, on the understanding that it can have very little effect on the way of things. Lanark is a kind of wise fool, who seems to rise to a position of some note in Unthank due basically to his intransigence rather than his perspicacity (Gray employs this idea in a more naturalistic short novel – *The Rise and Fall of Kelvin Walker*). It is because Lanark's understanding of the ways of Unthank is so imperfect and piecemeal (although the reader is privileged to an even lesser knowledge) that the novel maintains its mysterious enigmatic quality. To go further, it seems that knowledge is not necessary to understand Unthank – for there is no guiding logic or structure to the role of the creature (as Gray describes the intelligence or force that shapes his world). Unthank is constructed not as an alternative world, but as a compound of certain characteristics of the real world. From identifiable characteristics of Glasgow. But it is not a real city. It lacks that variety. Despite the fact that the imagined world of Unthank apparently, according to the text, occupies a seemingly endlessly expansive universe, it appears claustrophobic. This is mainly because the mise-en-scène is limited by its portrayal through the distorting lens of Lanark's imagination, and, secondly, because, like all fictions, it works with a small set of characters and relies on repetition and echoes for its effect. Unthank echoes Lanark's paranoic claustrophobia as if it were a small community rather than a real city. Unthank is the dark village of Lanark's desperate imagination.

Details from the cover of Alasdair Gray's *Lanark*

Lanark's initial sojourn in Unthank grows gradually more desperate.
The world seems locked in chaos, people are inflicted with strange
diseases. Eventually, at the point of Lanark's final despair he is led to
a location that is clearly modelled on Glasgow's Necropolis:

> ...he climbed the railings and waded upward between the
> trunks. The lamps in the streets behind showed a dim hillside
> laid out as a cemetery. Black gravestones stood on the snowy
> paleness and he climbed between them, amazed that the ground
> of this place had once swallowed men in a natural way. He
> reached a path with a bench on it, brushed snow from the seat
> with his sleeve, then knelt and banged his brow hard there three
> times, crying out from the centre of his soul. 'Let me out! Let me
> out'...
>
> The summit was a circular plot with a ring of obelisks round
> the edge and a cluster of them in the middle. They were old and
> tall with memorials carved on the pedestals. He was puzzled by
> the light. It was a glow like the light from a steady fire, it lit
> nothing over five feet from the ground and cast no shadows,
> and Lanark walked round the central monuments without
> discovering a source. The glow was brightest on a pedestal near
> the place where he had entered the ring, so he examined it for
> a clue. It was a marble block erected by the workers and
> management of the Turks Road Forge in gratitude to a doctor
> who had rendered them skilled and faithful service between
> 1833 and 1879. Lanark was reading the inscription for a second
> time when he noticed a dim shadow across the centre of the
> stone. He glanced over his shoulder to see what cast it and saw
> nothing, though when he glanced back it looked like the
> shadow of a bird with outspread wings. But the colour deep-
> ened and he saw that the shape forming there was a mouth three
> feet wide, the lips meeting in a serene, level line.[3]

Lanark's fate is to be swallowed by the mouth and resurrected in a
complex something like a hospital known as the Institution. That
both the exit and entrance to Lanark's new manifestation are based
on real models is made clear by the naturalistic fictional account of
Thaw's life in an identifiably real Glasgow (the reason why the
Glasgow of Book One is so clearly identifiable and meticulously
detailed, is precisely for this purpose – to make more explicit the
metaphors.) To what extent this part of Gray's novel is autobiographical is arguable, but his description of Riddrie, of the Forth and
Clyde canal, or of Whitehill school are very much as I remember them
– his personal topography is not identical to but overlaps with my
own and for this reason my reading of the novel can hardly be truly
objective. And this, in spite of the fact that Gray or Thaw's reminis-

cences are, supposedly, of a period some twenty years previous to my
own childhood. For so little had changed, it seems, from the Glasgow
of the thirties to the forties to the fifties to the early sixties. Yet only
five or so years later things would be different. In a sense (although
it is a pervasive mythology that each generation is the end of an old
order) these were the last years of the old Glasgow, before the full
impact of the Modernist revolution, and it is this Glasgow which
Gray uses to inform his fantasies.

   This correlative is always an active ingredient in the novel,
therefore, making books three and four more than fantasy, but an
actual reworking of a natural world For example, in his account of
Mrs Thaw's illness and death:

>   They entered a vast ward in the Royal Infirmary flooded,
>   through tall windows, with grey light from the sky outside.
>   Mrs. Thaw leaned on her pillows looking sick and gaunt yet
>   oddly young...Mr. Thaw said, holding his wife's hand and
>   looking through the nearby window, 'You've quite a view from
>   here'. Below them stood the old soot-eaten Gothic cathedral in
>   a field of flat black gravestones. Beyond rose the hill of the
>   Necropolis, its sides cut into the porches of elaborate mausole-
>   ums, the summit prickly with monuments and obelisks. The
>   topmost monument was a pillar carrying a large stone figure of
>   John Knox, hatted, bearded, gowned and upholding in his right
>   hand an open granite book. The trees between the tombs were
>   leafless, for it was late autumn. Mrs. Thaw smiled and whis-
>   pered wanly, 'I saw a funeral go in there this morning.' 'No, it's
>   not a very cheery outlook.'[4]

Or in Thaw's conversation with his childhood friend, McAlpin:

>   They stood under an electric pylon and looked across the city
>   centre. The wind which stirred the skirts of their coats was
>   shifting mounds of grey cloud eastward across the valley.
>   Travelling patches of sunlight went from ridge to ridge, making
>   a hump of tenements gleam against the dark towers of the city
>   chambers, silhouetting the cupolas of the Royal Infirmary
>   against the tomb-glittering spine of the Necropolis. 'Glasgow is
>   a magnificent city,' said McAlpin. 'Why do we hardly ever
>   notice that?' 'Because nobody ever imagines living here,' said
>   Thaw. '...think of Florence, Paris, London, New York. No-
>   body visiting them for the first time is a stranger because he's
>   already visited them in painting, novels, history books and
>   films. But if a city hasn't been used by an artist not even the
>   inhabitants live there imaginatively...Imaginatively Glasgow
>   exists as a music-hall song and a few bad novels. That's all we've
>   given to the world outside. It's all we've given to ourselves.'[5]

The Institute is clearly modelled on the Royal Infirmary and the Necropolis of *Lanark* on Glasgow's Necropolis (Glasgow Cathedral also figures, transmogrified, in Book Four) and one is entered from the other – the Institute, following the nature of the hospital, cut off from the real world by a passage through the novel's metaphoric synopsis of death and disease. For, whereas in real-life Glasgow the city slums infected their inhabitants with typhoid or cholera or dysentery or, even very recently, with a variety of minor verminous infestations and infections, Unthank inflicts several stranger complaints on its inhabitants. This becomes clear when Lanark is interviewed on his arrival in Unthank. There is a hard patch of black skin on his elbow: 'We call it dragonhide, a name more picturesque than scientific...It's a common illness, as common as mouths or softs or twittering rigor...Diseases identify people more accurately than variable factors like height, weight, and hair colour.'[6] Diseases have different but remarkable effects – mouths may result in the appearance of small talking orifices on parts of the body, rigor is 'crystalline hypertrophy of the connective tissue' making the body as brittle as ice or glass, dragonhide (clearly a development of the eczema suffered by Thaw as a child) is an infection that results in the afflicted gradually turning into various forms of reptiles or crustaceans. Here Gray's vivid, wayward imagination serves a clear purpose – for these inflictions appear to be pathological but their cause is not clearly defined. They seem to be somehow intrinsic to human nature – brought about, for example, by excessive stifling of human emotions. Similarly, in the Institute, treatment is unusual – doctors play music or read poetry to their patients; and usually unsuccessful – Lanark discovers that patients who cannot be cured are used to provide heat and energy or food for the Institute, while those who survive become doctors and feed off the others. In Gray's Unthank, as in the world of dreams and nightmares, everything becomes whole – the Institute is equivalent to the city, disease is the normal process of living, the world exists only to reflect personal failures and fears. In this way, there is a clear connection to be drawn between *Lanark* and the personalised horrors of Muir or Gibbon. Sometimes his descriptions of Unthank seem clearly based on the Glasgow of the depression years – as this passage which invokes George Square:

> The city did not seem a thriving place. Groups of adolescents or old men stood in occasional close mouths, but many closes were empty and unlit. The only shops not boarded up were small stores selling newspapers, sweets, cigarettes and contraceptives. After a while we came to a large square with tramcars clanging around it. The street lamps only lit the lowest storeys of the surrounding buildings but these looked very big and

ornamental, and people sheltered between pillars on their
facades. Some soot-black statues were arranged round a central
pillar whose top I couldn't see in the black sky.[7]

Similarly, this description of a Lanark's lodgings in Unthank could be
reminiscent of Bolitho's slumland – or, indeed, a more contemporary
Glasgow tenement:

> The next tram took him along a succession of similar tenement-
> lined streets. The stop where he got off had tenements on one
> side and a blank factory wall on the other. He entered a close,
> climbed ill-lit steps to a top landing and let himself quietly into
> the lobby of his lodgings. This was a bare room with six doors
> leading from it. One led to Lanark's bedroom, one to the
> lavatory and one to the kitchen where the landlady lived…The
> kitchen was a clean, very cluttered room. It contained arm-
> chairs, a sideboard, a scrubbed white table, a clumsy gas cooker
> with shelves of pots above it. An iron range filled most of one
> wall and there was a sink and draining board under the
> window. All horizontal surfaces were covered with brass and
> china ornaments and bottles and jam-jars of artificial flowers.[8]

Lanark also takes and transfigures the traditional industries of
Glasgow – steelmaking and shipbuilding – in his construction of the
Unthank dystopia – '"The Forge over the road is wanting men".
Lanark laughed harshly and said, "You want me to make components
for the Q39".'[9] So, Unthank, is a sort of hotchpotch of the elements
of the old Glasgow to Thaw or, indeed, Gray himself. After Lanark's
departure to the Institute, however, things change. He meets Rima,
who has also escaped from Unthank, and who resembles a girl he
knew in his previous incarnation as Thaw. He saves her from the
Institute, and they set out on an epic journey through a strange,
unsteady world in which time is relative. This is an infinitely more
modern world than that they have left. They cross strange zones
linked by endless giant motorways along which enormous trucks
carry dangerous waste products from undefined processes. It is
almost as if they are doomed to live the Modernist nightmare.
Eventually they arrive in Unthank. Lanark is now introduced to the
upper echelons of society which are a perverse parody of municipal
politics. Lanark has further adventures to undergo – including a visit
to another city, Provan, that seems to represent Edinburgh – and also,
due to the relativity of the time structure of the narrative, becomes,
almost immediately, a father – although he is denied the possibility
of domestic bliss which is grossly parodied in this section as a
nightmarish version of family life.

Most importantly, Unthank revisited by Lanark is transformed
and revitalised in some way. It is not impossible to discover portents

of the New Glasgow in this reconstructed vision – as in, for example, Lanark's return to the Necropolis:

> Lanark and Rima climbed slowly and painfully in watery green light. Ritchie-Smollet came patiently behind, humming to himself. After many minutes they emerged into a narrow, dark, stone-built chamber with marble plaques on three walls and large wrought-iron gates in the fourth. These swung easily outward, and they stepped onto a gravel path beneath a huge black sky. Lanark saw that he was on a hilltop among the obelisks of a familiar cemetery.
>
> After they had gone a little way Lanark stopped and declared, 'This isn't Unthank!'
>
> 'You are mistaken. It is.'
>
> They looked down a slope of pinnacled monuments onto a squat black cathedral. The floodlit spire held a gilt weather-cock above the level of their eyes, but Lanark was more perplexed by the view beyond. He remembered a stone-built city of dark tenements and ornate public buildings, a city with a square street plan and electric tramcars. Rumours from the council corridors had made him expect much the same place, only darker and more derelict, but below a starless sky this city was coldly blazing. Slim poles as tall as the spire cast white light upon the lanes and looping bridges of another vast motorway. On each side shone glass and concrete towers over twenty floors high with lights on top to warn off aeroplanes. Yet this was Unthank, though the old streets between towers and motorlanes had a half-erased look, and blank gables stood behind spaces cleared for carparks. After a pause Lanark said, 'And Unthank is dying?'
>
> 'Dying? Oh I doubt it. The population has shrunk since they scrapped the Q39 project, but there's been a tremendous building boom.'
>
> 'But if a place is losing people and industry how can it afford new buildings?'
>
> 'Ah, I know too little about chronology to say. I feel that what happens between *hearts* matters more than these big public ways of swapping energy.'[10]

Or his return to the square:

> They got off the bus in a large square Lanark knew well, though it was brighter and busier than he remembered. He gazed at the statues on their massive Victorian pedestals and reflected that he had seen them before he saw Rima. The square was still enclosed by ornate stone buildings except where he and Jack stood before a glass wall of shining doors. Above this

great horizontal strips of concrete and glass alternated to a
height of twenty or thirty floors. Jack said, 'The job centre.'
'It's big.'[11]

Uncannily, Gray, in this and in other sections, presages the New
Glasgow. For *Lanark*, is about both the old and the new – or rather,
about the transition from one order to another. The city, as portrayed
in books three and four of *Lanark* is in a state of continual flux, which
is rather unsettling for the reader. This sense of change, of lack of
direction and stability, could be seen as the essence of the burgeoning
post-industrial Glasgow of the seventies onwards. Yet if Lanark's
Glasgow is redoubtedly new, then Thaw's Glasgow is the apotheosis
of the old. Gray is also a painter of some note. One of his paintings,
Cowcaddens 1950, painted in 1964, is, to me, the perfect image of the
Glasgow I remember from my childhood. In it, a variety of scenes of
Glasgow life are portrayed, taking place within a contrived landscape
of streets that seem to twist into each other. In this way it is
reminiscent of those medieval paintings of saints showing them
several times along the same path representing different stages of
their life. Menacing black clouds and Munch-like contortions of
figures and landscape abound, but there are lights in high tenement
windows and (as in *Lanark*, perhaps) a hint of some new light dawn-
ing on the horizon. Some children run about and, at the extreme top
left of the painting a gas streetlamp shines against a black sky. This
old lamp, viewed from the perspective of a child, seems to awaken
some memory in me of my own street in Dennistoun all those years
ago. The same effect can be seen in both the cover illustration of
Lanark and the plates that serve to introduce each book, drawn by
Gray. Several scenes are counterpointed with each other and scenes
from classical art, reminiscent of Durer, are mingled with a common-
place Glasgow iconography – the Clyde, ships, cranes, the City
Chambers, the Cathedral, the Necropolis. Gray's peculiar use of
perspective informs the writing of *Lanark* too. Literally, in, for example, Book Four, when Lanark and Rima journey along a strange
complex of motorways towards Unthank. On one occasion, they
discover, one side of the road is uphill, the other downhill. Weird
differences in the passage of time take place, and at one stage they
come upon themselves, still frozen on a spot they had departed some
time in the past. More generally, however, Gray's Unthank is viewed
with this particular, peculiar use of perspective. It is fragmented, as
if in a nightmare or dream. Rather than the single perspective of the
camera lens or Farrow's video eye, the world of Unthank exists in
many different partial images. One of the questions that we might
justifiably ask, of course, is 'is Unthank hell?' Lanark says that it is
twice, once before he is swallowed, once before he loses Rima and

Alasdair Gray, *Cowcaddens* 1950

Sandy. In a sense the answer is yes – but Unthank is also more than that. It is also an allegory of life in the city. *Lanark*, like *Deathwatch*, is about death. In a sense, all the events of the novel only exist to assimilate Lanark to the idea of his own death. The interludes that form the substance of the story are, as Lanark suggests, 'a brief rest from endless falling nightmare' in the gullet.

And it is a nightmare that we can all recognise, and Unthank is a state to which we all belong. I can instantly recognise the Glasgow of Gray's paintings. Similarly, for example, if I flick through Colin Baxter's romantic, pastellised details of Glasgow (echoed by other photographers such as Corrance and Ward)[12] I see only Colin Baxter. His art expels all sense of place. If I look through Oscar Marzaroli's[13] grainy black and white snapshots of adults and children or studies of Glasgow tenements, I see exactly the Glasgow of my own childhood. Yet this too is an illusion, for both are mediations. And both are products of a certain time – Marzaroli's striking snapshots resurrected by our intense curiosity for the fifties and sixties, Baxter's colourful details of buildings and landscapes part of a wider nostalgic impulse – not substantially different from his photographs of Edin-burgh or other cities. Surprisingly, having 'discovered', perhaps, the true colour in the streets and closes of the New Glasgow, other photographers have taken things a stage further and returned to an older form of photographic representation – tinting black and white photographs to give interesting colourful effects. Photographers in the last couple of years have had little regard for the wider social scene but have been intent on representing the city synecdochally, through collections of ever smaller details – reducing the city further towards pure design.

Yet, although I am aware of the genesis of these representations, Gray and Marzaroli touch me in a way that I cannot easily explain. Perhaps because we have a common inheritance – their Glasgow is mine too – or because they constitute another mythology, a mythology to which my own imperfect constitution offers little resistance. This is true of *Lanark* also – a work which I find offers me a little more at each reading. Maybe this is because I find the community of Unthank a particularly potent metaphor for the city and Gray's ingenious way of representing the wider notion of city life through the limited perceptions of his protagonists both perplexing and satisfying. In order to fully appreciate the success of *Lanark*, one need only compare a lesser work of the last few years – Agnes Owens' *Gentlemen of the West*. The cover for this novel, drawn also by Gray, features the similar constituents to *Lanark*, the Necropolis, a city centre pub, random characters – albeit in a more naturalistic form – yet the fiction itself is profoundly unsatisfactory and unconvincing. For it is Glasgow – supposedly a real, harsh Glasgow of dossers and drunks – presented literally as a village, almost in the form of a kailyard community. This is city life described by the unknowing – with no depth of perception of the fragmentation of real city life, which is precisely the effect gained by Gray's judicious use of metaphorical communities. This is why, of the various writers who have come out of Glasgow in the last few years, Alasdair Gray is, in my opinion, on the basis of the achievement of *Lanark*, not only the best but the most relevant to the argument of this essay.[14]

The Bright Side of Town

Where can we search for the genesis of Gray's Unthank ? Well, try to imagine, if you can, catching the last bus to Easterhouse from Buchanan Street bus station, as I did, nearly twenty years ago. Beery men with carry-out bags, teenage girls done up to the nines chatting vulgarly about boyfriends, young neds with Celtic or Rangers scarves, a curious pensioner returning home. The conductor gives you not a ticket but half your fare back.

The route takes you via Royston Road, Garngad, the disastrous Red Road flats, gasworks, the stinking course of the canal, skirting Blackhill to follow the route of what is now the motorway, and turning into Gartloch Road via the golf course, past Barlinnie with its grey imposing wall, three stern rectangular blocks with tall gaunt chimneys overstating its function – a factory for processing men unseen by prying outside eyes.

As you climb up this road, into Ruchazie, a real-life panorama of the city unfolds to the south, over the homogeneous masses of Carntyne and Shettleston, at night as dark, dull and dismal as Gray's Unthank. Yet to the south a light, a fiery red sky can be seen. An impressive red glow, masking the dotted neon street lights and the floodlights of Parkhead. This is...was, in its heyday, to the rest of Glasgow, the permanent reminder of the clanging hammers and singeing furnaces of the Parkhead Forge.

The Parkhead Forge was founded in a small village just outside Glasgow around 1837 by Reoch Bros and Co. In 1842 it was bought by Robert Napier to make parts for steamships. In 1853 it was bought by William Rigby and he was joined in partnership by William Beardmore in 1862. By the end of the Victorian period, Beardmore's Parkhead Forge was not only neatly situated towards the centre of the rapidly expanding city of Glasgow, it was at the centre of heavy industry in the West of Scotland and, thus, of the British Empire. The Forge produced quality shipbuilding parts and locomotives for export throughout the world. Glasgow, with Beardmore's at its centre, feeding the expanding shipbuilding industry, was, at least in the popular imagination, the 'Workshop of the Empire'.[1]

A large part of John Maclean's speech from the dock, on the occasion of his trial in Edinburgh in 1918 (after the famous 'I am not here, then, as the accused; I am here as the accuser of Capitalism dripping with blood from head to foot') is dedicated to the situation of Parkhead Forge during the war and the so-called 'ca-canny' policy of the workers. Maclean was primarily concerned, as he saw it, with the 'economic war' that was to follow the Great War, but the crucial point was that he dared to question whether, during wartime or any other time, the interests of the nation, of Beardmore, the owners, and of the workers could truly be held as identical. This is, no doubt, one of the unwelcome truths that led to his internment – but it is also a truth that is generally elided by the mythology of The Workshop of the Empire.

The Parkhead Forge is gone, the walls crumbling, the vast wooden shuttering demolished, the massive gates forever closed. The curving steel rails etched into the streets, like Glasgow's countless tramlines, gone to smelter themselves.

Instead, today, take another vista. Approach Parkhead from the east, via Shettleston and Old Shettleston Road, old tenement areas once crowded with noise and smoke but now quiet and desolate – barely alive. There, on the site of the Parkhead Forge – you can glimpse it from a quarter mile away – is a strange structure indeed. A series of glass pyramids appear, reflecting the mid-afternoon sun (if we didn't know better we would suspect that the monstrous St Enoch's Centre had carelessly deposited a few of its offspring here). The framework is not burnished steel or cast iron t-joists, but constructed from tubular aluminium arranged in trihedrons. Modular, hi-tech, a million miles from the reality of rusty sweat and bubbling pig iron.

This is the Forge shopping centre, retaining the name and the industrial connotations from the original site. At the entrance, in bronze, to remind us of the connection, a statue of an aproned blacksmith at his anvil. Paradoxically, the connotations are all wrong. The blacksmith is not a labourer but an artisan, his place is primarily rural not urban, his produce specific and small-scale, not all purpose. Yet the Forge is proud of its name, its supposed real connection with history, with the people – as if to buy a packet of cornflakes or dried prunes were social history in the making, an ideological statement rather than a banal necessity of life.

Many years ago, as a small boy, I remember seeing in the corner shop, on the highest shelf where they were kept, one of those unusual long exotic boxes of dates with the scalloped round ends and the evocative picture, in orange and black, of a camel and three palm trees, sprouting from a common root, silhouetted against the sunset.

I remember asking my mother what these strange fruits were, where this magical land was? She bought a box once and showed me the ugly, sticky, packed fruits of the graceful, elegant palm. I realised at that time that I was being sold, not a product, but a little packaged mythology. In the Forge shopping centre, too, under the centre pyramid, are three large palm trees in a central reservoir, their message not apparent until one is aware of the peculiar marketing ploy used to sell the Forge to its clientele. For a visit to the Forge is no ordinary experience, it is, like so many elements of the New Glasgow, an adventure. It is *a trip to the mysterious east.*

The metaphor is extended in the advertising material for the centre. There are allusions, for example, to Aladdin's cave, to mysterious treasure – as if shopping were not a free barter for goods but the rabid collection of booty. Nothing could be more paradoxical, or unusual, than that this corner of Glasgow, the poverty-ridden, traditionally downtrodden east-end, should now be redefined as mystical, mythological, mysterious. There is a sort of perverse orientalism at work here – a kind of pastiche that is incapable of recognising its own irony. The pyramid is, of course, a particularly large and ostentatious tomb.

This is the exotic east-end of Glasgow, and, despite the efforts of the GEAR (Glasgow Eastern Area Renewal) scheme founded in 1976 and one of the largest such schemes in Europe, little has been done, after the demolition of the worst slums, to make this a coherent and vital living space. In fact, despite the work of such projects as GEAR (and I have no wish to traduce their strenuous and well-meaning efforts) it is arguable if anything can be done in the present climate. If we look at the six aims of an effective renewal programme detailed by the housing expert David Donnison, for example – 1/ make a nicer place to live in 2/ provide targeted employment 3/ increase income for non-workers 4/ provide more opportunities for individual enterprise 5/ provide community-based services 6/ encourage a more representative population in all areas[2] – what is immediately apparent is that very few of these good causes feature on any current political agenda – and, it may be pertinent to ask, how could they with a government set on ghettoising the poor and unemployed, cutting benefits and local services, and segregating the classes? Donnison optimistically suggests that '"Glasgow's Miles Better"… could not have been so convincingly launched had the GEAR project not been at work for six years to bring some of Glasgow's revival to the east end.'[3] On the other hand, Struthers's campaign and the New Glasgow ideology eclipses such seeming benevolence. It is impossible to conceive of one iota of New Glasgow propaganda that perceives the real social and political needs of the people in Glasgow's east-end.

More damning by far than anything I can say are the hard facts
produced by Alan Middleton, another housing researcher, who notes
that, out of a sample of east-enders asked where they lived, no-one
said that they were in the GEAR area, only 14% said the east-end, and
more than half of them identified areas not recognised as valid wards
on the valuation role.[4] It would be hard to obtain stronger evidence
of a people so dispossessed. Their own communities and lives
cancelled out by officialdom.

And so, it would take, it would seem, not fourteen but fourteen
hundred years to radically alter this blighted landscape. If we venture
further, and head towards the city centre, the effect is worse. Past
London Road towards Bridgeton Cross there is merely a deserted
area of old warehouses, with rusty bars, barbed wire, and dandelions
growing from cracks in the wall. Further up past Shettleston Road,
towards Duke Street , you are confronted with the prospect of high
rise flats and the old grey fifties tenements of Haghill. There is a
wilderness of vacant ground and the remains of an old public
lavatory, which must have once, presumably, stood among tenement
houses, now with its railings broken and twisted and a gathering of
rubbish and dirt in its well. Further along there are a couple of public
houses standing alone, with sooty rendered walls, blacked and barred
windows and metal doors. One exudes a smell of sweat, beer and
disinfectant, the other is deserted, closed, but a painted sign on the
wall, perhaps hopelessly out of date, promises discos nightly, and late
opening until one-o-clock in the morning. But this landscape, more
than anything, is dominated by a massive wasteland, beyond Old
Shettleston Road, up towards the old railway depot and the main
Glasgow/Airdrie line. Hundreds of square yards of decay, tumbled
cairns of decaying masonry, black cinders, a great deal of dumped
waste and twisted iron, broken glass in abundance, and, here and
there, a few stalks of dandelions, dock leaves, or rosebay willowherb.
Past the old railway bridge, from whence the trains puffed right into
the precinct of the Forge, are a few advertising hoardings – one
features, as if complicit in some grand joke, the latest propaganda for
the east-end renewal scheme, a poster graphically portrays the rays
of an abstract sun, coloured in orange and yellow. The caption at the
bottom says 'Glasgow's East End – The Bright Side of Town'.

The monstrously implausible doublethink required, confronted
with such a gleaming hi-tech tribute to mindless consumerism set in
a desert, a wasteland rivalling that of the most luscious novelistic
imagination, to conceive of this as, literally, 'the bright side of town'
brings, in the bitter wind, genuine tears to my eyes. There is, to my
childish mind, the hurtful disappointment here of a promise broken.
Like Granada television's *Glasgow*, it holds the promise of a fun fair,

the glitter, the panache, but in substance is so little indeed. This is the saddest side of the New Glasgow. Coming here reminds me of the desultory ending of James Joyce's classic short story *Araby* which conveys some of this strange mixture of desire and disappointment: 'I lingered before her stall, though I knew my stay was useless, to make my interest in her wares seem the more real. Then I turned away slowly and walked down the middle of the bazaar. I allowed the two pennies to fall against the sixpence in my pocket. I heard a voice call from one end of the gallery that the light was out. The upper part of the hall was now completely dark. Gazing up into the darkness I saw myself as a creature driven and derided by vanity; and my eyes burned with anguish and desire.'[5] This effect is echoed by the most accomplished Glasgow short story writer of the present generation, Alan Spence, in his short story *Tinsel*, which describes a small boy, living in a typical tenement slum, who has decorated his room and kitchen for Christmas: 'When he pressed his face up close to the window he could see the back court lit here and there by the light from a window, shining out on to the yellow snow from the dark bulk of the tenements. There were even one or two Christmas trees up above, columns of palegrey smoke, rising from chimneys. When he leaned back he could see the reflection of their own kitchen. He imagined it was another room jutting out beyond the window, out into the dark. He could see the furniture, the curtain across the bed, his mother and father, the decorations and through it all, vaguely, the buildings, the night. And hung there, shimmering, in that room he could never enter, the tinsel garland that would never tarnish'.[6]

Reading these words, I find it hard to be impartial, for as a child I would, with my father, walk down from our room and kitchen in Dennistoun to the Barrows, with its bustling crowds, vociferous street traders, and gaudy stalls (more treasures of the Orient, as Granada's *Glasgow* would have it) to buy a book or a comic to read curled up in front of the fire back home. And Spence's phantom room reminds me of this, my own small tenement home. For we must remember that, to a child, the city is full of excitement and promise and that even a tiny room and kitchen in an ageing tenement, constructed in an earlier age to promote social division of the classes, is home, and, perhaps, at that time, to a small boy in Dennistoun, the bright side of town was fairly bright after all.

Born in the Shadow of the Fairfield Crane

The eighties have seen the development of a school of painters and visual artists mostly associated with the Glasgow School of Art, sometimes known as the Glasgow Boys (or the Glasgow Pups) – following on from a school of painters so named a century before – who have achieved international prominence through their work. These artists have been in the vanguard of contemporary developments in the art world and of the so-called return to figurative painting. Of them all, Ken Currie, a young craftsmanlike painter from Barrhead, has most directly employed the iconography and mythology of industrial Glasgow. As he reveals, his *mise-en-scène* is the bleak landscape of *Lanark* or the mysterious east-end:

> In evolving my earlier figurative work I began to compose figures in more industrial and urban settings, although no specific location was suggested. I explored industrial installations in the city. The mysterious buildings, machinery and railway sidings of the sprawling Ministry of Defence bomb making plant at Bishopton fascinated me, as I regularly visited a friend there. I was attracted to the atmosphere of derelict factories, abandoned industrial installations, areas of wasteland, empty houses and dying industries like the great black outlines of Parkhead Forge. I saw people moving amidst all this, going about their lives, surrounded by unremitting bleakness, and began to identify completely with their plight...(there are) locations to which I was to continually return – the monolithic Red Road flats, the shipyard gates all along South Street, the huge dusty Meadowside Granary and, across the Clyde, the stark outline of Govan Shipbuilders; the deserted Queen's Dock with its mysterious rotundas and the powerful shape of the Finnieston crane; Parkhead Forge, slowly fading away...[1]

Yet Currie derives his impetus not from the reality of this tortured landscape but from what he sees as its implications. For Currie the reality of Glasgow today is subservient to its history – and his realisation of the city is spun from the real, or imagined, past of the working people of Glasgow. Currie is inspired, in fact, by a particular tradition of European culture which is overtly political and oppositional:

> The whole revolutionary culture which flourished in Europe between the wars remains the richest and most inspiring reservoir of historical precedent and, naively, we thought it possible to reproduce that culture in Scotland in the nineteen-eighties. In perceiving what we recognised as a period of reaction in Britain, with the ascendancy of the New Right, we saw parallels in particular in Weimar Germany and realised that there could not be a better time in which to produce this new kind of painting. We realised that we had to become 'total artists' capable of everything from Rivera-like murals to hard-hitting realist easel paintings; from agitprop tableaux to epic theatre sets; from documentary photography and photomontage to scenarios for films; from painting banners to devising mass open air spectacles – we saw the artist at the hub of revolutionary change…It was a period of unrestrained idealism.[2]

It is not just idealism, however, that informs Currie's work but, more specifically, nostalgia (the period of European history he features, notably, is, apart from, perhaps, the *fin-de-siècle*, that most touched by nostalgia). Currie's work cannot be at the centre of revolutionary change in the reactionary and staidly conservative Britain of the eighties. The type of revolutionary art that he preaches, influenced, as some have suggested, by Diego Rivera, but also by several other figurative painters, is, arguably, peculiarly lame in this context of actually eliciting political change. At a cultural level, however, a popular socialist history and, particularly in Currie's work, the iconography of Scottish working-class history and, especially, the mythology of the so-called Red Clydeside, have been recuperated to have a specific symbolic interest. Typical of Currie's work and the major themes he investigates are the eight paintings which constitute the *Glasgow History Mural*, commissioned by the People's Palace Museum in Glasgow and still on display there. These paintings attempt, in narrative form, to portray a working-class history of Glasgow – or, more specifically, a history of political struggles. The panels are as follows:

1/ *Weaver's Struggles – The Calton Massacre*
2/ *Radical Wars – Let Truth And Justice Be Woven Together, Liberty Is Our Fabric*
3/ *Great Reform Agitation – Union Is Strength*
4/ *The Socialist Vision – Workers Of The World Unite!*
5/ *Red Clyde – We Can Make Glasgow A Petrograd, A Revolutionary Storm Second To None*

6/ Fight Or Starve – Wandering Through The Thirties
7/ The UCS – The Fight For Our Right To Work
8/ Unfurling Our History – Our Future.

As we can see, this radical and oppositional history of Glasgow is littered with slogans or clichés. It is typical of Currie's work that he, to continue the metaphor, weaves this verbal commentary through his paintings, depicted on banners or placards – quotations from Marx ('Workers of the World Unite') or from socialist songs ('The Internationale unites the human race') – the legend often obscured so that some extra cultural knowledge or an effort of interpretation is required. There is a clear element of intertextuality about these paintings, an extra dimension that the cognoscenti will read and understand. In this sense they do address a committed audience. It is also notable that the scenes depicted are not naturalistic but symbolic and crowded with figures and emblems. Throughout, juxtaposed, are scenes of traditional labour in the forges and shipyards and throngs of marching workers with their tools of trade, their banners and flags, all united by a common colour scheme – the red/ orange of molten steel – and the chiaroscuro of directional lighting.

Panel Six – *Fight or Starve – Wandering through the Thirties* – is typical of his style – 'an attempt to present an image of an era rather than an event...the path trod on by the Hunger Marchers transforms into an unrolled plan for the future.' Currie has drawn on archive film footage (a filmmaker is portrayed in the foreground of the painting) and, like all his work, it draws on a spirit of carnival and the theatrical inspired by the May Day rally – '...huge painted 'agitprop' lorries with floats...vast mobile painted portraits of Scottish heroes like Wallace, Burns and Maclean...banners that looked mobile mural paintings; songs, declamations, dancing, ritualised tableaux, film and photography shows, exhibitions'. This method, of intense symbolic representation of a period of history, or the 'feel' of an era, is particularly redolent in sentiment and nostalgia. Panel Five – *We can make Glasgow a Petrograd, a revolutionary storm centre second to none* – is also a good example of Currie's intentions: 'In this panel I tried to show the centrality of the legendary figure of John Maclean in the historic events on Clydeside after the First World War. Maclean was a remarkable figure – a teacher, a propagandist and gifted orator, Britain's leading Marxist intellectual at that time and above all a visionary. He was the only one of the Red Clydesiders who grasped the idea of Scotland's place in world revolution, so in this panel he is seen holding a globe, surrounded by representatives of international movements which had a profound impact on his thinking...Here, therefore, I wanted to show him at the hub of the revolution in Scotland, orchestrating the entire movement of history through the

Ken Currie, *The Glasgow History Mural*, panel four

rapids of revolutionary change.'[3] In the painting, the shadowy and
impressive figure of Maclean is centralised in front of a bookcase and
lit from above, the brim of his hat obscuring his eyes. In the
background we can glimpse dark skies silhouetting gloomy mills,
chimneys, and the mountainous hulls of ships. Followers surround
Maclean, their banners furling around them. In the bottom right
corner rather brutal-looking police constables, their faces obscured
by their helmets, attack the workers. Again, there is a more detailed,
specific reading for the labour historian – James Maxton, the famous
Clydeside socialist, is depicted, members of the Bolshevik Navy, the
I.W.W., etc.

The symbolic nature of the painting is obvious. It is clear that
Currie's Maclean is the idealised proletarian hero of mythology. The
image owes most not to the real remembrance of a working-class
Glasgow past, but to the re-working of the Maclean myth within the
Socialist and Nationalist literary and folk revival of the fifties and
sixties exemplified by Hamish Henderson's famous ballad *The John
Maclean March* :

> Hey Mac, did ye see him as ye cam' doon by Gorgie,
>> Awa ower the Lammerlaw or north o' the Tay?
> Yon man is comin', and the haill toon is turnin' oot:
>> We're a' shair he'll win back to Glesgie the day...
> Great John Maclean's comin' back tae the Clyde.
> Great John Maclean's comin' back tae the Clyde
> ...The haill city's quiet noo: it kens that he's restin',
>> At hame wi' his Glesgie freens, their fame and their pride!
> The red will be worn, my lads, an' Scotland will march again
> Noo great John Maclean has come hame tae the Clyde.
> Great John Maclean has come hame tae the Clyde.

Despite the optimism of the song, in international terms the surge of
socialist or revolutionary sentiment prompted by Maclean had a
limited effect. The mythology of Scottish labour history that has been
widely circulated (not generally, however, in schoolbook history
which follows the dominant ideology) tends to give the events of the
first quarter of the century a particular significance. This problem is
confronted by the historian, Iain McLean:

> On Christmas Day 1915, Lloyd George was shouted down by
> an angry hall-full of munitions workers in Glasgow, and he
> promptly suppressed the socialist newspaper *Forward* for re-
> porting the fact. On 3rd December 1918, a Marxist revolution-
> ary called John MacLean (sic), who had just been released from
> Peterhead Jail after serving only seven months of a sentence of
> five years' penal servitude for sedition, was drawn through
> cheering crowds in a triumphal procession from Buchanan

Street Station to Carlton Place. On 31st January 1919 – 'Bloody Friday' – a vast demonstration of unofficial strikers in front of the City Chambers in George Square was very roughly broken up by the police, and the next day six tanks lay in the Saltmarket with their guns pointed at the citizens of Glasgow. In the 1922 General Election, Labour won ten out of the fifteen seats in Glasgow, and the new M.P.s, several of them colourful leftist rebels, were given a tumultuous send-off from St. Enoch Station: 'The singing of *The Red Flag* was general'.

From these famous scenes, and many others like them, springs the legend of Red Clydeside. It is a powerful legend, which entranced many in its own time and has continued to do so ever since. It records how Clydeside was ripe for revolution throughout the First World War; how the revolution just failed to occur in January 1919; and how some of the revolutionaries entered Parliament four years later, still determined to wipe capitalism out. It is a stirring story, which impressed frightened members of the 1918-22 Coalition Government as much as it did the revolutionaries themselves. Nevertheless, it *is* a legend.[4]

McLean, in fact, marshalls fairly convincing evidence to suggest that the political impact to these events was severely limited, and that is, perhaps, in real historical terms, true. To deny the political importance in these terms of Red Clydesideism, however, is not to disparage it. At worst, it presents a particularly inspiring set of myths. It is oppositional, which is no bad thing, but mythology is endlessly reconstructed according to the tenor of the times. However motivating the legend of John Maclean may have been at the right time, in the right place, it falls oddly flat in today's ideological climate. This is partly because it is recuperated through nostalgia, partly, because it is a myth of community. The most notable characteristic of Currie's paintings is the way in which characters entwine, seem to form themselves into a homogeneous mass. Julian Spalding has commented on this: 'Currie's city is not a backdrop, but enmeshed in its citizens' lives; his people are not isolated, but contextualised. It is this that gives Currie's work its political dimension. Currie's socialism is not the bright optimism of the early twentieth century, the belief, so clearly expressed in the luminous, muscular paintings of Leger, that change must come. Currie finds his optimism in people's will to change, in their determination to understand what is happening to them, to gain knowledge and sight power.'[5] The context of contemporary society is not, however, one in which mass or popular movements have much meaning. Arguably, the Postmodern period, the dislocation of the subject, the rise of the New Right, the loss of faith in progress, or whatever, have led us into a period in which every individual is isolated, and many are, to the powers-that-be, inconsequential. The old *Scottish Daily Express*, in its headline, used to call itself, paradoxically, 'the voice of the silent majority'. One of the political consequences of the rise of Thatcherism is that the now silenced majority no longer have that voice. This is, inevitably, why Currie's paintings work as nostalgia pieces – as does *The Steamie*, for example – but have no political clout. Unfortunately in the New Glasgow, a particularly reactionary and puritanical Glasgow, the revolutionary myths of Red Clydeside are interesting, and entertaining, but redundant as real social comment.

Peter Howson is a painter with a peculiar prejudice who takes some of the consequences of Currie's work to another remove. The fundamental difference between Howson and Currie is that, whereas Currie is concerned with myths of community, Howson is concerned with the individual. Howson's characters, despite the context, seem invariably alone, Currie's are seldom isolated. Howson's work also figures within the distinctly masculine, macho image of the Glasgow hardman:

> The world that Peter Howson depicts is a decidedly masculine one: soldiers, boxers, body-builders, sportsmen. But his attitude towards it is not celebratory or triumphant, although it might seem so at first sight. On the contrary, Howson sees this overweening masculinity as flawed. Bulging muscles, posturing and aggression are seen as futile and destructive, if they lack the right environment and the right channels or are pushed too far: soldiers become mere sado-masochistic thugs, boxers mindless aggressors. In this world of men, women, if they are depicted, are seen as adjuncts, wives or lovers, with no independence.
>
> The futility and indeed tragedy of this one-sided masculine world is seen at its most stark in Howson's paintings of Glasgow dossers. In their youth they are still strong, still willing to defy the system that has rejected them. But as they grow older they grow weary, weighed down by the constant struggle to survive. Howson's sympathy is with the dosser, who, worn though he is by the hardships of his life, is still proud and defiant. These figures have heroic proportions and are boldly silhouetted against the evening sky or lamplight.[6]

Howson's *The Heroic Dosser* (which exists in several different versions) is almost apocalyptic in its intensity. The connotations of the painting are clearly of the sea. A vague fortress-like building or craft in the background seems to cleave through waves lit by moonlight or a lamp standard, the dosser, buttressed by enormous legs and clad in a bulky overcoat, is resolutely set at a railing or helm gazing with dull sockets for eyes into the dark. There is a mysterious quality here

which is absent from Currie's portraits of working class men or
women – Currie's *Woman From Drumchapel*, for example, directly
addresses the reader, defiant weariness or craftiness are perhaps
connoted by her expression but not heroism, at least not in the direct
or mythical sense employed by Howson. Currie, as usual, is concerned with what he sees as the real workings of the world and the
individual's place in them rather than in any mysticism. For Currie,
in fact, heroism is not really the prerogative of the individual. Yet
Howson takes on this difficult business in a thrawn, perverse and
oppositional way. Not only the idealised worker, but any individual
is entitled to the status of hero within his mythology. There is
something in this of the concept of the basic goodness of the common
man that comes through in the work of popular community poets
such as Freddy Anderson (author of the novel, *Oiney Hoy*) and the
burgeoning Writers' Workshop movement, but there is also, I think,
a suggestion of absolution through suffering. The difficulty of
realising this concept in a real-life context (remembering that it is
Glasgow's shame that there are many decent – and perhaps heroic –
men and women in Glasgow condemned, often through mental
illness, to the life of a pariah) lies in the metaphor employed – that of
life as a voyage. For a voyage suggests progression or at least
movement, and, arguably, that is precisely what is missing or denied
to the dosser inured to the fragmented and centreless life of the
homeless. For this reason, I think, Howson's paintings are thought-
provoking but not really revealing. For another reason, it could be
argued, in this approach there is too much of the dangerous ideology
of resignation.

There is another mythology apparent in some of the work of the
Glasgow school related to this – the notion of the autodidact or self-
made man. This builds on both a long Scottish tradition from Carlyle
or earlier and on the Socialist-orientated novels of writers such as
Jack London and Robert Tressell. It is also explored in relation to
Glasgow by Archie Hind in his successful novel *The Dear Green
Place*:

> In one of these council houses late on a September night there
> was a light still burning. It shone faintly on the window, a dim
> amber light which had taken its colour from the room and from
> the old parchment coloured lampshade. Within the circle of
> light which the lamp cast on the surface of a table a man sat in
> the room, trying to write.
> He was a short, dark, ...man, with coarse black hair, a shadow
> on his unshaven cheeks. His rolled up sleeves showed muscular
> forearms covered in dark hair which stopped sharply at the
> wrists. He was crouched over the paper on the table holding the

pen in his hand tightly...For a couple of hours – ever since the other people in the house had gone to bed – he had been sitting writing...At the side of the mantelpiece above one of the bookcases was a framed reproduction of one of Millet's toilers...Mat was 'burning the midnight oil'.[7]

Ken Currie's painting *The Self-taught Man* is a prime piece of mythologising in this tradition. It features a working class man, the commonality of his situation signified by his unprepossessing appearance – greased hair, furrowed brow, a cigarette in the corner of his mouth, a broken nose, sinewy tatooed arms. He is alone in a cell-like room lit by a unidirectional glare from a single lightbulb reminiscent of Picasso's *Guernica*. What looks like a klaxon on the wall compounds this harsh image. Through a small window behind him we glimpse the iconography of industrial Glasgow (dare one call it romance) – the prow of a ship against a smoky sunset, the garish neon of a public house. The man, seated at his desk, seems engaged upon a form of self-education although exactly what form this may take remains ambiguous. Around him are disposed what might be called various instruments of enquiry – a microscope, callipers, a globe, a star chart. These seem to suggest some general impersonal search for the commodity of knowledge, an almost metaphysical enquiry into the real nature of the universe. On the other hand, the articles in his hand may seem more mundane – a newspaper, a notebook, a cheap paperback copy of the work of Gramsci. This seems to suggest, of course, a different kind of quest. Presumably what is to be discovered here is a kind of knowledge both more personal and more political. This is a specific kind of education that will explain to him his own situation – presumably why Gramsci is foregrounded – and leads, at least to some form of self-realisation, at best to some positive action. To further flavour our interpretation, a vague outline of the dove of peace haloes his head.

What does all this mean ? It is quite difficult to say whether Currie accepts or parodies this notion of self-improvement – and this, indeed, is the problem with all of his work. The accepted answer is that his work employs pastiche – which does not have the reductive connotations of parody. Yet there seems to be a dangerous naivety implicit in this approach. *The Self-taught Man* can be clearly interpreted in one way: '...the shipyards symbolise the general state of heavy industry in Glasgow, but the traditions that still live on there among some of its workers, provide hope for the future. The workers who teach themselves about the forces that govern the world, who read about the world issues, who learn to place their own situation in a world context, are freeing themselves in spirit from their localised conditions. This according to Currie is the first step towards world

Ken Currie,
The Self-Taught Man

solidarity.'[8] There is a truth in this – in that what the working or the lower classes invariably lack in capitalist society is a form of knowledge, a knowledge lodged in the shibboleths of social advancement. There is also a way in which education is the wrong term, at least in the popular and incorrect sense in which it is perceived by vast numbers of working people – as a type of commodity to which only the elite have right of access (this is the most pernicious hegemony of the class system). But the idea of self-improvement is itself old hat, established in the political rhetoric of various incarnations of hard-left parties who will no doubt reap its benefits after the next revolution. Where Currie's appeal is particularly potent is in its managing of certain literary and artistic discourses and its romantic associations with the symbolic ephemera of a dying (and therefore glamorous) industry. In the end, however, Currie's representations are symbolic, they are not typical and they are certainly not an option in the real political world.

The Riveter, produced at the National Film School in 1985, is the first substantial piece of work by Michael Caton-Jones, who has since gone on to successfully direct several television productions. It is an accomplished piece, set in Glasgow, and operating very much within the same generic range as earlier Glasgow television drama. The setting is suitably squalid – the tenements, the pubs, the windswept

streets – but it betrays its more recent origin through two clever
directorial ploys. Firstly, there are Forsyth-like touches of the absurd
– taciturn highlanders in party hats, a decrepit vault with the sign
'Mecca Television' – and, secondly, there is an informed awareness
of the post-industrial landscape – the film opens with the harsh clatter
of the shipyards being cut down. A clear problem is established –
Danny McAuley, a riveter by trade, has been made redundant,
associated with the problem of unemployment it is revealed (but not
elaborated on) that his wife has left him. Danny has been left to bring
up a teenage son, Slim, on his own. Struggling to make ends meet, and
with an unrealistic dream of buying a car to impress Slim, Danny gets
mixed up with a bunch of petty crooks who seem to run the
neighbourhood. As things deteriorate, Caton-Jones introduces a
clever (but easily missed) allusion into the narrative. Danny watches
an old film which can be recognised as *The Maggie* – the classic Ealing
comedy directed by Sandy Mackendrick about the crew of a small
steamer and their quaint West Highland ways. Afterwards, walking
down by the docks he sees a small boat and somehow inspired, sells
a video recorder belonging to Young Eddie, the leader of the
hoodlums, collects Slim from school and sets off across the sea to a
small island (very like the Isle of Arran) to start a new life. The rest
is, in a way, obvious. Danny and Slim at first seem happy but then find
that they don't really fit in with the islanders (who are just as crooked
in their own way). Finally Eddie catches up with them and threatens
Slim, but Danny stands up to him and realises that he must face up
to things and return home. He is at last totally accepted by Slim and
the final scene shows them returning home, arm in arm, in a bus, to
sunrise over the gasworks.

This is such a nice little story, so well acted and directed, that it is
initially hard to detect the rather dubious ideology behind it. Firstly,
the problem that the story posits is, initially, created by Danny's
unemployment. Clearly, the resolution or solution would be employment or some escape from poverty. In this way Danny's problem
is a real-life problem and the solution, arguably, a political one. Since,
however, this is fictional narrative and not a documentary, this line
is not taken up – instead it is made explicit that this particular
problem has no resolution, at least within the scope of the narrative.
Instead, an alternative disruption/ resolution scenario is presented –
Danny is misguided, he is cynical ('everybody works for Eddie') and
hard-bitten, living on unrealistic dreams. Slim, paradoxically, in his
child's eyes, has an uncorrupted vision, things, he believes, could be
different. The resolution now is quite straightforward – Danny
simply has to learn to see straight and face up to things as they are.
Having confronted Eddie, he sees the illusory mythology of his dream

of idyllic rural life and returns home. Danny's fictional problems have been solved through self-realisation, although his real-life problems still exist, at least now they will be confronted.

Yet we are being subtlely sold a lie. The mythical idyll that Danny rejects is every bit as real as the constructed Glasgow of the film text which is itself the sort of perverse urban village of television drama. Danny's fictional choice is not, in effect, opting for reality, and there is something insidious about the sort of self-help policy this suggests – if you merely face up to your problems they will go away. The way, however, that the narrative favours the urban scenario and can make the city appear a more realistic option than the country is a hard-boiled representational tradition tied to a spurious association between urban representations and social realism. It is, however, just another mythology, and as such, has no more credence in the real world than any other ideological posture. In the end, the problem with Currie's self-taught man (self-education) and *The Riveter* (self-realisation) is that they ignore the fact that the problems of the oppressed are often created by forces so complex and powerful that they cannot be directly confronted or opposed by the individual. To suggest that they can bring us perilously close to the Victorian discourse of sweet charity and, in that way, Thatcherite Glasgow is not far removed from Shadow's Glasgow.

It is clear that Currie employs to some effect in his work not only the traditional songs of revolution and rebellion, but, especially, the work of the Scottish folksong revival that came about in the late fifties and sixties, with its political motivation, inspired by American folksong pioneers such as Woody Guthrie. Most of his works are anchored by carefully chosen titles. Panel Six of the *Glasgow History Mural* takes its title from Ian Campbell's *The Old Man's Song*, written to the old tune *Queer Folk in the Shaws*:

I wandered through the thirties, out of work now and again,
I saw the blackshirts marching, and the things they did in Spain,
So I reared my children decent, and I taught them wrong from right,
But Hitler was the lad who came along and taught them how to fight.

As a sort of personalised socialist history, this song serves Currie's purpose. He takes lines from the song – 'A brand new world was coming' and 'Well ah don't know how tae change things, but by Christ we've got tae try' – as titles of elaborate pencil drawings on the same theme. Similarly, another drawing – 'Life grew harder day by day, all along the riverside' – is inspired by the song *The Fairfield Crane* written by Archie Fisher, Ian Campbell and Norman Buchan. The Fairfield crane, 170 feet high with a lifting capacity of 250 tons, was reputedly the world's largest crane:

    I was born in the shadow of the Fairfield crane.
    The blast from the freighter's horn,
    Was the very first sound that reached my ears,
    On the morning I was born.

    I sat and I listened to the shipyard's sound,
    Coming out of the unknown.
    I was lulled to sleep by a mother's tongue,
    That was to be my own.

    And as I grew to one year old,
    I heard the sirens scream.
    As the city watched in a blacked-out night,
    The trembling searchlight's beam.

    And then one day when I awoke,
    To my first day of peace,
    I knew the battle to stay alive,
    Was never going to cease.

    I sat and I listened to my father tell,
    Of the Clyde that he once knew,
    Where you either sweated for a measly wage,
    Or you joined the parish queue.

    And as I grew up day by day,
    Down by the riverside,
    I have often heard my mother say,
    It was tears that made the Clyde.

This song is a masterpiece in its own terms, translating the burden of working-class history into terms both personal and symbolic. Yet it is a song located in the specific period of history. The overwhelming metaphor of the crane only works in terms of an industrial society and a living shipbuilding industry. With the yards deserted, the cranes stilled and floodlit as monuments to a dead industry, the song, once again, is reinterpreted by nostalgia. In fact, a nostalgia twice removed – for the period of its birth was in itself a period of hope and youthful idealism which is now fading into the past (this brings to mind the notion suggested by some critics of a sort of second order nostalgia – 'remembering when you remembered'). To some extent this can be seen also in another song that conveys the spirit of old industrial Glasgow in the same vein – Matt McGinn's *The Ballad of the Q4*, a song that, during the last serious flourish of the shipbuilding industry culminating in the UCS work-in, served as an anthem for the shipbuilders:

    The Mary and the Lizzie they were built right here,

But you'll never see the likes of them, I fear.
They were the finest on the silvery sea,
They were built by the hands of men like me.

So thank you dad for all your skill,
But the Clyde is a river that'll no stand still.
You did gey well, but we'll do more,
Make way for the finest of them all, Q4.

We have an order we'll fulfil,
With a touch of the master and a bit more skill.
When the backroom boys get on their way,
And the pens they'll be rolling till the launching day.

There's big Tom O'Hara with the burning gear,
The plumber and the plater and the engineer.
There's young Willie Wiley with his welding rod,
They're waiting at the ready for the backroom nod.

We'll burn and cut and shape and bend,
We'll be welding and riveting and in the end,
When the painter dabs his final coat,
We'll be launching the finest of the ships afloat.

We've worked and sweated and toiled and now,
See the expert's hand from stern to bow.
She's ready for the torments of the sea,
She's a credit to the Clyde and you and me!

Ian Watson, a Marxist critic, has written a detailed commentary on this song: 'In the chorus, the river symbolises the continuous development of the forces of production, whose progress is also measured in generations. The worker inherits his skill and then by historical necessity outstrips his mentor. In a simple and direct lyrical way the idea of heritage and progress are welded. The lessons and learned skills of the past are not rejected, but transcended, so the stepping-down image of the phrase 'make way' is to be understood dialectically… The rest of the song concerns itself with the production of the Q4 itself, the chorus repeatedly underlining the progressive continuity of the process through the image of the river. The second verse deals with the contract and the design; the third names the skilled tradesmen who make their contribution; the fourth covers the building process as far as launching; and the fifth presents the finished ship ready for sea-trials…The closing line unites in four stressed syllables the ship, the community, the workers and the songwriter… *The Ballad of the Q4* is a highly concentrated lyrical expression of an organic cultural whole. Its strength lies in its stress on one side of the shipbuilding process, but also in the fact that it 'works' *as a song*. Its secret lies in its concreteness and its simplicity; but, above all, its compactness.'[9] Watson is trying to say, in fact, that this song fulfils the most important condition, from his perspective, of a worker's song – its structure, and thus, by implication, its use, directly reflects the process of production which it mimics, giving the song and its performance a particular authenticity. Within its context, this is undoubtedly true, but the implication of McGinn's chorus, that continuance of the organic community is assured, unfortunately proved to be mere wishful thinking. There are no more Q4's built on Clydeside. In *Lanark* Alasdair Gray takes the succession of the great ships to its ultimate conclusion when Lanark is offered work on the Q39 which turns out not to be a great passenger liner but something more mysterious and sinister. Unfortunately, the best products of the intensely creative folksong revival of the sixties and early seventies are now themselves part of a dated discourse of industrialism, recuperated through nostalgic reconstruction. In some ways it is impossible to think of a folksong in an idiom that truly reflects the eighties, although Jim Brown's amusing little songs such as *The Waverley* and *The Sludge Boat Song*[10] may fit the bill – this being a sample of the latter:

> Auld Scotland's built some bonny ships,
> The QE2's a gem;
> But once they've left the River Clyde,
> They're seldom seen again.
> So give thanks, you Glesca people,
> Each man, each woman or wean,
> And don't forget the cludgie-boats
> Next time you pull the chain!

These make no pretence of confronting the great themes but gain their effect from the same remembering and celebration of old traditions and mouthing of the mother tongue that typifies *The Patter*. What I feel we witness here, is almost the insidious process of reconstructing a benevolent toytown Glasgow, its inhabitants – men, women and weans – absolved from any responsibility from the real processes of production or of government.

From the same tradition as these fairly contemporary Glasgow folksongs comes a recent book that attempts, with some but limited success, to oppose the unrestrained rise of the New Glasgow. The book is called *Workers City*[11] (as in *Finnegans Wake*) and consists of a collection of generally admirable pieces edited by Farquhar McLay. McLay's cynical dismissal of the 'Culture City' tag is committed, coherent and rings true:

> GLASGOW; EUROPEAN CITY of Culture 1990. The announcement came from the Tory Arts minister, Edward Luce, in October 1986. It had a sickeningly hollow ring to it. Looking

at the social, cultural and economic deprivation in working-class areas of Glasgow, and thinking about the rigours of the new Social Fund and Poll Tax to come, it sounded like blatant and cynical mockery. And indeed a wry smile was the most usual reaction when people bothered to take the slightest notice...In the light of the hard facts of life as it is lived by the people at the bottom of the heap in Glasgow, it is difficult to see the 'culture' tag as being anything other than a sham accolade to help grease the wheels of capitalist enterprise and smooth the path for the politicians. It is little wonder working-class Glasgow remains unimpressed. There is widespread acceptance that it has nothing whatever to do with the working- or the work-less-class poor of Glasgow but everything to do with big business and money: to pull in investment for inner-city developments which, in the obsessive drive to make the centre of the city attractive to tourists, can only work to the further disadvantage of the people in the poverty ghettos on the outskirts.[12]

But there is a fundamental misconception here: 'working-class Glasgow remains unimpressed' – on the contrary there is not, and never has been, any suggestion that the working-class majority of Glasgow have stood back, remained aloof or cynical about the merits of culture year. Instead, the active process of hegemony and the activities of the popular press have had the effect that amongst the general population of the city only a very limited opposition movement has arisen. McLay is indulging in wishful thinking. There is, also, as most observant readers will quickly pick up, a fundamental paradox in the title of the book which is hinted at by McLay: 'Workers City' (without the possessive, notice, presumably suggesting a city for, not belonging to, workers) is no longer characterised by workers, a significant minority of the class addressed by McLay are now, in fact, because of the forces of contemporary capitalism maligned in the book, unemployed. This is more significant than it at first appears. McLay continues with a sort of short history of the class struggle in Glasgow:

Of course it is no new thing for the city authorities to be in the camouflage business. They were in the same business in the 1920's, shouting about 'libels on Glasgow', when it would have taxed an ingenious mind to invent a libel more outrageous than the reality prevailing at the time... Sadly, however, no Scottish poet, novelist or playwright...was able to resist the political and cultural dominance of London in sufficient degree to be able to depict, in its savage and unsentimental totality, the only real challenge to this rampant capitalist oppression: the class war in

Glasgow.
For alongside the poverty and disease and wasted lives there
was the glory and heroism of those who resolutely engaged
reaction and put Glasgow in the vanguard of revolution, not
just here in these islands but throughout the world. The men
and women who rejected parliamentary opportunism and
sought to advance the people's struggle in the work-place and
in the streets...It is a story which continues into our own day.
It is not a libel on Glasgow but her vindication.
In contrast to this mythology of past deeds, the present political
situation, and its encumbent media culture, fares very badly. McLay
continues:
The lies and hypocrisy of mealy-mouthed councillors and
turncoat Reds can change nothing of that. Nor can the cheap
trickery of PR frauds blind us to the evils of the present. For
although modes of repression and control in State bureaucra-
cies may have changed, relying today as much on advertising
conmanship as on police coercion, and although the new
capitalist-controlled computer technologies exploit and im-
poverish and degrade us in ways were hardly imaginable even
fifty years ago, yet it is repression for all that, it is still
exploitation, it is still impoverishment, and it is still degradation... De-industrialised Glasgow is living in a distant scheme,
without amenity and without community, and waiting for the
Giro...and whilst working-class Glasgow is in a kind of death,
middle-class Glasgow is in the throes of regeneration. The
Labour Council knows where it stands. There is no capitalist
enterprise that will not be looked upon favourably if it comes
under scrutiny for a grant. Come on, they tell us, play the game.
The wine-bar economy is all we've got and it's blossoming, so
don't start knocking it for Christ's sake.[13]
Apart from McLay's anarchic paranoid suspicion, whether justified
or not, of all those who happen to be in power (not to mention all new
technologies), the most notable feature of this tirade is, firstly, the
distinctly dated political rhetoric of abuse – 'mealy-mouthed councillors' and 'turncoat Reds' – and, secondly, and importantly, the
mythologising of history. This mythologising, of course, takes the
form of an oppositional, left-wing reading of the events of the past
constructed to counter the dominant ideology. Thus, for example, the
rhetoric of red-Clydesideism is paramount within this discourse.
There is no denying that this kind of counter-history may be worthwhile and inspiring, but for all that it is as much a construction as
established historiography and the reason why it fails in its intended
purpose is explained very well by Patrick Wright: 'It should certainly

be acknowledged that the sort of historiographical activism which confines itself to casting light on what was hidden from history in earlier times can itself contribute to the maintenance of the often very different forms of domination which exist in the present...my point is that a simplifying nostalgia can replace any principled democratic consideration here, one that is happier with its romantic identification with the nineteenth century working class...than with the challenging and complex situation of the area's population now.'[14] Within the particular rhetoric of working class Glasgow examined here there is also, often, both a romanticising and a simplification. At its worst it displays its origins in street-level propaganda as in the various badly-written and inaccurate biographies of Muir, Baird, Hardie, etc produced in pamphlet form in the twenties and thirties;[15] at best it is only the beginning of an attempt at the type of alternative Marxist historiography suggested by contemporary work in popular culture.

This type of alternative history-making, however, displays the predominant weakness of conventional schoolbook history – the notion, suggested by Thomas Carlyle, that the history of a people is the history of a few significant individuals – thus, as we see in Currie's paintings, individuals such as Maclean are hero-worshipped almost to the extent of fetish. The corollary of this, that can also be seen, is the development of the figure of the idealised worker. But this sort of history, and the connotations it produces, at least for those with some background in popular movements, is now thoroughly lodged in the past. Another substantial and interesting article in the *Workers City* collection by James D. Young, a long-time socialist agitator and now a lecturer at the University of Stirling, best known for his book *The Rousing of the Scottish Working Classes* and now engaged in writing 'a history of working-class Glasgow', has recourse to Currie's murals to make a point:

> What Ken Currie's mural history of Glasgow conveys to us is that the Scots have been exiled inside their own country. For when a people have no real access to their own history, they are exiles. However, this mural history of Glasgow between 1778 and 1978 is proof of the profound changes occurring in Scottish artistic, cultural and political life. By forcing their way into the national culture, the murals of Ken Currie depicting the historic struggles of working-class men and women, together with other facets of contemporary working-class cultural activity, are feeding back into Scottish life and impinging on the political consciousness of socialists and trade unionists.[16]

Workers City purports to be the voice of 'the Real Glasgow', and this struggle for the possession of the privileged, genuine, discourse continues – with several diverse bodies claiming to represent the 'real' Glasgow, but, arguably, Currie's pastiche has no truck with reality, it is the past recuperated and reconstructed through a peculiar distorting lens. How can the iconography of Currie's paintings – glaring furnaces, gleaming wrought iron, sinewy workers, heroic miners – have any meaning other than a symbolic meaning for a society typified by de-industrialisation, mass unemployment, new technology, and Postmodern ennui. *Workers City* is a brave attempt at opposition to the New Glasgow movement but it is, comparatively, a failure, being bought and read by only a fraction of those who have seen Struthers's crass *Glasgow's Miles Better*. The reason for its failure is linked with the reasons for the failure of the whole socialist movement to mount any concerted campaign in these Thatcherite times: it addresses itself to an established and captive audience already enamoured of its pointed rhetoric, and it adopts a peculiarly old-fashioned (although, paradoxically, fashionable in the form of nostalgia, reduced to pastiche) *industrial* discourse to address a distinctively *post-industrial* society. Yet examples of this abound in contemporary Glasgow. For example, witness a newspaper report on the installation of a new community sculpture in Springburn:

> Vincent Butler has recently and successfully completed a bronze group entitled *Heritage and Hope* in Atlas Square, Springburn, Glasgow.
> Courageously commissioned by a panel from four local community councils, together with Mark O'Neill, the curator of the Springburn Museum, it has already been vindicated by its great popular success. The two figures depicted, those of a railwayman and a young girl, symbolise Springburn's industrial heritage as the largest centre of locomotive manufacture in Europe and also its positive approach to the future... Mounted on top of a red sandstone base, the young girl, who is depicted as reaching out to the future with all the exuberance of youth, is contrasted with the unknown railwayman whose more cautious pose is dictated by experience... the figure of the man with cloth bunnet pushed back over curly forelocks comes dangerously near to social realist formula art.[17]

This 'social realist formula art' *manque* fails, however, to make any real connection between the subject matter of a supposed glorious industrial past and the real hope for the future of an area desecrated by de-industrialisation and unemployment. In this case 'heritage' and 'hope' are not connected sequentially or teleologically in that one is derived from the other, but oppositionally, the two disjunctive sides of the scale. And that is the sad point, as the heritage bandwagon rolls out its clichéd rhetoric and dead industrial complexes parade themselves proudly before our eyes. It is, in contemporary Glasgow, a *danse macabre* – like seeing the same ruckle of girders, derricks, hoists and cranes that our forefathers toiled with rearrange themselves in absurd impractical forms. Similarly, a gable-end mural by Daniel Trevor in Maryhill entitled *Rebuilding Community*, features a troupe of builders who not only seem to be refashioning the rafters of the imaginary interior of the building, painted in *trompe l'oeil* fashion (the paradox is, of course, that the painted figures are also actually painting the tenement wall), but also constructing some sort of fête or circus in the cause of Culture Year. The irony of the juxtaposition is clear. McLay, in his introduction to *Workers City*, is sometimes aware of this paradox but in the end he, like others opposed to many contemporary social and political developments, is unable to find a suitable voice in which to express his misgivings. Socialism in Glasgow, or indeed the whole country, awaits the discovery of such a voice, but in the meantime McLay's injunction to not play the game is sound advice, at least to those of us who believe that even the most harmlessly transparent workings of ideology deserve close examination.

On the face of it, the most revealing cultural event of the last couple of years in Glasgow was the unveiling by the sculptor George Wylie of his most-renowned work. Utilising the symbolic structure of the Finnieston crane, Wylie constructed and suspended a straw locomotive, thus resurrecting, in the form of parody or post-industrial pastiche, the original purpose of the giant crane which served to load real locomotives from Beardmore's forge for export to the four corners of the world. The gross irony or effrontery of this whole affair was hardly commented on by the press although some critics were clearly aware – Cordelia Oliver commented, 'Tragedy was at least implicit in the event, for all its pleasurable excitement. One scarcely needed the revelation of the steel question mark artfully secreted in the straw belly of the locomotive, to understand that Wylie's artwork stood for Scottish industry as a whole in its present state of neglect and starvation'.[18] Encouraged by this success, Wylie, having symbolically reflected the death of the steel industry, turned his attention to the shipbuilding industry, and his next project was to launch, on the Clyde, a giant paper boat – 180 by 60 feet. The 1989 Glasgow Mayfest programme commented: 'an export cargo from the Clyde has been arranged and the *Paper Boat* will carry a big Question Mark around Britannia's shores, me hearties, to ask all landyuppers – just what has become of us as a Maritime Nation...eh?'[19] Wylie's paper shell was launched before an enthusiastic crowd on Saturday 6th May 1989. In front of the gaunt, gauche faces of Currie's workers, the New Glasgow juggernaut rolls on.

Out of This World

In the drawings by Muirhead Bone[1] of the Glasgow shipyards in the early twentieth century, the impression is one of crush and clamour, as each black skeletoid limb of the cranes, the winches, the stanchions, the derricks, criss-crossed against the smoke and cloud, competes for its rightful path, forming an almost completely abstract pattern of light and dark. Fifty years later, however, the pall is lifted, the Fairfield Crane casts only an insubstantial, phantom shadow over the banks of the Clyde.

The death of the Glasgow shipyards was presaged by George Blake's influential novel, *The Shipbuilders*,[2] published in 1935, during the depression. Blake's Glasgow is vividly portrayed, for example, in this passage, in which Leslie Pagan, a shipyard owner, looks over his city before departing: 'It was his own city, for better or for worse. Never could he escape it. By no adjustment of the selfish mind; by no prepared indictment of its social deficiencies, its ugliness, its smugness, its sentimentality, its brutality, its dirtiness, its wetness, its greyness, its grimness – by no elaboration of personal criticism could he escape its grip on him or his awareness of responsibility to it. A city that had had its day; a city built on exhausted coal-beds and empty shipyards; a city now of middle-men and Jews and pimps...'[3] Alan Bold, the writer and critic, comments that 'from such excruciating sentimentality it can be seen that Blake's novel is naturalistic rather than realistic. It is shot through with technical imperfections, for the proletarian dialogue is stagey and artificial and the cloyingly unreal relationship between Leslie and Danny is a false model of human harmony.'[4] Although there is a vein of sentimentality running through the novel, however, Blake's reputation relies on an approach that is decidedly less sentimental than many of his counterparts. More insidious by far is the nature of the central relationship of the novel, between Pagan and his employee, Danny Shields, which is an attempt, in a sort of ham-fisted way, to rationalise class relations during the depression. The very real tensions and differing interests of different groups, however, are not developed, although Blake does make a point about differing opportunities and aspirations in the conclusion of the novel.

In the novel Danny Shields is a riveter who has lost his job due to the closure of the shipyards. He is meant to epitomise, in some way, the simple, steadfast nature of the British worker. At the end of the novel, Danny is offered alternative employment by Pagan, with whom he has served during the Great War:

'Well, Dan?' said Leslie, wheeling to face his friend. 'There's only a minute or two to go.'

'I think I'll just stick to my trade, sir,' came the answer, respectful but dour...

The man would not, could not, understand that the game was up. If it were only a few shipyards closed down! But even in the time that he had been idle the monster men called Progress had overtaken such as Danny Shields and left them behind, rejects, on the deserts of industrialism. Now in the place of the riveter was the welder, joining the plates of ships with a melting jet of white flame; and no riveter of the old school could hope to graduate in the fierce new art. Now one man and a boy, working a machine, could do in the way of making hatches what it used to take fourteen craftsmen to do. Now boys manned piano punching machines, each halflin with his engine displacing twelve helpers. Another dozen helpers were out of work because a hydraulic machine, operated by a man and a boy, could bend ships' frames. One man, commanding a single-drill punch, displaced six of his kind. So the number of men employed in the yards fell by one half in the ten years from 1920 – and would go on falling.

If there was only time to drive these facts into the thick head of Danny Shields! If only the man could see what was happening about him and could realise that in the good earth, English or otherwise, lay his only hope! But it was too late...[5]

Blake ends the novel on this pessimistic note. A few years later, in 1944, the novel was made into a film directed by John Baxter, best known for *Love on the Dole*. The film fits nicely into a genre of British films in the thirties that have been identified as fulfilling the hegemonic function of both working to reinforce the idea of a national identity and to deny the very real differences and tensions between the classes. The film begins with a high panning shot from a shipyard crane, the voice-over, in the form of a poem, aided by innovative montage techniques, purveys a straightforward message – 'The story of the British Isles is a story of great seamen and great ships...The British Isles are bound together in pride ('pride', as we discover, rhymes with 'Clyde')...We built an Empire with ships...ships to bind together the peoples of the world, to fight if necessary for the common man wherever he may be found'. This perspective, of course, denies any national or local concerns in the matter. Similarly, although there is clear introduction of class difference in the relationship between Danny Shields, the riveter, and Leslie Pagan, the shipyard owner – their families and home lives are directly compared – the film reconciles these differences in terms of common interest. The classes, in fact, are united in order to counter a menace that comes from without: 'There's more in this than you and I and Pagan's, there's a nation...To hell with party politics – this is something far above all that nonsense...It's not our fault, it's not even the fault of the government. It's a direct result of the world slump.' The theme of the foreign enemy is, however, developed by Baxter to give the film a very different slant to Blake's novel. In fact, the film really only begins where the novel ends – for the solution to the problem of the slump proved amazingly simple for Baxter – working only six years after the publication of the novel, but six years in which the world had been turned upside down. Firstly, Baxter follows the narrative impulse of the novel – Danny sticks to his trade, there is an impressive montage scene in which the background of the tenements, and scenes of deprivation are superimposed on the faces of the poor and, juxtaposed, Pagan pondering. But this is not the end. Pagan is determined. After going to visit parliament ('Churchill was the only one who made sense!'), he prophesies war. Orders for destroyers arrive to save Pagan's, and Leslie and Danny are again united in the common fight. Allied to this is another, sentimental, plot. Danny's son, Peter, after being jailed for his involvement with the Sing-Sing Boys, a street gang, goes to sea on a ship, the *Milano*, built at Pagan's, and dies a hero, manning the pumps so that they can 'bring the old ship home'. In so doing he saves Leslie's son. The film ends with Mrs Shields, who has left Danny earlier in the film, returning to the shell of their bombed tenement and finding, in the ruins, Peter's toy boat. The sentimentality, however, also serves to mask the more serious purpose of the film. The sophisticated montage techniques lionise the figure of the worker (and also the voice-over: 'they're always ready to work, they've never lost a simple faith') but also serve to restrict him to only one of limitless possibilities – his predetermined fate. In the film as well as the novel, Danny is doomed forever to 'stick to his trade' – he is also notably less well served by the film medium as to the reader, who has no recourse to his inner thoughts, he appears clownish and servile.

The same montage techniques feature predominantly only a few years later in an important piece in a different genre – John Grierson's important seminal documentary *Seawards the Great Ships*, probably the best known of the canon of documentaries produced by the Films of Scotland group originally in the thirties (stimulated by the Empire Exhibition) and again in the fifties. Despite its innovative and powerful appeal and important place in the history of Scottish film, *Seawards* can now be viewed perversely as the swansong of a declining industry. Colin McArthur perceptively pinpoints this paradoxical nature: 'The mythicising of the processes and personnel of the Clyde shipyards, the elementalism and giganticism of the visual and verbal imagery ('mighty', 'titanic','the welder is king', 'rigidity that will withstand pounding oceans') – reminiscent of the stakhanovite art of the Soviet Union – seem shabby and hollow in the light of what has become of the Upper Clyde. Starkly in retrospect, the breast-beating and tub-thumping of *Seawards the Great Ships* offers no comfort to Clydeside workers or guidance as to the historical processes which have put them out of work.'[6]

Despite Blake's dire message at the end of a novel penned in the mid-thirties, or Grierson's inflated rhetoric of the fifties, however, the sad story of the death of the Clyde has been reprised many times since, in Bill Bryden's *Willie Rough*,[7] Caton-Jones's *The Riveter*, or in the real-life tragedies of the sixties culminating in the workers' occupation of Upper Clyde Shipbuilders. The axe continues to fall, but it is fair to say that we no longer feel the chop. The docks up towards Finnieston and Govan have fallen into disuse and disrepair, left sorry and stagnant, and then, after the final death throes of the industry, in the eighties, filled in, their square-cut shapes lost to the memory of the landscape.

In 1857, Alexander Smith wrote his famous poem, *Glasgow*, an excessive evocation of the first era of industrial society:

> Draw thy fierce streams of blinding ore,
> Smite on a thousand anvils, roar
>   Down to the harbour-bars;
> Smoulder in smoky sunsets, flare
> On rainy nights, with street and square
>   Lie empty to the stars.
> From terrace proud to alley base
> I know thee as my mother's face.

This meaning, the intensity of personal identification with the powerful imagery of heavy industry, is lost completely in post-industrial Glasgow, and an altogether different paradigm comes to bear on the perceived identity of a city which no longer owes its substance and prosperity to a clear industrial function within a greater geographical entity. Post-industrial society, of course, was an expression coined by Daniel Bell, the American economist, in the sixties to refer to supposed changes in the social structure brought about by the demise of the industrial society of the twentieth century (as opposed to the family capitalism of the manufacturing society of the last century). We can also employ the term post-industrial, however, in its wider sense to suggest the reconstitution of the image of a city once dependent, both metaphorically and metonymically, on the real industrial modes of production. How this can be done is a central problematic in the constitution of the New Glasgow.

An example of this reconstitution was evident in the events of the summer of 1988 during which, across the river from the site of the old Queen's Dock where now stands the Scottish Exhibition and Conference Centre, acres of desolate dockland once dedicated to the shipbuilding industry, were set aside for another, very different, purpose.

During a very few months in this fairly average summer, on the banks of the river Clyde, the Glasgow Garden Festival flourished. The advertising slogan for the festival was 'A Day Out of This World' (*The Sun*, we were also told, was 'a daily out of this world'). This catchpenny was also employed by the television advertisement for the festival which, in its way, epitomised the concept of escape and adventure at the heart of the festival marketing. It featured characters who represent both, on one level, the typical family, and on another level, were transparently based on the fictitious heroes of the popular 'Indiana Jones' films. The festival itself was *the great adventure*, escape to, and from, the other world. For the advert the animation was worked from a line drawing which was only partially coloured in – allowing the characters and their surroundings to progressively metamorphose into various features of the festival which merged together (a characteristic also of the newspaper advertisements for the event) emphasising the festival as a *total* experience, and allowing the images to coalesce in a flurry of blossoms – the garden logos. An image highly stylised yet coherent.

The adventure theme was especially apparent in a series of fun rides offered on the festival site which can be seen as getting progressively more extreme – a stationary BR locomotive cockpit, a traditional Glasgow tram, a miniature railway, the Clydesdale Bank revolving tower – and culminating in the spectacular Coca Cola ride. All this, of course, is travelling without a real purpose, purely for the sake of leisure – or adventure. Nothing actually got you anywhere – the trains returned along their circuitous serpentine path, a quayfront tram ride only went one way, and its route was a direct reflection of the buses (trams twenty years ago) that followed the southern boundary of the site along Govan Road. This aspect of the location of the Garden Festival was revealing – for many years commuters travelled along this route without being aware of the existence of this dockland site (hidden from prying eyes). Similarly, inside the festival

The Glasgow Garden Festival with the Finnieston crane in the background

site you could remain unaware of the outside world – unless, of course, you refused to play the festival game, and kept your bearings by occasional glances through chinks in hedges and railings. Once part of industrial Clydeside, it shut its doors to the shipbuilding industry ages ago and lay derelict behind its perimeter wall for years. Then, for one short summer, this narrow strip of land was transformed. However, although the site formed part of the south bank of the river, its main vista for the Garden Festival was located on the other side of the Clyde, from the railway line that led from the city centre to Partick in the west. Leading from the erstwhile Finnieston station, now named Exhibition Centre, a long pedestrian tube walkway took you to the recently built Scottish Exhibition Centre, from where the scene opened up to encompass Bell's Bridge which led you directly across to the Garden Festival. Today still, welcoming you at the station, a specially commissioned mural provides a historical site for the festival itself. Designed by the Scottish artist Willie Rodger, it consists of 29 consecutive graphic panels charting the development of Glasgow from a rural village through commercialism and industrialisation culminating in the Garden Festival and, therefore, the return of post-industrial pastoralism. It syntagmatically forms a perfect cyclical narrative which positions, it seems, the festival itself within the historically inevitable and thus presents it as metonymically representative of the greater regeneration of Glasgow. To place the festival within this clearly industrial context with its unfashionable Modernist uncritical view of progress is paradoxical. The circle is broken. As the bulldozers move in the garden will wither and the site, thus initiated, return once to the worldly principles of big business.

Imagine a typical visit to festival, on a typical summer's day in 1988. Arriving on the festival site, the first thing that the visitor encounters is the High Street – a parade of souvenir shops set within a quite extraordinary structure, a sort of continuous scaffold or wooden framework with decorative features that constitutes a sort of skeleton. These are miniaturized versions of actual or supposed Glasgow buildings, from Victorian commercial edifices to dwelling houses, the ubiquitous tenement, paradoxically painted in a variety of bright colours rather than tenement grey. It is a contemporary cut-price version of the more substantial full-scale replica of medieval Glasgow erected for the 1911 exhibition.

Notably, this phantom village contains many clocks fashioned out of wood: they are all set, implacably, at different times. There is no way of telling the time at the Garden Festival – as if the great adventure must exit outwith time. Like the skeletoid structure of the phantom village, the experience is strangely ethereal and the visitor is instantly positioned in a vague otherworldly Glasgow by the almost-familiar outlines of the High Street. It is overwhelmingly reminiscent of Noddyland, a ghost borough of benevolent municipality – so toylike that it requires a shake to remind oneself that these are scaled-down representations of the real Glasgow: the university (which reflects its real life equivalent across the river Clyde), the city chambers, tenements. Like some sort of lost Elysium, this 'out-of-the-world' uncannily reflects the real world stripped of its corporate political and socio-economic reality.

To some extent, everything in the festival is out of scale – giant taps and teapots, dwarf bonsai trees. The macrocosm is represented by natural minutiae – there is a globe made out of different grasses, and a sunken rockery with shrub and lichens forms an aerial representation of the counties of Argyll and Bute. There is a sort of miniaturisation of Scotland – an attempt to condense elements of Glasgow and Scotland into the signifying fabric of the festival. This is reminiscent of Colin McArthur's perceptive account of the Empire Exhibition,[8] which develops the fundamental opposition of progress *vs* tradition which peripheral societies and cultural often find operates to their cost in terms of favouring nostalgic, mythological constructions of the past over the real demands of the present. The efforts of the 1938 exhibition to situate Scotland within the context

The Glasgow Garden Festival – Eros with the university, the new Forum hotel and
a replica of the top twenty feet of the Tolbooth steeple in the background

of contemporary industrial society, he suggests, was modified by the
use of blatant Scotch mythology – the Clachan (a constructed
highland village) – which drew on a nostalgic longing for a mythical
pre-industrial past operating within the discourse of otherness investigated by Fanon, Said, etc. The Garden Festival bows towards
this tradition with features such as Para Handy's cottage (based on
the famous stories by Neil Munro featuring a West Highland steam
puffer and its crew). But the effect is very different – there is no real
attempt to relate mythology to real life. The dominant discourse is
nostalgic in a way that relates not to a supposed lost rural past but to
comic book fantasy. It is mythology twice removed from its source.
Similarly, although the Clachan was populated by real people playing
out supposedly authentic parts, Para Handy, Sunny Jim and company are, in fact, only fibreglass models – as are the 'windae-hingers'
and other figures in the High Street. Phantom inhabitants of the
phantom village.

The paradox of the 1938 exhibition is not so evident within the
Garden Festival itself, however, because the Garden Festival is
symptomatic of a wider historical and cultural paradox. This is
evident if we take it in a historical context. The Garden Festival is
third in the line of great festivals or exhibitions with which we have
charted the progress of the city at fifty year intervals – 1888, 1938,

1988 (there were also the exhibitions of 1901 and 1951). Each is a particular reflection of the dominant concerns of the time. If we examine the site plan for each of these occasions some trends become evident.

Firstly, lost from the Garden Festival is the theme of the international – especially of Empire. Glasgow is no longer, as in 1888 (and in 1901), the industrial centre of North Britain (sic), as in 1938, second city of the Empire, it merely *is itself*, at this moment in time, and can be accepted as such. Likewise, the Garden Festival is ephemeral rather than monumental. There are no halls devoted to industry or commerce (or palaces, as in 1938). There are open spaces, tents, arenas and continual passages or mazes. There are also spaces labelled 'science', 'technology', etc – but these are less clearly delineated, moving out from the central hub (metaphorically the petals of a flower) they merge into each other. Neither is the visitor so clearly categorised. There is an impulse towards constant movement and changing vistas.

Wandering through the festival it is hardly surprising that I should pause to consider the way in which the unique Glasgow tradition of festival is part of my own personal, family, history. I know that I still have a small medallion, purchased sometime in my childhood, (probably at the Barrows) when I used to collect coins, from the 1901 exhibition (the year, perhaps, when my grandmother, my father's mother, was born – there is some uncertainty about the exact date) that features an elevation of the Kelvingrove Art Gallery. I remember my astonishment that such a familiar building (I often went on school trips there) should be preserved for posterity in this way. It was only many years later that I learned that the building had actually been constructed for the exhibition. I know that my grandmother, thirty-seven years later, visited the Empire Exhibition (I have no evidence that my father, nineteen years old at the time, ever did) and she may, as a child of indeterminate age, have also attended the 1911 exhibition.

However, if today we return to the site plans of the great exhibitions, again we can see the progression from 1901, machinery, to 1938, engineering – the addition of the man-made element of bricolage, to, in 1988, and on a smaller scale, technology. But the festival is not dedicated to the gods of industry – it is more a celebration of the human form – health, well-being, nature, landscape, etc.[9] For example, there are the Eye and Ear gardens featuring strange sounds and exotic images, and various play areas for children offering a variety of different physical experiences. The predominant theme is leisure as opposed to industry. In 1901 and 1938 the exhibitions laud the achievements of industrial Glasgow on sites – Kelvingrove and Bellahouston parks – dedicated to leisure. The Garden Festival is an offering to the god of Leisure situated on a site once the hub of industrial Glasgow now laid waste and recuperated once more by the thirst for consumption – not the need for production. The Garden Festival does not represent but replaces industry. Therefore, as we have already noted, it can be seen as the first of (perhaps a succession of) great post-industrial exhibitions.

The essential difference is that the Garden Festival is not so obviously thematic. It is not informed by one coherent impulse – the grind of mighty machines or the bustle of Empire. Neither is there any one dominant design initiative (such as art deco in 1938). Apart, for example, from the strange concept house (impermanent) or the idiosyncratic Rudolf Steiner little house the buildings are predominantly pastiche – Laing's baronial suburbia, half-log cabins, even, in the phantom village, grandiose pseudo-entrances with plywood cornucopias. The *experience* of the festival is itself not coherent – instead it seems to build on vague memories of past adventures – the Funfair, the Seaside, the Adventure Playground, the Natural History Museum. The glue that holds these elements together (and eventually places them vicariously within the overall paradigm of adventure – the Indiana Jones experience, as it were) is nostalgia. Nostalgia is omnipresent at the Garden Festival. Overtly, in the tram car rides, the Glasgow patois, or, more tangentially, within the context of the mythology that places Glasgow, within Scotland, within some sort of magical fictitious childhood. In this way nostalgia serves, within the overall experience of the festival, to both reassure and unsettle. The Garden Festival experience is, in fact, composed of other secondhand experiences – it is not *new*. It is a bit like continual visits to the carnival with somebody else's granny.

And yet it is an experience that I will remember vividly, as will countless thousand others and even today, with the Garden Festival long gone, we can return to the souvenir programme to remind us, take us back to that experience (although the glossy 'travel brochure' illustrations of sun-kissed children, etc owe little to the real experience.) Yet, when I do so my eye is drawn not to the glossies, but to the poem by Stevenson that serves as a foreword:

> Where the roads on either hand
> lead onward into fairy land
> Where all the children dine at five
> Where all the playthings come alive

The windae-hingers that populated the phantom village of the Garden Festival were, to me, these playthings. The image of them, each dark day after the Garden Festival had been put to rest, awakening to cavort in the ghostly framework of imagined Glasgow inspired the title of this book. Elizabeth Wilson, in her book *Hallucinations*[10] refers to the 'uncanny' as meaning when something

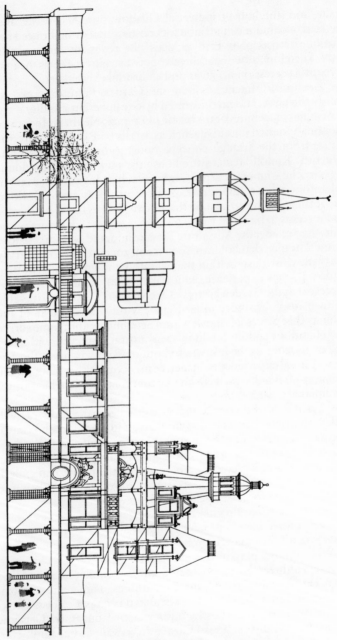

Architect's design for 'The Phantom Village'

inanimate suddenly appears alive. She also refers to what she calls 'living dolls' – those mechanical dancers who appear in streets and pedestrian precincts, their faces painted, their eyes covered by dark glasses, moving inch by inch like puppets or robots. Go to Argyle Street in Glasgow each weekend and you will see them too, almost frozen, earning their meagre living from these tiny, inhuman actions. And one stage further down the slide, in Central Station, the homeless and destitute sit motionless, sometimes posing as freeze models, hoping for a few pence to enable them to survive the great city for one more night. And out in the schemes, the countless thousands sit in front of their television screens or stare from a window – the silent majority whom Culture City passes by but who constitute, nevertheless, real Glaswegians. If I construct my meaning metaphorically in this book it is because I cannot forget these images. That is why Glasgow is the Phantom Village.

However, in that particular summer, the paradox of holding a garden festival in a city in which a small percentage of the population actually own a garden, was neatly resolved by the mythology of the New Glasgow which subsumed the Garden Festival and all it stands for. The Garden Festival was destined to be borne on the tidal wave of enthusiasm for the revitalised Glasgow, the recuperation of the city's image and the 'Miles Better' campaign. Its success, perhaps, was merely the inevitable conclusion of that remarkable self-fulfilling prophesy first uttered some six years ago. And, with this in mind, the most interesting spaces in the Garden Festival were those in which the nature/ culture divide was at its most paradoxical. The marina, into which old three-masted ships sailed, which smelled of great oceans, but which, in reality, was a little bit of industrial dockland redefined for the riverboats or the sleek streamlined dinghies and sailboards of the leisure industry, or the allotment[11] type plots of the various societies – regimented little slices of a rural past hemmed in by the urban present. One of the interesting things about the housing schemes in their infancy was that they infringed on the real countryside. In praise of space and greenery, bottom flats were given large gardens, in the hope that they would sprout grass or trees or roses. Sadly, these peripheral spaces were claimed by culture – or at least the barren estates or philosophies that inspired them. Like Checkland's upas tree each terraced block took root and, slowly, the dream was lost.

In post-industrial Glasgow there is something about the way that the elemental nature of the land is challenged, then repossesses, is redefined, and spaces moulded to ideas or purposes in, if you like, a more random process of the type suggested by Rodger. In this way I remember an industrial resource of an earlier era. Once the Monklands Canal cut its way deep into the centre of Glasgow. As a

boy, I used to walk along its banks with my father, its banks
crumbled, its original purpose defunct. I remember one day going far
along, much further than I had been before and coming upon the
ruined shell of an old factory, inside, amidst the dust, a rusty block
and tackle hung still. Today, on this spot, overlooking the cathedral
and the Royal Infirmary, the urban motorway sweeps down the hill
in the path of the old canal. From the east, you can drive into Glasgow
in minutes, past giant housing schemes – Easterhouse, Garthamlock,
Ruchazie, Stepps, Cranhill – skirting past Provanmill, Riddrie,
Blackhill, and down into Dennistoun, eventually falling into line with
what was, in my childhood, the beginning of Alexandra Parade. The
urban motorway was, of course, the great white hope of the Modernist rebuilding of Glasgow in the sixties, connecting the peripheral
housing schemes and New Towns to the city. Today its primary effect
is to allow the city centre to be traversed in only a few minutes. Yet
these are significant minutes. As I enter the city, only yards from
where I was born, in Rottenrow Hospital, my old school, my first
university and even the Registry Office in which I was married, my
own life passes into sight and, as the wheels relentlessly rotate, for a
moment, it is as if I am actually perfectly still and the city is, in fact,
unfolding in front of my eyes, the continuous city of *Deathwatch*, or
the topsy-turvy city, viewed from a constantly changing perspective,
of Book Three of *Lanark*. When Jean Baudrillard drove through
America he reflected on the desert unfolding with 'the timelessness of
film'. The urban motorway almost does the same for the urban
environment.

Similarly, Martin Culverwell notes the peculiar character of the
urban motorway in Birmingham:

Cities were originally designed for stopping. Birmingham is
designed for passing through. You enter and leave a town or
city, and the moment of entry is marked by a halting of the flow
of traffic. In the pre-industrial city this point was marked by the
edifice of the city gate, the barrier between inside and out where
exchange and trade took place. With industrialisation the walls
and gates disappeared and the point of entry and exit was
marked by a new edifice, an imposing building that is still
important to the identities of modern cities – the railway
station. Birmingham used to have two railway stations, the
redesigned car city has none, just a series of platforms at one end
of a huge shopping centre – the Bullring. Instead the motorways
and flyovers continue right through the heart of the city and the
city gates have reappeared, multiplied and mobilized. The car
driver is someone who has obtained their own city gate and
transports it to wherever they drive. For the pedestrian, de-

prived of the key to the city, the experience of Birmingham city centre is a very different one... Birmingham city centre appears as a city turned outside in. Virilio asks whether the city can still be said to face us, whether it has a facade any longer. He goes on to suggest a new urban order based not on construction and substance (buildings and highways) but on communication and time (information technology), where today's monuments 'are no longer visible but inscribed in the (computer) terminal's obscure luminosity' and 'Idleness – the monumental wait for services in front of machinery, everyone waiting for (tele)communication'.

This conceptual redefinition of the city also has important psychological consequences which relate quite clearly to our own personal perceptions of everyday experience and construct in special ways our own mental geographies of urban space:

> Virilio's urban order requires a new temporal map of the city, where 'the urgency of work time plays the part of a *time centre* while unemployment and vacation time play the part of the periphery – the *suburb of time*'. The other facet of this is that everyone has their own map of the city, and the factors differentiating them are far more diverse than that between employed or unemployed or drivers and pedestrians. Gender, race, class, disability and age will all determine different experiental maps of the city centre, which continues to be the site of struggles against esclusion and for space. The city centre is not just a place to visit; it is still lived in, and redevelopment has clearly had a profound impact on homes and communities laid waste to facilitate the uninterrupted passage of cars.[12]

This is clearly a description that equally well applies to Glasgow. Particularly in respect to the now absolute differentiation between the core and the periphery which also serves to explain the nature of the inner-city dweller, popularly identified as a member of the 'yuppy' class, who has infiltrated the Merchant City. These protagonists of city style inhabit, it would seem, an imaginary space in which work and leisure are not differentiated, in which the imagined city is the real city. This is truly the New Glasgow – the city in which representation becomes reality. In fact, in some ways, Glasgow seems intent to fully simulate itself – like Lewis Carroll's giant map that covered the whole empire and was left in place to rot into fragments on the ground – and continually new methods of representing the city are discovered. Glasgow Online is a project that employs a computer software package generically called hypertext (a system that allows the user to access information not just via a hierarchical menu but in a more random way, by moving both horizontally and vertically around a more amorphous

mass of information). Glasgow Online employs both text and graphics
(the title screen, for example, uses Art Nouveau script) to construct its
picture of Glasgow. Sitting before the screen, the user can vicariously
visit the constructed Glasgow of the computer's data files – like some
minute homunculus injected into the dreamy paths and alleys of an
artificial brain. This is Glasgow as Information City – the substance of
the city relayed by the insubstantial, invisible body of an electronic
impulse.[13]

And what else is in store for the year of culture ? An amateur Glasgow
artist, Edward Chisnall, best known for a short-lived, tortuous cartoon-
type strip in the *Evening Times* on the history of Glasgow, has designed
twin towers – an 85ft clock tower and a 45ft bell tower – which he plans
to have erected in the city centre. Strangely, they seem from his own
drawings to be scaled-down versions of the upper half of the Tolbooth
(as in the Garden Festival) and the umbrella at Bridgeton Cross. There
may be dubious historical value in such a blatant form of pastiche or
simulation, but the lesson of the Garden Festival may be that what we
can expect to emerge from the fertile soup of culture year may only be
Glasgow reproducing itself in miniature. For, similarly, enthusiasts can
now buy small porcelain tenements, genuinely crafted, detached and
glazed in pastel shades – a toytown icon as typical and representative of
Glasgow as a plastic Rabbie Burns Cottage in a snowstorm is of the
greater Scottish myth. And the next stage, the paper tenement, which
you make yourself (and therefore has some virtue as a craft object)
snipping out as you go, if you fancy, your own paper inhabitants.

Also, at the end of 1988, a charitable company, 'The Words and the
Stones', was set up to construct a major exhibition for 1990. This was
planned to utilise the connecting underground warehouses and archways, redundant since the heyday of Victorian industrial expansion,
which run down to the Clyde from Central Station. Initial reports
suggested that this exhibition would apparently include 'escalators
down from platform 13 of Central Station to a 'mini-Glasgow' with its
streets representing periods in history'. Six periods of history would be
represented: 'The myths and legends of origin, The Norman and
medieval town, The 17th and 18th century enlightenment, The 75 years
of industrial dominance, the post-second world war era, The Next
Wave.' (This begged several questions – did the war kill off industrial
Glasgow? What is the 'Next Wave'? Who were the Normans anyway?)
No doubt the opening of this exposition in April 1990 – at a cost of over
three million pounds – will answer these and other pertinent questions
that should be addressed to such a major undertaking. Yet the imagination almost baulks at this prospect. What will happen when the
escalators stop churning their four-pound-a-head passengers, when the
engines up above cease to clatter their way south with a payload of

tourists or commuters, when the lights go out and the seal is set on the man-made cellar? What tiny ghosts will tread the miniature avenues and alleys of this phantom village? When we have encapsulated perfectly for eternity, or for merely a moment, the life and times of a city. Trapped in the perfect blindness of an unlit cavern, or pinned and preserved in the ceaseless luminous gaze of the camera flash, the meaning is exactly the same – representation without interpretation. Glasgow preserved for all time in the perpetual present tense.

However, as the opening date of this extravaganza approaches, the plans have changed somewhat. The exhibition is now renamed 'Glasgow's Glasgow' and its remit has altered. As well as homages to Glasgow's industrial past, it will now feature substantial leisure facilities – a bar, theatre, cinema, etc – and offer a range of interactive experiences for the curious – 'Use a periscope in Great Western Road and meet Lord Kelvin, Join the UCS work-in, Watch Benny Lynch in his prime, Fly through the city on computer' – and exhibit a range of treasures – 'from a Fabergé egg made for the Tsar of Russia to a Shanks toilet made for the people of Glasgow'. *Glasgow's Glasgow* offers, it seems, the complete fantasy for the New Glaswegian – to actually visit, in microcosm, Glasgow's grand, resurrected past. This strange ambition to literally visit the past, as if in a time machine, is a common contemporary feature of such phenomena as theme parks and heritage centres, feeding off what some critics such as David Lowenthal have identified as an intense personal longing for the experience of the past born of the fear that the past may be lost forever (as if, *pace* Annan or Shadow, it can ever truly be preserved). Colin Sorensen has clearly pointed out the worrying paradox in this tendency:

> ...they are places out of time – anyway, out of *this* time. They are visits to times past. They allow, encourage us to play, for a time, in another time. In order to do this, some of them, rather worryingly to some of us, play *with* time. Death and decay, it seems, denied. Strangely and paradoxically in the context of institutions normally preoccupied with the passage of time, these phenomena are not allowed to occur. This denial of the realities of time, this artificial omission of any interval between then and now leads to the ready assumption, indeed the implication that then and now are very similar, and that *we* and *they* are, except for a few superficial differences, very similar also.[14]

This very real danger seems to me important, for the city's history, however we construct it, must be seen to have economic, political and social consequences for the way we experience the city today. Working from different perspectives, we may have differing views on how this process has operated, but it seems important that we

preserve some notion of historical process, and to lose that notion in
a dream of vicariously *belonging* to the community of the past perhaps has unfortunate consequences.

Apart from *Glasgow's Glasgow*, several other events planned for
1990 seem to carry the same heavy ideological cargo. As well as John
McGrath's *John Brown's Body*, a history of the Clydeside working class
(apparently based on Foucault's *Discipline and Punish*) written to be
performed at the new Tramway theatre, a major production by Bill
Bryden, the playwright and director best known for his earlier sentimental account of the political struggles in the Greenock shipyards in the
early years of this century *Willie Rough* (Rough is both the alter ego of
Bryden, a son of Greenock, and the epitome of the common working
man), is planned for the autumn. An epic history of the shipbuilding
industry called *The Ship*, it promises to blend drama and reality in a
unique way – as part of the plan is to incorporate a small-scale
resurrection of the Clyde shipbuilding industry and construct an actual
ship (presumably of girders and steel plate rather than of paper) during
the performance.

The Ship is described by the advance publicity as: 'One of the great
events of 1990! At its height, Glasgow was building or repairing an
average of 13 ships a day. *The Ship* is a theatrical tribute to the
greatness of the shipbuilding industry in the west of Scotland. The city
has commissioned Bill Bryden, associate director of the National
Theatre, and William Dudley, award-winning stage designer, to
mount this special production. Music is being composed by John
Tamms. The cast will include 20 of Scotland's top actors. They'll
perform alongside 10 shipyard workers – welders, riveters, joiners,
platers – who each evening will build and launch a ship, *The Princess
of the Fleet*. To find the right location for this massive production,
every working and redundant care and maintenance yard on the
upper and lower Clyde has been explored, derelict factories and
warehouses investigated.'

The dereliction of the site is perhaps mirrored by the dereliction of
real history that pervades this approach. Robert Hewison comments
that: 'Post-modernism and the heritage industry are linked, in that
they both conspire to create a shallow screen that intervenes between
our present lives, and our history. We have no understanding of
history in depth, but instead are offered a contemporary creation,
more costume drama and re-enactment than critical discourse'.[15] As
each small remaining portion of Glasgow's industrial legacy is
rediscovered and recuperated for this purpose we may question the
validity of the histories we construct. Like the timbers of Nelson's
flagship, continually replaced as they rot so that soon none of the
original material will remain, the real fabric of Glasgow's past is

being subtlely reconstituted. But then again, is there any real past ? There is not one history of Glasgow but many, and history is not an absolute but has political, ideological and moral dimensions. The history of the city that we choose is important because it is a part, also, of our own identity.

Je Me Souviens

In his brilliant and seminal study, *The Image of the City*,[1] Kevin Lynch refers to Shipton's account of climbing in the Himalayas. Approaching Everest from the south side, Shipton immediately recognised the peaks and saddles that he had viewed from the north side. The Sherpa accompanying him, however, long familiar with the area, had never realised that these features, viewed from either side, were the *same* features. Lynch takes this analogy to apply to our perception of the city, in that the city, in its mass of component parts, does not necessarily constitute a homogeneous whole to its inhabitants. Rather there are hidden forms and meanings in the city that may be revealed or appear to us in different circumstances and from our own individual perspectives. The very relative nature of our perception of the city and the roles we play within it is, in fact, demonstrated supremely well by Sean Damer's study of a 'dreadful enclosure', an area of Govan known as Wine Alley.[2]

Wine Alley, an area of fairly typical slum housing, and its inhabitants, were subject, during the sixties and seventies, to a process of perjorative labelling by both the authorities, in the form of the Housing Department, and the other inhabitants of Govan, who tended to use Wine Alley as a scapegoat for the inadequacy of their own living conditions – plotting themselves as decent and respectable as opposed to the 'riff-raff' of Wine Alley. A close examination of the situation, however, revealed that the 'riff-raff' themselves and the 'dreadful enclosure' itself, despite its association with crime and drug-addiction, were by no means as black as they were painted, and, in fact, the individual inhabitants of Wine Alley were aware of the fact that, individually, they did not deserve their reputation. What they were not aware of, however, was that the same might apply to their immediate neighbours. The result of the labelling process, therefore, was that the inhabitants of Wine Alley lived in mutual distrust and suspicion of their neighbours. This is the same sort of process that has operated in recent years in council housing 'ghettos' such as Blackhill. Because the image perpetuated on behalf of the inhabitants is at odds with their own knowledge of themselves, they are effectively dissociated from their environment and their own city. In this way, the city, or part of the city, becomes not only an instrument of categorisation but also a form of knowing, a peculiar perspective on life and living.

Yet, how can we fix the image of Glasgow ? How can anyone construct a city from a mass of grainy impressions and insubstantial memories ? This is the question that Jonathan Raban ponders in his book *Soft City* :

> To call a city a slough of despond, or a great wen, or a cesspool, is to give it a functional identity, to fix it in the mind as surely as Bradley Headstone is fixed in Dickens's novel. The city, like the people in it, lends itself to this sort of moral abstraction. Oddly enough, cities, for all their bigness and complexity, get tagged with hard-edged images much more readily than small towns. What mental picture is conjured by, say, Chicago or Sheffield? Isn't it more definite, more dominant, than that of Banbury? A line of cattle trucks, a lamplit street, a waterfront of cranes, are emblematic substitutes for the contrary lines of millions of individual lives. Moral fervour – seeing a particular city as especially evil, a sink of quite unprecedented iniquity – may be a simple convenience, a way of glueing together those visual fragments that compose the city in our head. The sheer imaginative cumbersomeness of the city makes us frequently incapable of distinguishing its parts from the whole; and moral synedoche, the utopia/ dystopia syndrome, is part of our essential habit of mind when we think about it.[3]

In a sense, Raban is only developing the dualistic model of the city, which operates as a representational metaphor, to refer to a form of perception. The implication of this, I think, is that the meaning of the city as we construct it is, because of our own nature, intimate or personal, and metonymic in practice (because of the nature of representation) but, also, in the end, totally moralistic. We construct our image of the city from a metonymic set of icons which stand for the component parts of the city fabric but also, in the wider sense, for concepts that inform our everyday lives – work, leisure, community, neighbourhood. We do not encounter the city in order to tell us where we live, it is in order to tell us how we should live.

How can the New Glasgow, the Glasgow of the 1980s and 90s, inform us in this way? What is new or different? What makes Glasgow a better place today, what can make us, as Glaswegians, better people? Probably very little indeed. Today, on the Garden Festival site returning to its desolation, the Phantom Village, full of empty quotation, has become the deserted village ('where wealth accumulates, and men decay') and towering above it is the Finnieston crane which I remember visiting as a boy, with the ambition of every

Mayfest poster, 1987

little boy – to climb the long ladder to the top secluded cabin, safe from the hammer's ring, to take in both hands the controls and move the giant with a lurch and a shudder into action. Yet today no human hand will grasp the rails the controls are still, welded into a homogeneous mass. This is a dispossessed giant, still sentinel to a land gone to waste. Stand at the central cross and view the High Street, tilt the head a little further, the plywood fenestration, the windae hingers, all gone, returned somewhere to their elemental clay. All that remains, the emptiness of the grey skies of massing clouds, the perfect loop of a scavenging seagull. Whispers of mortality. The old totems have been allowed to return.

I can remember my father here, by the banks of the Clyde, almost synecdochally. The peak of the cap he always wore, as all bald men did at one time. The stiff, shiny knees of his working trousers when he came back from the late shift. The strong cigarettes he smoked, with a ginger-bearded sailor with 'Hero' on his hat on the packet, and the endless sea, evocative of foreign strands. There is a peculiarly specific Glasgow lore he was heir to, and I can remember some of its features, especially those steeped in tragedy or the exotic: Willie Woodburn suspended *sine die* (as in Adam McNaughtan's song), John Thompson, the Celtic goalkeeper tragically killed on the field of play, Manaletto, the bullfighter gored to death shown on television by John Grierson, Jim Reeves in a plane crash, *The Spaniard who Blighted my Life,* Chung Ling Soo who died trying to catch a bullet in his teeth. Perhaps to me, as to all small boys, my father was something special, but he also was something more. My father was an average, respectable man. He was balding in his middle-age, but as a boy he had curly black hair and perfect white teeth. As a young man he was an accomplished footballer and could have became a professional – but the war put an end to that. He served for several years in the desert in the Royal Artillery, mostly as a despatch rider (he told me that once he rode over a hillock and came upon a German camp. He turned round and rode away and never saw them again). He went to Italy and I still have a faded, torn photograph of him playing for the Roma football team. After the war, after a time repairing lawnmowers and an unsuccessful attempt to become a bus conductor, he found work in ICI's paint works and worked shifts there for many years. In 1966 he received a silver watch for twenty years' service, one of the sort with the painted luminous dial that makes a geiger counter tick furiously. He didn't drink, except on very rare occasions, his only hobbies, as I knew him, were horse-racing and football (he was a closet Rangers supporter although, so keen was he to shelter me from any form of bigotry, that I didn't discover this until I was ten years old), he devoted his life to his family. And more than this he showed me around Glasgow, took me to the canal, to Glasgow Green, the People's Palace. He knew the ways of the city as no-one else did (my mother was English, a foreigner to all intents and purposes). As a small boy he took me down the exciting and strange shores by the banks of the Clyde, to cross the river back and forward on the ferries (the only one remaining today, after the construction of the Clyde tunnel is the Yoker/Renfrew ferry). Travel without a purpose – except to breathe the sea air, or the stench of the Clyde, hear the clanging hammers of the shipyard, the welders and the cutters going to work, although these trades, and the shipyards themselves, were already declining at the time, to see the tugs or puffers steaming upriver, to see the weird orange-rusted meccano-set frameworks of the car ferries or the revolving buckets of the dredgers. And when I couldn't be there, first-hand, to see these things, I could think on a rarer treat. Sometimes, we would go to the Kelvingrove Museum where there was a most amazing collection, in glass cases, of these ships, tugs, river boats in miniature.

There is an interesting section in Gilbert Adair's book, *Myths and Memories*,[4] in which, following the example of Georges Perec's essay, *Je Me Souviens*, he lists his memories of years past in a form seemingly random but somehow structured. As I think back to my childhood in Glasgow, the memories struggle back in this semi-random fashion. I have taken the liberty of including here, in Adair's fashion, some of these memories. I remember...

I remember each Friday, when my father came home, going through his pockets and finding one bar of Duncan's orange cream.

I remember going to the co-op for potatoes and putting them into a dirty green latticed plastic bag.

I remember that our third storey window was very, very high up – higher than any other building – for a small boy. You could watch adults and children coming and going around the sweetie shop across the road.

I remember when I was Film Boy at school.

I remember hearing a street-singer in the back courts.

I remember being hit in the face with a football when I was little, and washing off the stinging grit round the edges of my cheeks and chin.

I remember one day on my way to school going up Ark Lane and there, on the pavement, being molested by some boys and spitting and hissing at them, was a swan that had somehow lost its way, it seemed, from Alexandra Park (I had often asked my father on the way back from the park where the swans went at night – and at one time, when very young, I had the strange notion that they were kept by the park keepers behind a solid mahoghany door at the corner of Craigpark.)

Years later, I read Lowell's version of Baudelaire's poem:

> I saw a swan that had escaped its cage,
> and struck its dry wings on the cobbled street,
> and drenched the curbing with its fluffy plumage.
> Beside a gritty gutter, it dabbed its feet,
> and gobbled at the dust to stop its thirst

and remembered it.

I remember once going to the hill above the Monklands Canal to fly a kite. When I stumbled I found a nine-sided threepenny piece in the long grass. Later I found a ball of leaves with scores of little silvery caterpillars in it.

I remember my father used to say 'in the name of the wee man' which was the catchphrase of the comedian Tommy Lorne.

I remember once standing in the middle of the street with my father to see an eclipse (I don't remember the eclipse) and, one night, looking up at a lamplighter lighting the gas globe at the corner of the street and seeing the moon directly alongside, much larger than I had ever seen it before or ever would again. Years later I remember seeing an engraving by Daumier of a man seated at a desk in front of a window with an enormous moon in the background.

I remember the One-O-Clock Gang.

I remember when I was a small boy my father bought me a pair of boxing gloves. They smelled of leather and the red dye came off on your face. I remember thinking that they had no real use – only to shadow box, fantasy fighting. Of course, their attraction, their beauty, lay not in fantasy but in reality, because they were scaled down versions of real boxers' gloves – bought in a sports shop not a toy shop.

I remember Bible John.

I remember avoiding all the cracks on the pavement on my way to school. Later I realised that I had been a victim of false doctrine and stepped on all the cracks.

I remember sitting on my mother's knee and the smell of her hairspray.

I remember counting to a thousand in bed at night waiting for my father to come off the back shift.

I remember that a boy in my class drowned in the canal when the ice broke and the teacher asked us each to bring in sixpence for a wreath.

I remember wearing a sloppy joe.

I remember seeing a poster in the railway station with mountains and flowers and brightly coloured people in a strange dress with the caption 'Scotland', and asking my father where this was.

I remember going to the Lifebuoys, wearing a hat, a blue jersey and a brass badge, and marching around and singing *Land of Hope and Glory*.

I remember going to the meat market to see the pigs and the sheep and, occasionally, the bulls in the ring, and that there was a lot at the back with old cars and buses for sale for practically nothing.

I remember *You Cannae Shove Your Granny Aff a Bus*.

I remember going to Haghill Park to see a football team called Dennistoun Waverley who hardly ever won.

I remember one morning, sitting on the couch when my father had gone down to the corner shop, hearing a noise behind me and thinking he had sneaked in to surprise me. When I turned round I saw a huge dalmatian that had, somehow, wandered in from the street.

I remember that my father one or twice took me to his work – the ICI paint factory – and showed me the machines that made paint and the billiards and table tennis tables in the canteen.

I remember that I used to go to Kelvingrove Museum and Art Galleries (built for the 1901 exhibition) often with my class at school or with my father. One evening, my parents said they would take me there – I could hardly believe that this was possible, so close to bedtime – and we arrived there to find it closed. Instead, they took me to the carnival at the Kelvin Hall. I didn't want to spoil their little joke by telling them that I was mildly disappointed.

I remember that cars only very occasionally would find their way up the hill to Eveline Street, but best of all I remember the horse and cart that brought the hot, black steaming briquettes. I wondered how the men delivering them didn't burn their hands.

I remember when I was older reading that you could find fossils in coal bunkers. Ours was on the landing below but it was only full of thick black dust.

I remember at school singing 'I'm Captain Jinks of the Horse Marines, I feed my horse on corn and beans' along with a squeaky middle-class voice from a square loudspeaker.

I remember going to Alexandra Park, and lots of things that appear in Stephen Mulrine's *Glasgow Number Seven*:

When we were wee
it wis aw berr feet
an who likes candy
an nane o yir cheek
an see us a lenny
an dreepin aff dykes
an kick-the-can
an shots oan bikes
wis rerr
When we wur wee
it wis holes in yir sannies
an egg-in-a-cup

fur tea at yir grannies
an sauce oan a piece
pit that in yir belly
K D R F
an chickie-mellie
dje derr?
When we wur wee
it wis durty rotters
an melt ye wan
an tears an snotters
an doggin it
an dae whit yir tellt
an single woodbines
an six o the belt
no ferr
When we wur wee
it wis ghosts an docs
an kuller earwigs
an big black clocks
an Ally Park
an hame tae yir maw
an Teeny Leek
an Heid-the-baw
wis therr
When we wur wee
it wis gaun yirsel
an honey perrs
an taste the smell
jis bein therr
wis gey near hivven
bit wee an aw
wis Number Sivven
ur merr

but I never went anywhere barefoot – or ever dogged school.

I remember my father taking me to a comic shop at the bottom of Dunchattan Street to swap Batman or Superman or Justice League of America comics. I remember that one box contained adult comics that often featured buxom young woman with ripped clothes and pierced skin enjoying the attentions of bestial-looking soldiers or alien monsters. Sometimes I had nightmares about these.

I remember that my favourite comics featured Bizarro, an imperfect Superman created by accident who dressed like the superhero but did everything the wrong way round – like setting the alarm clock to go to bed.

I remember getting nits and washing my head in an evil-smelling solution.

I remember going to the dentist and being put to sleep with gas. I dreamt I was in a hellish place constructed of red and yellow lights and loud noises. Eventually I saw a chink of light enter through my eyelids and I knew I was alive.

I remember at the Barrows seeing fishermen put their hands into buckets of squirming maggots.

I remember I had a pet mouse until one day I saw little wriggling things in its tray. My father told me it had to go away although I never found out what he did with it.

I remember the sweetie shop across the road sold Lucky Bags and white sugar mice.

I remember on one very rare occasion my father was late home from work and I waited at the window for what seemed like an eternity until I saw him coming round the corner of Dunchattan Street and Eveline Street.

I remember the only time I saw my father the worse for drink (he rarely drank but sometimes kept a couple of green beer bottles – that had to be opened with a bottle opener – in the kitchen) was one day, when he was taking some kind of pills and he had a couple of whiskies and was very sick.

I remember that ginger bottles had cork tops that sometimes went pop.

I remember that my father had varicose veins. One day we went on a Works Outing and he burst them playing football and had to be taken to hospital. My mother and I went home on the bus and I ate a big packet of sweeties and was sick.

I remember I had a budgie called Billy and a hamster called Hammy.

I remember that a neighbour's budgie laid an egg and I took it to school to show to my class. When I got home it had cracked.

I remember that at the works Christmas party I always got a pen and pencil set because I was a studious child.

I remember once, when my father was going to work I put on his cap back to front. Later he told me he was walking down the road when a man said 'Hey Jimmy, are ye gaun oot or comin' hame?'

I remember asking my father how it was that so many people knew his name was Jimmy.

I remember that Lulu came from Dennistoun like me.

I remember, one birthday, getting a little box camera and going with my father, in a freezing wind and drizzle, to the very end of Alexandra Park, to take photos, and listening to the Molendinar burn, running underground beneath metal grates.

I remember Pat Roller and Lobey Dosser.

I remember when I was about ten years old encountering the maxim that whatever you most fervently wished would never happen always did. This totally shocked me. It was so contrary to what I believed to be a commonsense philosophy of life. I spent several years trying to disprove this, to find a logical loophole. Of course, there was none, for it was not predicated on logic. I remember especially that it haunted me one day when I was sitting on a bus home from school and despairing. I knew from the very first time I heard this maxim that it meant my father would die.

I remember most of all not one but many occasions standing alone, hidden behind the bedroom curtain, gazing down from my perch, like Chaucer overlooking the gates of London, on Eveline Street and all its coming and goings.

These are some of my memories. Some of what makes me me. Yet what purpose has this personal apocrypha? It has no real structure other than what order I give it on the page. It is determined by the frailty, the idiosyncrasy and the pathology of my memory. If it has meaning, then that meaning is only personal and hidden even from my own consciousness. It owes nothing to coherent intelligent thought, to logic, or argument, to explication. It owes nothing to the present – only to the past. Nothing to historical substance, only to imagination. I am, in fact, keenly aware that it constitutes a mythology of its own, undoubtedly tainted by sentimentality. The interpretation of this kind of writing, also, is intensely personal, dependent on the reader's familiarity or unfamiliarity with the details of time and place evoked or implied by the reminiscences. It is also notable that it a comparatively recent psychopathologic model that equates reminiscing with therapy (thus reversing, in some ways, the original model of nostalgia as disease).

I remain unconvinced, therefore, of the merit of these remembrances, but they are included here because there is a sense, I perceive, in which their crazed logic constructs and limits my own version of Glasgow – the version, in fact, that this book, in its own way, projects. For, if my memories of childhood are memories of those encounters with a forbidden knowledge, with my loss of innocence, then, appropriately it seems, they come from a period when the city itself, at least from my personal perspective, was on the verge of change. It has always seemed to me that, just as Edinburgh changed from a medieval city somewhere around 1820, in the 1960s Glasgow ceased to be a Victorian city (in a social, rather than an architectural sense). My memories seem to me to be, for a comparatively young man, still those of an old order. I cannot, in the space of this essay, develop this point, but I will say that there is a sense in which the vagaries of memory seem, instinctively, to beg an interpretation which may, in certain circumstances, be illuminating. In praise, therefore, of coincidence, I would like to relate two particular true stories from my own memories.

The first takes place at an uncertain age. I remember I had to go to the eye hospital (I have always been short-sighted although, as long as I can remember, I have had a phobia about my eyes and would never let anybody touch them). My father took me by the hand and led me up the road past my school – it was deserted and hushed although it was a schoolday – and past the old ruined air-raid shelters in Ark Lane, all the time telling me stories and chatting away. I was soiled with tiny tears and frail with fear. If I hadn't had a tight hold of my father's hand I would have blown away like a dandelion clock. If it hadn't been for my father's ineluctable will I would not have gone. The fact that I had no choice was a vague comfort. The hospital was as bad as I had imagined. After sitting interminably in a waiting area with dirty painted wooden panels and frosted glass, I was invited to a large chair where horrible instruments were fitted to me and strong, stubby fingers forced my eyes open and squeezed stinging gel into them. When I left I imagined I could actually see everything more clearly than I had previously. The foreign tenemented streets seemed interminably interesting. My father's strong warm hand was secure and welcoming, his pace as steady and regimented as before. I refused to get a bus home – the long walk now seemed full of unexpected joys. I was going home.

On another occasion, years later, when I had become a student, I was sitting in the old grand reading hall of the Mitchell Library on one of the massive polished tables below the great dome far above with its distant columns and rococo flourishes. I had selected one old volume from the scrapbook of pasted strips that was the catalogue at that time, to be retrieved from the vaults. It was a scholarly text which attempted to show that the story of Orpheus was of Latin rather than Greek origin. Faced, in this enormous repository of words with one significant element of a larger arcana, I suddenly felt dizzy. For some reason I began to imagine that I was blind and that the book, the table, were fading into obscurity in front of me. Packing my few papers I hurried out of the library, relieved to see that, outside in the autumnal city air, it was still light. I wandered slowly up to Charing Cross and down Sauchiehall Street as twilight came and a few people scuttled home from work or headed towards pubs or the dancing. Somehow I felt elated. In the nooks and crannies of the buildings above the starlings were going to roost, as they did every night, despite the attempts of the city fathers to chase them away, making an awful noise. Marching triumphantly down the centre of the street, I doffed my metaphysical hat to them. For a while, at least, the whole city, it seemed, had turned its fickle attention to me.

What do these stories mean ? In both there is a sense of escape, of misery and despair turning to elation or joy. More than that, there is in both a sense of belonging, the neighbourhood, the city, the sinister streets transformed to something more benevolent – as if, as for Shipton's Sherpa, I had seen both sides of the peak and recognised them as one. They are both about returning home, both about the meaning of home.

We all have a history, although our past is always shaped by the personal and impersonal prerogatives of the present. As I have constructed my own personal history it is irrevocably intertwined with that of Glasgow – the facts about my father or my mother (more complete but more distant, a foreign country) are, as I have demonstrated, not outstanding or revealing in themselves, although unique. The details of my grandfather, Thomas Spring's, life are a complete mystery (such a shadowy insubstantial figure he seems to have been that no-one in my family, not even my grandmother when alive, had anything of consequence to say about him). I only know that he came to Scotland from Bray in Ireland sometime at the beginning of the century (the Springs are quite a prominent family in Ireland, but, as yet, I haven't even visited the country). One detail I do recall is that he is buried in Springfield Cemetery whose boundary wall runs beside Celtic Park football ground (as a teenager I sometimes went to matches here). When my grandmother died she was buried next to him here, even though the cemetery was long closed, and the gates had to be opened and a path trod through the overgrowth to the graveside where I had to hold one end of a slender cord as the coffin was lowered. My face was stung by the freezing rain. My one abiding image is of the very elderly minister at the graveyard, his face so emaciated and skeletal that one could imagine he could quietly slip into the wet turf himself, unnoticed. My grandmother, who I simply remember as an old woman who kept a budgie (strange that the various times we spoke when I was a child and a teenager should register so little), I know, was born in Falkirk as Annie Green, and later, after marriage, became Annie Green Spring – a name which augurs an extraordinary coincidence, for in California there is a popular drink called Annie Green Spring's Tonic Wine. It is mentioned in Lisa Alther's novel *Kinflicks* and in at least one other literary work whose name I have forgotten. Some time in the past, my aunt wrote to the company who replied, apparently, that they had no knowledge of the origin of the name but, in recognition of the fact, sent over a crate of the wine. I once had a bottle and, eventually, I drank it all. It had rather a sweet, sickly taste.

But within this digression, perhaps, the point I am trying to make

is that we all have a personal history of a sense – however partial or
fragmented. Part of that history, also, is a sense of belonging. In the
words of the most famous of Glasgow songs, by Will Fyffe, there is
also a message about belonging:

I belong to Glasgow,
Dear old Glasgow Town.
But what's the matter with Glasgow?
For it's going round and round.
I'm only a common or working chap,
As anyone here can see,
But when I get a couple of drinks on a Saturday,
Glasgow belongs to me.

There is a very strange effect in these words (apart from the dubious
stereotypical drunken Glaswegian) that seems to emanate from the
nature of the relationship between the individual and the city. The
natives of many cities may come from that city, but it is a peculiarly
Glaswegian (or perhaps Scottish) habit to 'belong' to your home
town. It is this form of words that allows, in fact, the specious
inversion of the song whereby, in an ecstatic epiphany, the whole city
actually 'belongs' to the narrator.

Belonging to Glasgow, perhaps, should offer more than such a
temporary elevation. To its sons, the city must mean more than just
the sum of its parts and, I feel, although it may be an illusion, that
there is a greater meaning that Glasgow has to offer me. To conclude
my study of Glasgow, it is necessary to delve more deeply into the
personal, the particular. It is easy to picture Joyce, in exile, peering
through his frosted round spectacles to picture each of the shops in
Sackville Street. His is a perfect picture of his city, but it is a fictional
one. Mere visualisation is not enough for what I wish to say. The
distant view may distort – as a camera can perform the trick, with a
certain lens, of manipulating relative sizes. It is necessary, to complete
my own imperfect picture of Glasgow, to go back home.

Until the Day Break

And can one return to one's childhood home? I ask that question again. To seek what really exists – that substantial reminder of the past embedded in brick and stone rather than the ether of memory – and to articulate what is perhaps best left to the free rein of the imagination, I did attempt to go home. One mild winter's day I caught the number 90 circular bus in Farmeloan Road, through Dalmarnock and Parkhead, past the Forge, the bright side of town, through Haghill and along Duke Street to Bellgrove. This is a brief account of my journey home.

I enter the heart of Dennistoun for the first time in many years. Walking up the road I pass big houses, Victorian villas lost in time, consigned to a part of the city now out of fashion. Some have been renovated but others are still decrepit and silent – no aged inhabitants peeping from behind greying chintz drapes. There is a procession of such homes, each unique. One has an appended staircase with what looks like a little timber-framed conservatory in the sky. I remember as a boy imagining this little magic room with, perhaps, its magic toys, or nooks and crannies. I remember that years ago these pavements were laid with flintstones – but the flints are gone, except in some of the back lanes, where you can walk between the houses hidden behind high walls. Unlike our own tenements these houses never intruded into public space. From my own room and kitchen I could only imagine how many rooms, corridors or staircases they contained. I knew that these spaces were the preserve of fiction. Children in all the books I read, with their school uniforms, their nannies and their plummy English accents lived in houses like these. Twice a week I walked along here to the public library until I had exhausted every shelf.

But, as I reminisce, my heart suddenly misses a beat. I seem to have come too far. Within minutes from one boundary to another of my prescribed country. But I haven't transgressed, nor has any strange transformation of topography or geometry occurred. The truth is that the margins of my childhood memory have hopelessly extended through the years. My childhood home is claustrophobically small –

so small that my thirty-four year old body now seems uncomfortable in this little neighbourhood. I wander past a few more houses and stumble left down the hill. I almost lose my bearings. The parallel streets I expect are no longer there – instead I find myself entering into a new compact housing scheme built on several levels. Instinctively I follow a path down some steps, through an archway into an unexpected space.

Here, suddenly, it becomes clear. The open, extending, externalised space, the inexorable unfolding of the tenement grid, the whole world of my childhood, has now been absorbed, redefined and contained in this cloistered, internalised courtyard within a little scheme designed in brick to simulate a type of village Scottish vernacular. The stepped pathways, through archways, between recessed walls and square mullioned windows lead to this quiet, isolated central square. Each egress is marked by an arched structure of smoky-black wrought iron, as insubstantial as the gaudy painted lattices of the phantom village, a sort of minimalist traditionalism pointing to a communal right of way.

Then I realise, with a shiver of panic, that I can see no Eveline Street named here – although other nameplates echo familiar childhood names. I scout around but I cannot find it. Eventually I locate myself in the very centre of the square at a small sculpture and a noticeboard situated as if for the communal oyez. It is blank and the wood is streaked and pitted. The whole square is silent. I wonder if I'm intruding. I wonder who the inhabitants of this deserted village are. Suddenly a dog starts barking from nowhere. It doesn't stop until I leave.

I ponder for a moment to consider where I have been. This neat, pleasant, deserted little scheme has been constructed out of a myth of community. In the simulated vernacular style to give it a specious patina of age and tradition, it has replaced the appalling age-old slums of my boyhood. Eveline Street, which once strode up the hill, has not been accommodated within this scheme – indeed, it is impossible now to imagine enough space to contain it. I exit by another boundary – Ark Lane, bordering the Tennent's brewery. Once a fairly major thoroughfare, it has now regressed to its original purpose – an actual lane, leading pedestrians up from Duke Street. On the wall of one of the newer blocks is a plaque marking the birthplace of William Miller (who wrote *Wee Willie Winkie*) – a touch of tradition that would have been irrelevant within the living fabric of the tenement tradition; now only coherent when the past has been eternally condemned to the land of imagination. Likewise, only just round the corner is situated one of these monumental sculptures that keep cropping up – a circular bronze relating a history of Wellpark, erected by Tennent's whose massive brewery skirts the western boundary of this land – again irrelevant when the brewery itself was walled with stone and barbed wire, noisy and smelly, a source of employment, money and damned pleasures. Now the brewery itself is only a monument of shiny silver piping, higher than the clouds, itself. Founded in the eighteenth-century, it is a part of an old Glasgow tradition now.

And so my childhood home has been erased from the landscape. Not even remembered, as far as I can see, except for the insubstantial redefined street names, in the fabric of this section of the New Glasgow. Instead, what has been constructed here is another community, based on another mythology, although of the same tenor. I occasionally wonder what has happened to my old neighbours, my schoolmates, but there is no clue here.

The crumbling sandstone walls, the endless middens, are gone, and frankly I can only be relieved about this. I truly believe that I have no real sentimental attachment to these times. Nor, perhaps to my loss, could I ever indulge fully in the facile musing of stairheid nostalgia. In retrospect, my memories of childhood are twofold – those of envy and those of shame. In retrospect, the faces of Muir's slum-dwellers become clear, because, as Muir correctly surmises, they are in possession of a very particular knowledge. Envy, the first of these, is, to my mind, quite clear. It was not hard to be envious of those who had more, of the people I never saw who inhabited the big houses behind the high walls at the top of the hill. When, as an eleven year old, I passed the selection exam and went, as a bursary boy to Allan Glen's School, I had to meet these people, from Bearsden or Milngavie, and pretend I was the same as them – although, of course, I wasn't, for I was heir to a knowledge they would never possess, and they had an easy understanding that I could never master. Shame, the second, is not so easy to come to terms with. I think it is correct that I lived in a slum, although it would be wrong to pretend that my parents were really poor. They were respectable, worked hard and kept an immaculately clean room and kitchen on the third floor of a tenement block. But, in today's terms at least, a slum it was, and living in a slum for a child is a strange mixture of revulsion and wonder. Slums are hemmed in by their backyards and middens – places where all that we divest returns to its elemental state, borderlands between nature and culture. I had a delicate stomach, and, like Thaw, I wouldn't eat very much that didn't have the impartial and artificial texture of plastic. I was always afraid nature might catch up on me. I remember too, the lavatory, down a flight of stairs, that we shared with three other flats. Sometimes damp, often dark – a sort of cell that you didn't have the privilege of inhabiting alone. You put toilet paper

The Necropolis

on the seat, touched as little as possible, averted your eyes from the floor unless you caught a glimpse of an earwig or something worse. You had to lock the door with a massive key from the inside in case anyone came. That was the worst, hearing the footsteps, wondering if they would peep through the keyhole, which seemed like an apparatus designed to make your most private functions public. And so, you acquired a certain knowledge from living there that set you apart from those who didn't. But this in itself was not something of which I was ashamed. I was ashamed because I couldn't tell anyone where I lived, and it still hurts to do so now, because this was home, and it was the home of my parents, and because they and I deserved better. But we didn't get it from the old Glasgow, and what we would have got from the new was never revealed, because, for my father, and thousands like him, it would soon be too late.

With this in mind I set my face further west. Up to the top of Ark Lane, past the little blue shop, once owned by a man whose name was John Pirie, where I once bought sweets and packets of stamps for my album, past my old school, Golfhill, a typical Victorian red sandstone edifice with symmetrical playgrounds marked 'Boys' and 'Girls'. Opposite there is a tiny strip of semi-landscaped grass, with occasional benches. Under here lie the remains of the old air-raid shelters, now unseen. I cut across the grass to the perimeter wall, greasy in the damp December air. After a minute I find a foothold and launch myself at the top and mantelshelf up, feeling as guilty as a naughty schoolboy. Hitching my jacket I dreep down and land with a thud in the precincts of the Necropolis.

Here, under the overcast sky, everything is a textured shade of grey as if viewed through a Marzaroli photograph. I am almost alone – but not quite. Some children are climbing to the top of a hexagonal mausoleum, and cannot find a foothold on a white marble pockmarked madonna with a patina of streaming rain stains. Eventually they climb and descend and run away with a few cries in a language which would not have passed my boyhood lips. I instinctively wander towards a black angel – a sculpted seraph on the top of a monumental plinth who has collected the memories of a hundred years of industrial grime and lost, over the same time, one arm and one leg. He stands out, bowed, his wings hunched behind him, as a silhouette against the cloud.

The vista here is truly amazing. The north-west is again dominated by the Infirmary but by its more modern grey concrete counterpart constructed in long horizontal slabs, the tower blocks at Sighthill, some now graced with a random pattern of coloured panels; Red Road, the housing scheme of Garngad, and, above all, to the north, the motorway, following the old ways of the canal, a continual

movement against the stillness. To the south there are the silvery
tubular matrices of the brewery and billows of silver smoke and the
smell of barley and hops. Then, more immediately, there is the
cathedral with its green copper roof and a graveyard even older than
the Necropolis, and Provand's Lordship. Tradition has it that an
underground tunnel links the old house to some exit on the hillside.
This little part of the big city is where Glasgow began, along the banks
of the Molendinar where Mungo reputedly had his cell and set up the
church which grew into the Cathedral of Saint Mungo, thrusting a
staff into the ground which took root and grew into a tall ash tree. In
the nineteenth-century the growing strain of mass immigration and
industrial expansion destroyed the rural idyll. Cholera, typhoid and
dysentery bubbled up in the Molendinar as it retreated, under the
weight of civilisation, further underground. On the little hill by the
cathedral, partially quarried and partially forested, the fir trees shed
their needles and died. In 1831, John Strang addressed an appeal to
the Glasgow Merchants' House for the construction of a cemetery
and pleasure garden on the site of the old Fir Park: 'A garden cemetery
is the sworn foe to preternatural fear and superstition... In bending
over the grave the afflicted soul naturally seeks refuge in the arms of
its Creator, and through the mere conviction of earthly frailty, are its
hopes raised to a better state of being thereafter, and its trust in
heaven is established and increased...the grave which points out the
termination of this life's miseries on the one hand, and the beginning
of a blessed immortality on the other, might be made so attractive as
to become an occasional retreat and an occasional solace to the
citizens of Glasgow...Why should not the secret voice which whispers to us while gazing on a grave, that the ashes beneath are destined
yet to spring into life, be more frequently listened to at the tomb of
our fathers, at that spot, in fact, which is at once the shrine of memory
and the altar of hope?'[1] And so the Necropolis was born out of the
urgent need for more hygienic burial grounds, the frantic quest of the
middle-classes for monumental immortality in an age of uncertainty,
and the peculiar Victorian fascination with the trappings of death.
And, thus, the clear association, from the beginnings of the Necropolis, of remembrance with pleasure. Vicariously, amongst the
last remains of strangers, we can turn our thoughts to the sentimental,
or the morbid, remembering, and indulging in a form of personal
mortification while flirting with the wider mythology of community.
In this way, the purpose of the Necropolis, as it was originally stated,
and, perhaps, as it is today, as the visitors flock back, is not all that
different from the purpose of Annan's photographs which now grace
the wine bars and restaurants of Culture City.

    The Necropolis is also a key constituent in the symbolic structure of *Lanark* . Lanark returns here towards the end of the novel:

> The clergyman led them down dim seedy paths past the porticoes of mausoleums cut into the hillside. Gleams of light from below lit corners of inscriptions to the splendid dead:
>
> '...*His victorious campaign*....'
> '...*whose unselfish devotion*...'
> '...*Revered by his students*...'
> '...*esteemed by his colleagues*...'
> '...*beloved by all*...'
>
> They crossed a flat space and walked along a cobbled lane. Ritchie-Smollet said, 'A tributary of the river once flowed under here.'
>
> Lanark saw that a low wall beside him was the parapet of a bridge and looked over onto a steeply embanked road. Cars sped up this to the motorway.[2]

Gray's description rings true – although I have never visited the place at night when the neon spotlights, slotted into artificial monumental monoliths, shine into the sky. Instead, on the day of my visit, the tombstones are lit with an even light, created by the clouds and mist, which accords each remembrance its own portion of light. Such powerful icons seem to deny their cultural derivation – although they are in kind totally different from those continental graveyards, with their carved wooden crosses, dried flowers, and old photographs of the deceased. Variously, some of the inscriptions read:

William McEwan, died 7th December 1849'
'Them also which sleep in Jesus will
God bring with them'.

Charles Tennant of St Rollox, died 1st May 1838 erected by a few of his friends as a tribute of respect.

Robert William Innerarity,
died 28th January 1837
'Blessed are the dead who
die in the Lord'.

Sacred to the memory of Alex Wilson Esq.
died 20th November 1840
'For if we believe that Jesus died and rose
again even so them also which sleep in Jesus
will God bring with him'.

Duncan McPhail died aged 71
Dugald   27
Duncan   25
Dugald   77
Marion   73

Angus	46
John	52
James	52
Duncan	1
Duncan	44
Donald	9
Flora	1
Albert	26
Donald	5
Flora	13
Alexander	36

Robert Stewart of Murdostoun, Lord Provost
of Glasgow 1851-1854, died 12th September 1866
'We sorrow not even as others which have no
hope. For we believe that Jesus died, and
rose again, even so them also which sleep in
Jesus, will God bring with him'.
                                        1 Thess IV 13-14

Sacred to the memory of John Gilmour, John
James (who died in infancy), Christina Gladstone,
William Somerville, their father, Janet Gilmour,
their mother
'Until the day break and the shadow flew away'.

In real terms the difference between these and Gray's imagined texts
may seem minimal. Gray has resorted to structured quotation in
order to emphasise the uniformity of the remembrances, the anonymity of the dead, and the insincerity of the rhetorical eulogies. Perhaps
these non-fictional examples, with the addition of names and dates,
fulfil the same purpose. Yet there is an extra sense of poignancy to be
derived from these, because of their very nature. Gray employs
literary parody which invests his examples with implied meaning. My
selection is more iconic. For one hundred and fifty years these words
have remained here, etched in stone, unseen, for all I know, until I,
without the aid of chisel or mortar, have embedded them into my little
narrative, presumably for some purpose. Yet they defy interpretation
in the normal way. Rather than suggest or explain anything, they
simply deny. What strikes me more than anything else is the utter
emptiness of the discourse to which they belong. There can be nothing
more ridiculous, confronted by this mass of textual evidence, than for
anyone to think that history is inscribed in the works or the
remembrances of great men. Although these texts are chosen randomly, they are typical, and like the Necropolis, an inscribed text on
the greater city landscape, they have only one sparse message. What

information do we glean from them, name, perhaps place, profession. But more than anything, the sheer cumulative display of death – no matter what age, no matter what year, the uncompromising exercise of mortality. All the great merchants and traffickers and their monuments wrought from age old stone, are settling into the same turf sod.

The metatext, the quotations from scripture, with their insistence on resurrection (at odds with the gradual decay of the stone texts, as the sandstone swells and flakes below inscriptions and the tendrils of ivy prod into the folds and tucks of mausoleums – the utter irreconcilability of the living and the dead is the most notable feature of graveyards) is, on the other hand, completely impersonal – appended after death, owing nothing or giving nothing to the individuals interned within the parameters of the archaic inscription. Here we can see, not the remembrance of individuals, but merely the instruments of constraint – the facts that define and categorise them, the religious sentiments that condemn them to endless redemption.

The novel *Lanark*, too, ends here, as Lanark, suffering from a *taedium vitae* (which is, after all, a form of nostalgia) after his many wanderings, returns to look down on a city torn apart by natural catastrophe and civil strife expecting to encounter some grand apocalyptic ending. The truth, he discovers, is infinitely more terrifying:

> The figure bowed again and said, 'You will die tomorrow at seven minutes after noon.'
> The words were almost drowned by a squawking gull turning in the sky overhead, but Lanark understood them perfectly. like a mother's fall in a narrow lobby, like a policeman's hand on his shoulder, he had known or expected this all his life. A roaring like a terrified crowd filled his ears; he whispered,
> 'Death is not a privilege.'
> 'The privilege is knowing when.'
> 'But I...I seem to remember passing through several deaths.'
> 'They were rehearsals. After the next death nothing personal will remain of you.'
> 'Will it hurt?'
> 'Not much. Just now there is no feeling in your left arm; you can't move it. In a moment it will get better again, but at five minutes after noon tomorrow your whole body will become like that. For two minutes you will be able to see and think but not move or speak. That will be the worst time. You will be dead when it stops.'
> Lanark scowled with self-pity and annoyance. The chamberlain said, respectfully 'Have you a complaint?'

'I ought to have more love before I die. I've not had enough.'
'That is everyone's complaint. You can appeal against the death
sentence if you have something better to do.'
'If you're hinting that I should go in for more adventures, no
thank you. But how will my son – how will the *world* manage
when I'm not here?'
The chamberlain shrugged and spread his hands.
'Well go away, go away,' said Lanark more kindly. 'You can tell
the earth I would have preferred a less common end, like being
struck by lightning. But I'm prepared to take death as it comes.'
The chamberlain vanished. Lanark forgot him, propped his
chin on his hands and sat a long time watching the moving
clouds. He was a slightly worried, ordinary old man but glad to
see the light in the sky.[3]

Lanark, in the City of the Dead, looking out over a city of internecine
strife, is denied the lightning bolt, the storm, the raging against the
wind, the apocalypse. His fate is, tragically, only to join the anonymous, forgotten dead, to freeze in the land of the frozen, to be
resolved, like Don Juan, into just another statue in a forest of stone.
And so is the fate, in the New Glasgow, of all those who oppose its
inevitable logic – the slum-dwellers, the windae-hingers, the dossers,
the steel workers, all frozen in time, not the object of veneration but
sacrifices to the cause – reconstituting the old Glasgow in favour of
the new.

The apocalypse is not expected in the year of Culture City,
although in the past there have been storms, hurricanes, floods. They
seem to come in the middle months of the dark bleak Scottish winter.
What better time to begin to celebrate the New Glasgow than the
most revered of Scottish festivals, when the shops shut, the buses stop,
the pubs close (for the only time in the year except, perhaps, Fair
Monday) and the whole workings of the city pause, for a moment, to
reflect:

> On the last Hogmanay night (New Year's Eve), as on all its
> predecessors, no matter how dourly and darkly I take my
> pleasures, the same way some people keep snakes for pets, I
> once again, with a great upsurge of savage joy, recalled another
> verse of mine and practised what I preach, namely:
> > O this is the time for all mankind
> > > To rejoice without a doubt
> > – And break the neck of the bottle
> > > If the cork will not come out!

And that is precisely how Scots do bring in the New Year. They
gather in the public squares of their cities and towns, and as the
bells ring out the Old Year and ring in the New, they empty their

bottles and smash them on the street. On this most recent Hogmanay I was one of a company of many uproarious hundreds doing this in George Square, Glasgow, undeterred by the fact that a day of gale and sleet was giving way to snow and ice and that hundreds of people in Glasgow alone had been rendered homeless by blown-down houses or injured in the streets by falling chimney-pots and torn-off slates.[4]

This is Hugh MacDiarmid's New Year, and he seems to think well of it, despite the casualties. And if we remember *The Steamie,* and Magrit McGuire's joyful parting then we may assume that, in Glasgow, the New Year is, at least, a time to forget our troubles, a time for the myth of community to become reality. On the contrary there is another interpretation of the celebration of the New Year; that it is the most sordid of Scottish festivals, and Glasgow the most dreadful of cities at that time. There is little of the excessive, the sentimental, the violent, the absurd and the stupid that will not be part of thousands of dreadful little scenes played out in the city on the night of Hogmanay, when we foolishly consign ourselves to the oblivion at the bottom of a whisky bottle and pretend that the wounds we have nurtured over a full year have mysteriously healed. Hogmanay in Glasgow is a festival of illusion, of false hopes and broken promises. Alan Spence has a short story called *Auld Lang Syne* in which he greets the New Year in Glasgow: 'Last day of another year and I sit at the window looking down over Hill Street, out over the city, Glasgow. Directly opposite, across the road, a row of grey tenements, crazy-tilted chimney pots, a tangle of television aerials. Further along, the red brick block of the cancer hospital. From here, if the lights were lit, I could see right into the houses and into the hospital wards...From down the road comes a soft chiming of bells from the church of Saint Aloysius. The chimes are a tape-recording, played through speakers high up in the church tower. This is the bell that never rang.'[5]

And so finally, at the end of this narrative, to hear, perhaps, the bells that never ring, on the 31st December 1989, the end of the decade (in popular opinion, although technically, perhaps, an extra year is required), a mild but grey day, I set off by bus from Edinburgh to Glasgow on my last journey to the New Glasgow. On the journey I start talking to the man seated next to me. His name is Ho, from Kuala Lumpur, and he has only just arrived in Scotland. His intention is to spend one day in Glasgow and to see the sights. I try to explain that he has picked the worst possible day of the year to see anything but nevertheless I try to describe the city and explain what he might see, a task I find incredibly difficult (despite the time I have spent writing about Glasgow). As we speed down the motorway through

Easterhouse, Stepps, Garthamlock, Ruchazie, Cranhill, Provanmill and Blackhill I warm to the task, although the socio-economic deprivation of the east-end housing schemes are not part of the Glasgow my friend from the even farther east has envisaged. As we enter the city we catch a glimpse of the cathedral and pass the Royal Infirmary, an impressive site. He thinks that it may be a college so I explain its function. Then, embarrassingly, I get mixed up between antiseptic and anaesthetic, Lister and Fleming. As a tourist guide, I realise, I am a flop. Eventually we arrive at the bus station. It is a quiet, gloomy day in Glasgow too. Shops are closed. I take him down to George Square and St Vincent Place, but the Information Bureau is shut too. I make some fairly feeble suggestions about what he might do (he doesn't seem interested in pubs or restaurants, the obvious refuge) and leave him there in the centre of the square. Strangely the most interesting feature here is only temporary – the giant television screens erected as part of the massive celebrations planned to greet Glasgow's year of culture – advertised as the the Greatest Hogmanay Party in the World.

The rest of my day is fairly unexciting. I wander around the Barrows and consume a little New Glasgow style and a fish supper, then visit my in-laws. In the evening, along with my wife, I take a taxi into the town centre (as we drive in the driver gets a call for Scottish Television – the task is 'to take the Scottish cup back to Paradise'). We meet some friends and have a drink. Midnight approaching, we end up in a small pub near the river where the landlord provides us with a supper of sandwiches and chicken. Not so far away, at the Greatest Hogmanay Party in the World, in George Square, the mayor of Paris, Jacques Chirac, is passing on the keys of culture to the city via a television link-up, and Robbie Coltrane is cracking jokes at the stroke of midnight (a slight mistiming that was to cause a controversy later). For my part, ticketless and unable to get within spitting distance of the square, I wander down to the Stockwell Bridge, where a piper is regaling a small audience, and watch the fireworks in Glasgow Green. Incendiary Glasgow, circumscribed by fire, as culture year explodes into life: a display of wanton destruction in the aid of illumination that would surely not disappoint the world-weary Lanark.

And here I stand, amongst the others, and celebrate the new Glasgow, and cast my mind back to the old Glasgow. Exactly twenty-one years ago, on Hogmanay, 1968, after the sentimental formalities following the bells, my father took ill; he found he couldn't properly move his right arm. Five weeks later he lay in the Royal Infirmary in the antiseptic ward overlooking the Necropolis. Unknown to anyone, including the doctors, a small recalcitrant cell in his brain had formed a deadly tumour. They moved him to the neurological hospital at Killearn, converted from old airforce barracks, closed only a few years later, where he lay in a long ward with another fifteen male patients in various stages of serious illness.

When I last saw my father, he could only move his eyelids, the rest of his body was completely paralysed. A totally naked man with his head shaven was having a fit in the next bed. When we left the hospital, waiting for the hourly bus, I had lemonade and a caramel wafer in the cafeteria. I was only thirteen. My father died ten days later and was buried on my fourteenth birthday, the ninth of March, 1969.

There is nothing at all virtuous in watching anyone die, as Farrow discovers when, his eyes offending him, he prefers continual darkness to light. Lanark, at least, has the real privilege of dying alone, but his frozen stare, for the eternity of two minutes, is more than just a dying – it is a deathwatch over the city of Unthank, which, after all, is the purpose of the novel, for literature fixes what in memory fades, is insubstantial, is nothing. Twenty-one years on I can only wonder, and I still often do, what thoughts passed through my father's head at that time, for his Glasgow was my Glasgow and the Glasgow of countless thousand others – living, breathing real Glaswegians – yet their thoughts are as silent now as words from the hollowed epitaphs of tombs. And so, as the phantom bells ring in the New Year of 1990 and Glasgow delivers its offspring – the leaner, neater, more cultured city for these times – I, personally, ask to be permitted to retire from the celebration and sit it out hopefully, like Lanark, my weather eye set dispassionately on the light. For me, and many other Glaswegians, our memories are only a legacy of lost years. From my perspective, high in the city of the dead, far from the excesses of Culture City, the little beetling, rude, crazy metropolis below, its sooty face scrubbed clean, like a recalcitrant schoolboy forced to visit a wedding or a funeral, will always be the Phantom Village.

References

Deathwatch

1. Shadow (Alexander Brown), *Midnight Scenes and Social Photographs, being descriptions of the streets, wynds and dens of the city* (Glasgow, 1858).
2. Ibid., v.
3. Rev D MacColl, *Among the Masses, or, Work in the Wynds* (London, 1867), pp. 29-30.
4. Shadow, ibid., pp. 108-109.
5. Ibid., pp. 110-111.

We Only Live To Take Our Ease

1. The various published editions of the collection are detailed in J A Fisher, *T. Annan's Old Closes & Streets of Glasgow: A Guide* (Glasgow, 1977).
2. John Tagg, 'God's Sanitary Law: Slum Clearance and Photography', in *The Burden of Representation* (London, 1988).
3. *Photographs of Glasgow* , published in 1868.
4. Thomas Annan, *Photographs of the Old Closes and Streets of Glasgow* 1868/1877 , with a new introduction by Anita Ventura Mozley (New York, 1977).
5. Reprinted in 1976 by the University of Glasgow Press.
6. Andrew Noble, 'Scottish Writing and the Nineteenth-Century City' in ed. George Gordon, *Perspectives of the Scottish City* (Aberdeen, 1985), p. 85.
7. Malcolm Chapman,*The Gaelic Vision in Scottish Culture* (Edinburgh, 1978).
8. George W Stocking Jnr, *Victorian Anthropology* (Chicago, 1987), p. 251.
9. Kenneth M Boyd, *Scottish Church Attitudes to Sex, Marriage and the Family 1850-1914* (Edinburgh, 1980), pp. 107-108. See also Thomas Chalmers, *The Christian and Civic Economy of Large Towns* (Glasgow, 1821-6, 3 vols), and Ian Levitt, *Poverty and Welfare in Scotland 1890-1948* (Edinburgh, 1988).
10. A Sabbath School Teacher (William Logan), *The Moral Statistics of Glasgow in 1863* (Glasgow, 1864), pp. 16-17.
11. W Naismith, *City Echoes; or, Bitter cries from Glasgow* (Paisley, 1884).

12. Ibid., p. 154.

13. Ibid., pp. 175-176.

14. Ibid., pp. 177-178.

15. Ibid., pp. 205-206.

16. Reprinted by the Molendinar Press as *Glasgow a hundred years ago* (Glasgow, 1973).

17. Frank Arneil Walker,'The Glasgow Grid', in *Order in Space and Society* (Edinburgh, 1982), ed.Thomas A Markus, pp. 155-199.

18. Frank Worsdall, *The Tenement as a Way of Life* (Edinburgh, 1979), ix.

19. Jacques Donzelot, *The Policing of Families* (London, 1980), first published 1977, pp. 42-43.

The Glasgow that I Used to Know

1. Glasgow Corporation Housing Department, *Farewell to the Single End* (Glasgow, 1976).

2. See Fred Davis, *Yearning for Yesterday - a Sociology of Nostalgia* (New York, 1979), and David Lowenthal, *The Past is a Foreign Country* (Cambridge, 1985), pp. 10-11. Davis comments that, 'nostalgia thrives on transition, on the subjective discontinuities that engender our yearning for continuity', p. 49.

3. Robert Hewison, *The Heritage Industry: Britain in a Climate of Decline* (London, 1987), p. 134.

4. Both are quoted in Farquhar McLay (ed.), *Workers' City* (Glasgow, 1988).

5. Willie Gall, *The Sheer Gall of It! The Wit of Glasgow* (Edinburgh, 1988).

6. Cairns Craig, 'Fearful Selves: Character, Community, and the Scottish Imagination', *Cencrastus* , No. 4 (Winter, 1980-81), 29-32.

7. Gall, ibid., p. 7.

8. Cliff Hanley (ed.), Glasgow – *A Celebration* (Edinburgh, 1974), p. 14.

9. Although not acknowledged individually, most of the following short quotations are from various editions of the *Evening Times* .

10. John Struthers, *Glasgow's Miles Better* (Glasgow,1986).

11. Stephen Games's documentary, *The Reversible Mackintosh* ,was broadcast on Radio Three in 1984.

12. Frank Walker, 'A Mackintosh Temple for the City of Culture', *Scotsman* (27th March, 1989), p. 9.

13. Michael Munro, *The Patter* (Glasgow, 1985).

The Construction of Consensus

1. Ian Jack, 'Reinventing Glasgow', *The Independent Magazine*, (4th February 1989), 22-29, p. 29.

2. Quoted in Enid Gauldie, *A History of Working-Class Housing 1780-1918* (London, 1974) p. 74.

3. See Anthony S. Wohl, *The Eternal Slum* (London, 1977). Wohl notes that 'illness was one of the basic causes of working class pauperism...between 1850 and 1880, the argument that 'health is money, as much as time is money, and sooner or later sickness must be paid for out of the common fund', became almost a stock-in-trade of the housing reformers' arsenal of arguments.' p. 66.
4. See John Barry Cullingworth, *A Profile of Glasgow Housing - 1965* (Edinburgh, 1968), and *Scotland's Older Houses, Report of the Sub-Committee on Unfit Housing* (Edinburgh, 1967). Some form of legislation against overcrowding had been in effect for some time (arguably since the days of the famous ticket houses) but it was not particularly effective. The Housing Act of Scotland 1935, for example, allowed up to four children under 10 in each room of a house.
5. Bo'ness Rebels Literary Society, *The Rebels Ceilidh Song Book, No.2* (Bo'ness, 1985), pp. 28-29. Compare Adam McNaughtan's *They're Pullin' Doon the Building Next Tae Oors*: 'Now many folk have laughed, and they've said that we were daft, / No tae go where everything was new and neat. / But we're happy where we are, think we're better aff by far, / Wi a pub on every corner of the street.'
6. Sally Magnusson, in *Scotland on Sunday* (7th August, 1988), p. 10.
7. David Pae, 'The Factory Girl' in *The People's Journal*, Feb. 1864, p. 2. Cited in William Donaldson, *Popular Literature in Victorian Scotland* (Aberdeen, 1986), pp. 90-91.
8. Quoted in John Hill, '"Scotland doesna mean much tae Glesca": Some Notes on "The Gorbals Story"', in Colin McArthur (ed.), *Scotch Reels* (London, 1982), pp. 100-111. Hill points out, astutely, that *The Gorbals Story* takes bourgeois family drama as a model but reverses its function.
9. For these and others reviews of the play, see Robert McLeish, *The Gorbals Story*, introduction by Linda Mackenney (Edinburgh, 1985).
10. See Hal Foster (ed.), *The Anti-Aesthetic* (Port Townsend, 1983).
11. See Fredric Jameson, 'Postmodernism, or The Cultural Logic of Capitalism', *New Left Review*, 146 (July/August, 1984), pp. 53-93.
12. See Mike Davis, 'Urban Renaissance and the Spirit of Post modernism', *New Left Review*, 151 (May/June, 1985), pp. 106-113.
13. The answer to this question, as far as all fashion-conscious Glaswegians are concerned, is Partick Thistle. Rangers are the team in Glasgow with big money and a big reputation, but they remain irrevocably Modernist, and Celtic, Clyde and Queens Park do not figure in the fashion stakes.

Cancer of Empire

1. William Bolitho, *Cancer of Empire* (London, 1924).

2. Ibid., pp. 13-14.
3. Ibid., pp. 34-35.
4. Ibid., pp. 37-38.
5. Sidney Checkland, *The Upas Tree* (Glasgow, 1976).
6. Lewis Grassic Gibbon and Hugh MacDiarmid, *Scottish Scene* (London, 1935), pp. 114-115.
7. Edwin Muir, *Autobiography* (London, 1954).
8. Edwin Muir, *Scottish Journey* (Edinburgh, 1979, first published, 1935), pp. 115-116.
9. Ibid., pp. 112-113. This description could be said to be a general account of the depravity of city life, but it is very different in style and tone to, for example, his description of Scotland's second city, Edinburgh: 'The first sight of Edinburgh after an absence is invariably exciting. Its bold and stony look recalls ravines and quarried mountains, and as one's eye runs up the long line of jagged roofs from Holyrood to the Castle, one feels that these house-shapes are outcroppings of the rocky ridge on which they are planted, methodical geological formations in which, as an afterthought, people have taken to living.' p. 5.
10. Some details are from Alastair Borthwick, *The Empire Exhibition Fifty Years On* (Edinburgh, 1988).
11. J R Allan (ed.), *Scotland – 1938* (Edinburgh, 1938), p. 60.
12. Colin McArthur, 'The dialectic of national identity:The Glasgow Empire Exhibition of 1938', in *Popular Culture and Social Relations*, ed. Tony Bennett, Tony Mercer and Janet Woolacott (Milton Keynes, 1986).
13. Alexander McArthur and Herbert Kingsley Long, *No Mean City* (London, 1986), fp 1937.
14. Bill McGhee, *Cut and Run* (London, 1986; 1st edition 1956), pp. 6-9.
15. Ibid., p. 11.
16. Ibid.

Just a Boy's Game

1. McDougall's plays are set in the urban connurbations of the west of Scotland. I am well aware that *Just a Boy's Game* is specifically set in Greenock, which is not just an extension of Glasgow, but the main points about the hard man image apply in general to the industrial west of Scotland.
2. See Dave McKie, 'Death and the City: Media Representations of Urban Scotland', *Cencrastus*, 13 (1983), pp. 37-39.
3. Jimmy Boyle, *A Sense of Freedom* (Edinburgh, 1977).
4. S G Checkland, *The Upas Tree* (Glasgow, 1976).
5. Colin McArthur, 'A Man's World', *The Listener* (9th August, 1984), p. 27.
6. William McIllvanney, *Laidlaw* (1977), and *The Papers of Tony Veitch* (1984).
7. James Patrick, *A Glasgow Gang Observed* (London, 1973).

8. Ibid., p. 30.
9. Ibid., p. 31.
10. Bill Murray, *The Old Firm: Sectarianism, Sport and Society in Scotland* (Edinburgh, 1984).
11. See Tom Gallagher, *Glasgow, The Uneasy Peace* (Manchester, 1987).
12. I am aware that to some extent I am misrepresenting Protestant tradition in this respect, but I am looking at the situation from the point of view of the average, fairly non-committed Protestant. It is true that, for example, the higher echelons of the Orange Order, known as the Black Men, would claim an established ritualistic mythology as ancient and as valid as any Catholic rites. Certain fringe groups such as the British Israelites, in fact, would claim that Protestant tradition has historical precedence over Catholicism. For an insight into this area, I am grateful to the Ulster anthropologist, Tony Buckley.
13. Hugh MacDiarmid, 'The Dour Drinkers of Glasgow', in *The Uncanny Scot*, ed. Kenneth Buthlay (London, 1968), 93-101, pp. 96-99. MacDiarmid's best-known references to Glasgow are relentlessly uncompromising: 'All the buildings in Glasgow are grey/ With cruelty and meanness of spirit', 'The houses are Glasgow not the people - these/ Are simply the food the houses live and grow on / Endlessly, drawing from their vulgarity/ And pettiness and darkness of spirit/ Gorgonising the mindless generations, / Turning them all into filthy property/ Apt as the Karaunas by diabolic arts/ To produce darkness and obscure the light of day./ To see or hear a clock in Glasgow's horrible,/ Like seeing a dead man's watch, still going though he's dead./ Everything is dead except stupidity here.'
14. For a fascinating account of public houses in Victorian and Edwardian Glasgow see Rudolph Kenna and Anthony Mooney, *People's Palaces* (Edinburgh, 1983).

Unthank

1. Alasdair Gray, *Lanark* (Edinburgh, 1981), p. 19.
2. Ibid., p. 3.
3. Ibid., pp. 46-47.
4. Ibid., p. 191.
5. Ibid., p. 243.
6. Ibid., p. 21.
7. Ibid., p. 19.
8. Ibid., p. 12.
9. Ibid., p. 41.
10. Ibid., pp. 397-398.
11. Ibid., p. 434.
12. Colin Baxter, *Glasgow* (Glasgow, 1986), Douglas Corrance, *Glasgow* (Glasgow, 1981), and Robin Ward, *The Spirit of Glasgow* (Glasgow, 1984).

13. Oscar Marzaroli, *Shades of Grey: Glasgow 1956-1987* (Edinburgh, 1987).
14. Another Glasgow writer who has received some acclaim, but whose work I have not chosen to deal with here, is James Kelman. Kelman's strength is his propensity for the rendition of dialect - often described as naturalistic, but, in actuality, more an effect of his use of language. His work has developed and at its best is extremely effective. See Edwin Morgan, 'Glasgow Speech in Recent Scottish Literature', in J Derrick McClure (ed.), *Scotland and the Lowland Tongue* (Aberdeen, 1983), pp. 195-208.

The Bright Side of Town

1. See Michael S Moss and John R Hume, *Workshop of the British Empire* (London, 1977).
2. Ed. David Donnison and Alan Middleton, *Regenerating the Inner City - Glasgow's Experience* (London, 1987).
3. Ibid., p. 274.
4. Ibid., p. 14.
5. James Joyce, *Dubliners* (London, 1967; first published 1914), p. 36. It is worth noting, simply for curiosity, that Joyce did visit Glasgow as a boy, an event recorded by his brother Stanislav. Apparently, it rained all day.
6. Alan Spence, *Its Colours They Are Fine* (Edinburgh, 1983), fp 1977, pp. 20-21. The collection is obviously influenced by Joyce.

Born in the Shadow of the Fairfield Crane

1. Ken Currie, 'Statement on the Development of My Work 1980-1988', in *Third Eye Centre, Ken Currie* (Glasgow, 1988). This book has no page numbers.
2. Ibid.
3. Ibid.
4. Iain McLean, *The Legend of Red Clydeside* (Edinburgh,1983), p. 1. James Young, however, argues that the movement was successful in mobilising mass support against the war, militarism, and poor housing: 'In contrast to the few historians who have questioned the argument that the labour unrest on the Clydeside constituted a serious threat to the established social order, the authorities soon identified 'the state of irritation which quickly spreads beyond the boundaries of the establishment where the trouble first arose to other works, and frequently from adventitious causes wholly unconnected with the origin or merits of the dispute it becomes elevated into a question of principle affecting all employers and munitions workers generally throughout the district', James D. Young, *The Rousing of the Scottish Working Classes* (London, 1979), p. 191.
5. Julian Spalding, in National Galleries of Scotland, *The Vigorous Imagination* (Edinburgh, 1987).

6. Ibid., p. 78.
7. Archie Hind, *The Dear Green Place* (Edinburgh, 1984; first published 1966), pp. 12-13.
8. Ken Currie , ibid.
9. Ian Watson, *Folk Song and Democratic Culture* (London,1986) pp. 102-104.
10. For a review of Brown's work, see Watson, ibid.
11. Farquhar McLay (ed.),*Workers City* (Glasgow, 1988).
12. Farquhar McLay, introduction to *Workers City* , ibid., pp. 1-3.
13. Ibid., pp. 1-3.
14. Patrick Wright, *On Living in an Old Country: the National Past in Contemporary Britain* (London, 1985), pp. 243-244.
15. From this same tradition, however, arose Tom Johnstone's interesting but flawed account of working-class history in Scotland: Tom Johnstone, *The History of the Working Classes in Scotland* (Glasgow, 1946).
16. James D. Young, 'Culture and Socialism: Working-Class Glasgow, 1778-1978', in McLay, ibid., p. 143.
17. Richard Jacques, 'Springburn symbolised in bronze', *Scotsman* (29th March, 1989).
18. See Murdoch Nicolson and Mark O'Neill, *Glasgow: Locomotive Builder to the World* (Glasgow, 1987), p. 43. This account of the history of the locomotive industry in Glasgow was actually inspired by Wylie's straw locomotive.
19. Recently, Wylie, along with the engineer Tom Craig, has had the idea of constructing a mammoth sculpture, *The Glasgow Flourish*, a 200 ft high arch that will span the Clyde at a location near the Garden Festival site, with a suspended pendulum (cf Foucault's) as the river flows timelessly by. Already this extravagant idea has been exhibited in the form of a model and well received at *L'Europe des Createurs* in Paris – a showcase for innovative architecture projects. Another project Wylie has in mind for the Finnieston crane is a 'Dear Green Aeroplane', the framework covered in leaves.

Out of This World

1. Some of the drawings of Muirhead Bone illustrate *The Upas Tree*, ibid.
2. George Blake, *The Shipbuilders* (London, 1986), fp 1937.
3. Ibid., pp. 279-280.
4. Alan Bold, *Modern Scottish Literature* (Harlow, 1983), pp. 232-33. There is also an interesting account of the novel by Manfred Malzhan in 'The Industrial Novel' in ed. Cairns Craig, *The History of Scottish Literature* (Aberdeen,1987), pp. 229-242: 'The central figures are boss and worker, an odd couple branded by history as anachronistic remnants in a changed environment...what is lamented is the passing of a pioneer age, a world that had scope for heroic achievement, giving way to a kind of progress that seems as

unpalatable as inevitable... the question 'Was the glory ever real, except as a story told to a child?' is merely rhetorical.The function of myth – and *The Shipbuilders* is an attempt at myth-creation – is to provide patterns for the ordering of experience', p. 231.

5. *The Shipbuilders*, ibid., p. 151.
6. Colin McArthur, 'Scotland and Cinema: The Iniquity of the Fathers', in *Scotch Reels* (London, 1982), pp. 40-69.
7. Bill Bryden, *Willie Rough* (Edinburgh, 1972), first performed at the Royal Lyceum, Edinburgh, February 1972.
8. Colin McArthur, ibid.
9. An uncritical, but reasonably detailed account of the exhibitions is given by Perilla and Juliet Kinchin, *Glasgow's Great Exhibitions* (Oxford, 1988).
10. Elizabeth Wilson, *Hallucinations: Life in the Post-Modern City* (London, 1988).
11. For an useful definition of the function of the allotment see David Crouch and Colin Ward, *The Allotment: Its Landscape and Culture* (London 1988), p. 5: 'These images come together in an allotment *idea*. The word 'allotment' is curiously abstract: a legalistic term meaning simply 'a portion', but it is shorthand for a number of images of people, places and activities. It is loaded with assumptions, attitudes and experience that bring us back into our own culture, whether or not we are plot-holders. The word occupies an obscure corner in contemporary culture,but an absolutely interesting one. It may imply something out of the way, passing out of ordinary experience, overcome by the real concerns of the late-twentieth century. But it is also tinged with nostalgia for the world we think we have lost, an image of humility from the days when our grandparents would urge us to: 'Use it up and wear it out/ Make do or do without.'Yet it also implies the idea of something 'worthwhile' to occupy the weekend, a concern with the quality of the food we eat, an attractive alternative culture.'
12. Martin Culverwell, 'Drive in Birmingham', *Cultural Studies* , vol. 1, no. 2 (May, 1987), pp. 255-258.
13. Glasgow Online – 'The Electronic Window on Glasgow' – is produced by the Department of Information Science, University of Strathclyde, and can be purchased from them in disk form.
14. Colin Sorensen, 'Theme Parks and Time Machines', in Peter Vergo (ed.), *The New Museology* (London, 1989), pp. 60-73. On the matter of time machines, see also David Lowenthal, *The Past is a Foreign Country* (Cambridge, 1985), pp. 14-21.
15. Robert Hewison, *The Heritage Industry* (London, 1987), p. 135.

Je Me Souviens

1. Kevin Lynch, *The Image of the City* (Cambridge, Mass.,1962).
2. Sean Damer, 'Wine Alley: The Sociology of a Dreadful Enclosure', *The Sociological Review* , vol. 22, no. 2, New Series (May, 1977), pp. 221-248. Damer's work has now been published as a full-

length book by Edinburgh University Press. Wine Alley also
features in an Alan Spence short story, *Silver in the Lamplight*:
'Winey was short for 'The Wine Alley' a small pre-war housing
scheme backing on to a railway line. Although the actual houses
were better than where Aleck lived, the tenements much cleaner
and each flat with an inside bathroom, the place itself had some
reputation for thuggery and violence.' *Its Colours They Are Fine*
(Edinburgh, 1983; first published 1977), p. 74.
3. Jonathan Raban, *Soft City* (London, 1974), p 82.
4. Gilbert Adair, *Myths and Memories* (London, 1986).

Until the Day Break

1.   John Strang, *Necropolis Glasguensis; with observations on Ancient and Modern Tombs and Sepulture* (Glasgow, 1831), pp. 57-
59.
2. Alasdair Gray, *Lanark* (Edinburgh, 1981), p. 399.
3. Ibid., pp. 559-560.
4. McDiarmid, ibid., p. 99.
5. Alan Spence, *Its Colours They Are Fine* (Edinburgh,1983; first
published 1977), p. 198.

Index